STUDIES IN THE ECONOMIC HISTORY OF THE PACIFIC RIM

Trade across the Pacific will be one of the dominant forces in the economy of the next century. Is the economic importance of the Pacific Rim really a recent phenomenon?

The origins of this 'Pacific Century' date from as early as 1571 – the founding of the harbour of Manila, centre of a huge exchange of Spanish American silver for Chinese silk. Yet the study of the world's largest maritime trade route has been, until recently, neglected in favour of Atlantic history.

This collection reflects the birth of Pacific Rim history. It addresses the development of the Pacific Rim over four centuries, combining broad historical syntheses with a range of essays on specific topics, from trade with Hong Kong to British overseas banking. It will form a major contribution to this rapidly expanding new field.

Sally M. Miller is Professor of History and Editor of the John Muir Center for Regional Studies at the University of the Pacific, California. **A.J.H. Latham** is Senior Lecturer in International Economic History at the University College of Wales, Swansea. **Dennis O. Flynn** is Professor of Economics at the University of the Pacific, California.

ROUTLEDGE STUDIES IN THE GROWTH ECONOMIES OF ASIA

1 THE CHANGING CAPITAL MARKETS OF EAST ASIA
Edited by Ky Cao

2 FINANCIAL REFORM IN CHINA
Edited by On Kit Tam

3 WOMEN AND INDUSTRIALIZATION IN ASIA
Edited by Susan Horton

4 JAPAN'S TRADE POLICY
Action or Reaction?
Yumiko Mikanagi

5 THE JAPANESE ELECTION SYSTEM
Three Analytical Perspectives
Junichiro Wada

6 THE ECONOMICS OF THE LATECOMERS
Catching-Up, Technology Transfer and Institutions in Germany, Japan and South Korea
Jang-Sup Shin

7 INDUSTRIALIZATION IN MALAYSIA
Import Substitution and Infant Industry Performance
Rokiah Alavi

8 ECONOMIC DEVELOPMENT IN TWENTIETH-CENTURY EAST ASIA
The International Context
Edited by Aiko Ikeo

9 THE POLITICS OF ECONOMIC DEVELOPMENT IN INDONESIA
Contending Perspectives
Edited by Ian Chalmers and Vedi Hadiz

10 STUDIES IN THE ECONOMIC HISTORY OF THE PACIFIC RIM
Edited by Sally M. Miller, A.J.H. Latham and Dennis O. Flynn

11 WORKERS AND THE STATE IN NEW ORDER INDONESIA
Vedi R. Hadiz

12 THE JAPANESE FOREIGN EXCHANGE MARKET
Beate Reszat

13 EXCHANGE RATE POLICIES IN EMERGING ASIAN COUNTRIES
Edited by Stefan Collignon, Jean Pisani-Ferry and Yung Chul Park

14 FIRMS AND TECHNOLOGY IN THE REFORM ERA
Yizheng Shi

STUDIES IN THE ECONOMIC HISTORY OF THE PACIFIC RIM

Edited by
Sally M. Miller, A.J.H. Latham and Dennis O. Flynn

Routledge
Taylor & Francis Group
LONDON AND NEW YORK

First published 1998
by Routledge
2 Park Square, Milton Park, Abingdon, Oxon, OX14 4RN
Simultaneously published in the USA and Canada
by Routledge
711 Third Avenue, New York, NY 10017
Transferred to Digital Printing 2006
Routledge is an imprint of the Taylor & Francis Group, an informa business
First issued in paperback 2016

Typeset in Garamond by
J&L Composition Ltd, Filey, North Yorkshire

British Library Cataloguing in Publication Data
A catalogue record for this book is available from the British Library
Library of Congress Cataloguing in Publication Data
Studies in the economic history of the Pacific Rim/
edited by Sally M. Miller, A.J.H. Latham and Dennis O. Flynn
p. cm.
Includes bibliographical references and index.
1. Pacific Area—Economic conditions. I. Miller, Sally M., 1937– II. Latham, A.J.H. III. O. Flynn, Dennis
HC681.S78 1997
330.99–dc21 96–50306
CIP

ISBN: 978-0-415-14819-1 (hbk)
ISBN: 978-1-138-98315-1 (pbk)

Publisher's Note

The publisher has gone to great lengths to ensure the quality of this reprint but points out that some imperfections in the original may be apparent

For the
John Muir Center for Regional Studies
of the
University of the Pacific

CONTENTS

Part II Selected Economic Issues in Pacific Rim History

FIGURES

TABLES

CONTRIBUTORS

David A. Chappell is Professor of Pacific Islands History at the University of Hawaii. He received his BA (Syracuse) and MA (Stanford) in history and taught in the US Peace Corps in West Africa, thereafter earning a PhD in Pacific History (Hawaii) in 1991. He now teaches at the University of Hawaii, has published numerous articles on the Pacific Islands, and is preparing a book on Islander work and travel aboard Euroamerican ships.

Tsu-yu Chen is Professor of History at the Institute of Modern History in Taipei, Taiwan. She graduated from National Taiwan University, and received her PhD in history in 1980. She has published two books and more than thirty articles concerning international trade and industry in modern China and Taiwan. She is working on research on Japan's coal mining investment in China in the early twentieth century.

Karen Clay is Professor of Economics at the University of Toronto. She received her PhD from Stanford in 1994. She is currently working on an examination of the California Land Act of 1851.

Douglas Daigle is an environmental advocate and educator, and received an MA in Environmental Ethics from Colorado State University. Formerly, he was education director at the Pacific Environment and Resources Center and is currently with the Coalition to Restore Coastal Louisiana in Baton Rouge.

Paul D'Arcy teaches Pacific History at the Australian National University in Canberra. He earned his undergraduate degree at the University of Otago, New Zealand, and then did postgraduate work at the University of Hawaii in Pacific Islands history. His current research interest is on different cultures' uses of, and attitudes towards, the sea, particularly those cultures of the Pacific Rim.

Arthur P. Dudden is Professor Emeritus of History at Bryn Mawr College, having earned his PhD from the University of Michigan. He has been the Fulbright Research Scholar in Denmark, and the Founding President of the

Fulbright Association. His most recent books are *American Humor* and *The American Pacific From the Old China Trade to the Present.*

Dennis O. Flynn is Professor of Economics, University of the Pacific. He has published many articles on various aspects of early-modern monetary history including 'Comparing the Tokugawa Shogunate with Habsburg Spain: Two Silver-Based Empires in a Global Setting', in J. Tracy (ed.), *The Political Economy of Merchant Empires* (1991).

Annick Foucrier is Assistant Professor at the University of Paris-Nord. She earned her PhD at the École des Hautes Études en Sciences Sociales; her dissertation has won awards from both the Society for North American Studies and from the French Commission for Maritime History. She is presently working on a book about the French presence in California.

Lionel E. Frost is Senior Lecturer in Economic History at La Trobe University in Melbourne, Australia. He is the author of *Australian Cities in Comparative View* (1990), *The New Urban Frontier: Urbanization and City-Building in Australia and the American West* (1991), and *Coming Full Circle: An Economic History of the Pacific Rim* (with Eric Jones and Colin White, 1993).

Arturo Giráldez is Assistant Professor of Spanish at the University of the Pacific. He obtained a PhD in Spanish Literature at the University of California, Santa Barbara in 1990. He is currently completing a PhD dissertation in History at the University of Madrid on the Philippines trade in the early-modern era.

Frank H.H. King is Professor Emeritus, University of Hong Kong, and has most recently been Visiting Professor in the University of Reading, England. A graduate of Stanford and Oxford universities, he was an economist with the World Bank and director of the Centre of Asian Studies, University of Hong Kong. His research focus has been the monetary history of East and Southeast Asia and he is the author of a four-volume history of the Hong Kong and Shanghai Banking Corporation.

A.J.H. Latham is Senior Lecturer in International Economic History at University College, Swansea. He is the author of *Old Calabar 1600–1891*; *The Impact of the International Economy Upon a Traditional Society* (1973); *The International Economy and the Undeveloped World, 1865–1914* (1978; in Japanese, 1987), and *The Depression and the Developing World, 1914–1939* (1981). He was co-editor of *The Market in History* (1986) and co-author of *Decline and Recovery in Britain's Overseas Trade, 1873–1914* (1993). He is currently working on the history of the international rice trade.

John McNeill earned his PhD at Duke University, and is Professor of History at Georgetown University. His books include *The Mountains of the*

Mediterranean World: An Environmental History (1992) and *Atlantic American Societies* (1992). He has written articles on environmental history dealing with North Africa, China, Brazil, and the Pacific islands, among other places. His next book will be an environmental history of the world in the twentieth century.

Sally M. Miller is Professor of History and Editor at the John Muir Center of the University of the Pacific, having earned her PhD at the University of Toronto. She has authored or edited a number of books, including *The Radical Immigrant, 1820–1920* (1974), *The Ethnic Press in the United States* (1987), and *John Muir: Life and Work* (1993). She has held Fulbright appointments at the University of Otago in New Zealand and at the University of Turku in Finland.

David J. St Clair is Professor of Economics at California State University, Hayward. He is the author of *The Motorization of American Cities* (1986) and was the recipient of the Allan Nevins Prize in 1979. He received his PhD in Economics from the University of Utah.

R. Bin Wong studied Chinese and European history at Harvard University (MA and PhD). He is the co-author, of *Nourish the People* and of numerous articles. He has held research and teaching positions in the Society of Fellows of the University of Michigan; Institute of Economics of the Chinese Academy of Social Sciences; Institute of Oriental Culture of the University of Tokyo; and the École des Hautes Études en Sciences Sociales in Paris. He currently teaches history at the University of California, Irvine, where he also directs a programme in East Asian Studies.

ACKNOWLEDGEMENTS

The editors wish to thank the John Muir Center for Regional Studies of the University of the Pacific for its support in this project. They also express their gratitude to the various authors without whose efforts this work would have been impossible. The support of Dean Robert R. Benedetti of the College of the Pacific and Professor Ronald H. Limbaugh of its History Department enabled this project to move from its planning stage to its completion. Lastly, and perhaps most importantly, the staff of the Muir Center, especially Marilyn Norton for her unfailing helpfulness and good humour no matter how trying the moment might be, was indispensable in this entire endeavor. The editors of course bear full responsibility for any problems or errors in the work.

1

INTRODUCTION

The Pacific Rim's past deserves a future

Dennis O. Flynn and Arturo Giráldez

BACKGROUND

One cannot normally trace the origin of a major phenomenon in economic history, such as the transition from feudalism to capitalism, the price revolution, or the Industrial Revolution, to a specific place or time. Historical eras are multifaceted, convoluted, and therefore generally defy scholarly attempts to specify dates of origin. The birth of Pacific Rim trade is an exception to this rule: it dates from the founding of the city of Manila in the year 1571.[1] Substantial, continuous trade between Asia and the Americas did not exist prior to the founding of the city of Manila; Pacific Rim trade began in 1571, not earlier and not later. It seems strange that we are entering an era dubbed the "Pacific Century" in which trade around the Pacific Ocean has emerged as a dominant force in the world economy at a time when the academic world seems so disinterested in how Pacific Rim trade originated.

Lack of interest in the early history of the Pacific trade may be attributable to the conventional perception that, after a promising start, Pacific trade via the Manila Galleons faded dramatically following the first quarter of the seventeenth century. After all, the eminent French historian Pierre Chaunu (1960) claimed that the spectacular flowering of the Acapulco–Manila trade from 1571 through the 1620s was followed by abrupt, yet protracted decline. Chaunu's influential investigation was based upon records of official Spanish *almojarifazgo* tax receipts, which did indeed register decline.

Chaunu's allegation of a withering Pacific Rim trade does not correspond with contemporary claims that smuggling rose substantially as a proportion of total Pacific galleon trade, and Chaunu's influential conclusions also conflict with important scholarship since 1961. Han-Sheng Chuan (1969) offers an Asian perspective on the Galleon trade which contrasts sharply with Chaunu's Atlantic-centered orthodoxy. Chuan's study of documents in the Blair and Robertson (1903–9) collection led him to conclude that the Manila Galleons carried an annual average of 2 million pesos of silver toward China throughout the seventeenth century; he could find no evidence of a drop off after the 1620s. Professor Chuan's work has been mostly ignored, as far as we know, but recent research backs his contention that 2 million pesos of silver crossed the Pacific throughout the last three-quarters of the seventeenth century.[2] In sum, Chaunu's post-1620s decline in Pacific trade is a myth. Official tax records do reflect a decline in tax revenues, but official records capture only a fraction of actual trade activity. As indicated, smuggling comprised a rising percentage of Pacific trade during the seventeenth century. When legal trade is combined with contraband activity, the picture which emerges is an overall Pacific trade which continued at the level of 2 million pesos annually throughout the seventeenth century. The incorrect, conventional wisdom on this subject has contributed to a lack of interest in early Pacific Rim economic history.

Just how large was 2-million pesos in trade during the seventeenth century? If it is true that 2 million pesos in silver passed annually through Manila for more than a century after 1571, in other words, how might one assess the significance of this particular number? One bench mark against which we can compare 2 million pesos (over 50 tons of pure silver) is to compare it with the value of shipments between Europe and Asia carried by the Portuguese Estado da India, the Dutch East India Company, and the English East India Company *combined*; the surprising total here is again approximately 2 million pesos per year.[3] Knowing that these three behemoths carried mostly silver to Asia, as did the Manila Galleons, how can we justify the continuing attention upon these particular European institutions, while simultaneously ignoring the equally substantial Pacific leg of world trade? The answer lies, not in denying the significance of European–Asian trade, but rather in acknowledging that the history of Pacific Rim interchange is worthy of equal attention. The Americas and Asia have engaged in substantial direct trade for the past 425 years, yet the evolution of this trading relationship is not part of the collective consciousness of the scholarly world.

The impact of these vast exports of American silver on China's economy is a significant and interesting topic in its own right, but is not entered into here.[4] It may be helpful, however, to consider briefly a few important effects of the Manila trade on the American side. At the main square of Mexico City, authorities established a "Parian" (named after the famous Chinese neighborhoods in Manila), in which all kinds of products arriving via the Philippines were sold.[5]

The trade between Mexico and Peru also reflected the vitality of the flourishing Manila trade. Imports from China ruined the market for finished Spanish silk goods in Mexico, but the Philippine trade attracted large supplies of cheap silk yarn to Mexican manufacturers; in turn, a substantial portion of Mexico's thriving production of finished-silk output was thereby exported to Peru. A 1604 decree by the Spanish government was designed to suppress all trade between the two viceroyalties; the same law was reissued in 1609, 1620, 1634, 1636, and 1706, the repetition of which indicates the lack of control imperial authorities exercised over such distant markets. When Mexican silk fabrics were significantly blocked from the Peruvian market as a result of the 1634 decree, however, Mexico's powerful silk manufacturers were destroyed. The 1634 prohibition seems only to have stimulated trans-Pacific trade in finished silk products, as commodities from Manila comprised 90 percent or more of the goods traded between Mexico and Peru (Borah, 1954, p. 123). In 1735 two Spanish commissioners, Jorge Juan y Santacilla and Antonio de Ulloa, visited Central and South America and secretly reported on the illicit trade: "Juan and Ulloa saw Chinese porcelain for sale in the shops of Lima and Chinese silks were sold and worn quite openly from Chile to Panama" (Schurz, 1959, p. 370). Once again, such descriptions (many more of which could be offered) are inconsistent with the view that trade via Manila had experienced protracted decline during the previous century.

It has been stated already that the Pacific trade was motivated by profit-seeking commercial interests, yet this trade activity yielded some broader, long-term surprises on the Asian side. Manila was a conduit for biological exchange between the Americas and Asia. For example, the American sweet potato, maize, groundnuts, and tobacco were all introduced into Southern China via Manila. If we consider that the Chinese population boom from 1790 to 1840 is attributable in large part to the introduction of edible American plants, then we can begin to glimpse some truly historic ramifications of the Manila trade route (see Fairbank, 1992, pp. 168–169). Silver–silk trade profits definitely motivated the birth of Pacific Rim trade, and silver continued to play a prominent role all the way through the eighteenth century; but sometimes commercial interactions generate unexpected consequences which are not normally considered under the narrow rubric "trade issues." Humans, flora, and fauna migrated alongside commercial products. The result was a dramatically altered landscape neither intended nor imagined by contemporary commercial participants and their governments. The foregoing implies that early-modern Pacific commerce should be regarded as an extremely important force which helped shape numerous societies around the Pacific Rim.

Personal research on world silver flows, especially silver's journey via the Manila Galleons, prompted a search for books and articles which might provide an overview of over four centuries of Pacific Rim interchange. For years, scholars around the world have given the same answer: no long-term overview of the Pacific Rim exists in any language. This implied that there was no such thing as "Pacific Rim History." Failure to acknowledge an over-420-year trade relationship covering one-third of the globe's surface seemed like a glaring intellectual omission, so the University of the Pacific agreed to host the world's first conference on Pacific Rim History over the weekend of May 1, 1994. Fifty scholars from a dozen countries presented papers on diverse aspects of Pacific Rim History. A sampling of these essays (in revised form) comprises the body of this volume.

It is clear that Pacific Rim History is not yet mature enough to offer a true historical synthesis. If one common denominator arises, it is that China has been, and continues to be, a major focal point of Pacific Rim attention over the centuries.

The chapters of this volume are divided in two main categories: (1) General overviews of long historical processes, and (2) studies of more specific issues. In "Overviews of the Pacific Rim" the several chapters consider general historical trends spanning prehistoric times to the present. The interdisciplinary nature of the inquiry and the wide scope of these studies permit identification of some webs of complex relationships among Pacific societies. The section on "Selected Economic Issues" contains diverse chapters which focus on specific issues and demonstrate clearly some of the crucial links connecting societies in and around the Pacific.

OVERVIEWS OF THE PACIFIC RIM

In "No Empty Ocean: Trade and Interaction Across the Pacific Ocean to the Middle of the Eighteenth Century," Paul D'Arcy states that there have been few attempts to construct an image of the Pacific parallel to the works of Fernand Braudel for the Mediterranean and K.N. Chaudhuri for the Indian Ocean. D'Arcy deals mainly with exchanges between Pacific peoples before the establishment of a sustained European presence. The Pacific archipelagos were settled by peoples from South-East Asia during the Pleistocene Era 50,000 years ago. Due to cool temperatures, the sea-level was lower, which created narrower straits between land. This explains the occupation of America by humans who crossed the Bering land-bridge. The remainder of Oceania seems to have been colonized in a 2,000–year period beginning around 3,500 years ago. Relatively predictable current and wind patterns and clear skies in the Pacific Ocean facilitated navigation of canoes sailing into the prevailing south-east trade winds. The period AD 1100 to 1500 was one of inter-island voyages and therefore of disruption to established societies and trade networks; this appears especially to have been the case in southern Papua and some islands in Melanesia. Some also attribute changes in Hawaii and New Zealand to visitors from Tahiti. Use of the lateen sail expanded through South-East Asia and was used in Micronesia, which indicates contacts between the peoples of the region. Interaction between Eastern and Western Polynesia appears to have been rare, however, in the centuries prior to sustained contacts with Europeans. Eastern Micronesia also had limited contacts with other island groups. The Yapese Empire was a network of exchange between the eastern Carolines and Yap in Western Micronesia, which explains shared characteristics with populations living in that area.

Less evidence exists of contacts before the European arrival in the northern and eastern Pacific. However, DNA research indicates some common genetic material shared by American Indians and aboriginal populations in Asia, Polynesia and Melanesia. Also, unintended arrivals in the Americas by Chinese and Japanese sailors may have been possible. Some scholars perceive cultural similarities between China and Mesoamerica. Cases of links between East Asia and Peru and Ecuador and between Polynesia and South America do exist. Nonetheless, evidence connecting these areas could have been the result of sporadic events. Only Fiji, Samoa, the Tonga triangle, the Society Islands–Tuamotu area, and the Yapese Empire seem to have developed sustained relationships. For unknown reasons, contacts seem to have disappeared with the passage of time in other archipelagos. Island societies appear to have been in relative isolation, with populations adapting items and cultural traits according to local circumstances.

Hawaiian society experienced population expansion between AD 1100 and 1650 which entailed technological, social and political changes. The demographic increase was associated with agricultural expansion in the form of new fields at high altitude and irrigation in the valleys. Class societies, which replaced kin group organization, were related to agricultural developments. Competition for land caused warfare and the emergence of powerful chiefs.

There is a legend of white men arriving during the seventeenth century, which could refer to Spaniards from a lost Manila Galleon. European contacts with Tahiti are supported by the legend of a priest called Paao, who introduced the idea of human sacrifices into the religious practices of the islanders. Common words, technology and the possible introduction of the sweet potato and the coconut also indicate contacts.

In "Coming Full Circle: A Long-term Perspective on the Pacific Rim," Lionel E. Frost argues that proper understanding of the present and future of the Pacific Rim necessitates study of the Rim's long-term history. But history is itself dynamic; static histories sometimes confine as well as enlighten. An example is the traditional, Eurocentric view that economic growth occurred abruptly in particular places over relatively short periods of time, like the conventional interpretation of the Industrial Revolution in England. The poor performance of Asian economies during the first part of the twentieth century contributed to the perception that Asian societies were unable to grow, perhaps due to cultural-religious constraints such as the so-called Confucian ethic. Yet, some of the fastest-growing economies in the world today are located around the Pacific Rim. East Asian countries, Japan, South Korea, Taiwan and Hong Kong, and the coastal provinces of China and Singapore, Malaysia and Thailand are the protagonists of these seemingly startling developments. After the Second World War, Japan experienced an unexpectedly speedy recovery, due partly to importing investment and technology and partly to US military protection. US government expenditures also stimulated the growth of the American West, which in turn stimulated American trade with Asia. By 1987, 'America's Pacific trade was half as big as its Atlantic trade.'

Once considered incapable of growth, Asian societies have themselves become models of growth today. A more-balanced, less-Eurocentric study of history helps locate today's world within a broader perspective. In late-T'ang and early-Song China, as well as in Japan during the Tokugawa era, periods of substantial economic growth occurred without industrialization. Perhaps European and European-American prominence in the world economy should be considered a transitory (and relatively brief) phenomenon between such periods and the renewed dynamism in East Asia today. Thus, the Pacific Rim has come "full circle", with the "rise of the Pacific" interpreted as a "return to prominence". A long-term perspective reveals that economic growth was not a uniquely European phenomenon. The values of Confucianism are evidently adaptable to different circumstances, indicating that perhaps culture is a poor predictor of economic change.

More important than "culture" for understanding economic growth in East Asia is the role played by governments, which sometimes impede and other times facilitate market-based activities. The study of patterns of public–private interaction is an area where the Asia-Pacific region may offer, on the one hand, useful alternative models of economic development. The dramatic recent surge of Asian economies has had serious ecological consequences, on the other hand, which also must be taken into consideration. Damage to the environment is visible in urban areas where pollution, population growth, and poverty are pronounced. Again in this sphere, the role of governmental institutions is fundamental if urban population growth rates are to be sustained.

In "Peripheralization of the Center: A Historical Overview of Pacific Island Micro-States," David A. Chappell points out that, despite optimistic images of an integrated Pacific Basin economy, from the point of view of the insular micro-societies "the region shows far more incoherence, limitations and inequities than might be expected." In the eye of this economic vortex, the small insular societies have adopted strategies to accommodate themselves to a rapidly changing world.

For millennia the ocean was a barrier for the societies living around its shores. Five thousand years ago in the southwestern Pacific, the Austronesian peoples expanded in an eastward direction in order to occupy ocean archipelagos. These societies maintained links among themselves, but their self-contained world was out of reach of populations occupying the continental Rim. Notwithstanding the conquest of Guam in 1662, the Manila Galleons did not break the isolation of the Pacific Islands. Only after Cook's explorations in the eighteenth century did these insular societies increasingly become linked to the world economy. Hawaii was a stopping point for the merchants involved in the fur trade between the Pacific northwest and Canton; similarly, the Chinese market for sandalwood and *bêche-de-mer* incorporated other Islanders into a wider web of economic forces.

A radical transformation of island societies occurred after the European arrival. Island demographics changed due to alien diseases and immigration, commercial plantations multiplied and the archipelagos were divided among colonial powers. The Second World War and the subsequent Cold War left Island societies marginalized, but with increased knowledge of the material wealth of the outside world. With the exception of Melanesia minerals, however, most islands contain few resources and therefore can offer the outside world only strategic bases, migrant labor, and tourist resorts. In response to this situation, islanders have implemented an array of strategies representing "the cutting edge of global interdependence."

A new category in international law is a form of partial sovereignty called Free Association. The Cook Islands in 1965 and Niue in 1974 became Freely Associated with New Zealand; a Compact of Free Association also exists between the United States and two Micronesian states. Another strategy for modernization is called MRAB (migration, remittance, aid and bureaucracy), one effect of which is that there "are more Samoans in Los Angeles today than in Pago Pago." In order to increase revenues, some states charge foreign ships for use of their 200-mile Exclusive Economic Zones. Tax privileges and off-shore banks, tourism and, in some cases, labor-intensive manufacturing provide alternative avenues to economic development. To cope with the modern world, the islanders produce strategies consistent with their historical tradition of voyaging. According to Chappell, their " 'transnational corporations of kin' are building diaspora societies whose cores and peripheries meet at the airport."

John McNeill's "Pacific Rim Economies and Pacific Island Ecologies from Magellan to MITI" outlines the main ecological changes produced in the Pacific islands after 1521. In an ecological sense, the oceanic islands remained relatively isolated from the rest of the world after the initial settlers arrived and until the sixteenth century. The ecological impact on the islands during the first centuries of European expansion was modest considering that from 1521 to 1769 only 450 European ships crossed the Pacific. Although the 'Magellan Exchange' reached the Asian shores in the form of American plants like maize, potato, and cassava, the processes of change dramatically accelerated after Cook's voyages: "The 1760s were to the Pacific what the 1490s were to Atlantic America."

The first consequence of the European contact with islanders was a demographic catastrophe. In many islands population declined by 90 or 95 per cent; the numbers stabilized around 1880–1920 and subsequently grew. Diseases, enslavement and migration were factors in the decline. Labor migration contributed to the spread of germs around the Pacific, therefore increasing the death rate. The introduction of new crops and alien species, like grazing animals, mosquitoes and rodents, altered the island ecology in numerous ways. "All told, the arrival of Europeans, with their 'portmanteau biota' and their connections to the Rim, was a disaster for lowland organisms and soils in the Pacific islands."

European voyages and settlements were the unifying forces around the Pacific but the economic demand underlying the system lay elsewhere: "European and American merchants served as middlemen between Chinese markets and Pacific island ecosystems." The exploitation of the Pacific after Cook implied a depletion of resources on a grand scale. With the exception of whaling, the extractive activities were directed to the Chinese market. Sandalwood, sealskins, *bêche-de-mer*, timber and many other products were exchanged for Western manufactures and finally for Chinese silk and tea. There was a "triangular trade" linking the Pacific island economies to Europe, North America and China and, according to McNeill, "China's exports were the prize that energized the whole system." Suddenly societies which had been isolated for millennia found themselves linked to wide trade networks and huge markets with millions of people demanding products from their fragile ecosystems. The "Age of Cook" (1769–1880) was "a point of punctuation in the punctuated equilibrium of Pacific evolution."

From a closer perspective the Pacific Ocean evolution could be divided between an era of fast change (1790–1850) and one of a slower-paced transformation (1850–80). Changes in the China market had very much to do with this evolution. After 1850 Chinese demand was reduced due to a scarcity of Pacific products previously gathered, as well as the fact that tea could now be exchanged for opium after the British East India Company began growing it in Bengal.

Plantation agriculture and the transportation revolution accelerated environmental change. The Panama Canal lowered the costs of maritime transport; after the decline of shipping, air traffic became predominant. As a consequence, new biological invaders joined the already-colonized islands. Other factors leading to ecological change were forest clearance due to the establishments of plantations, subsistence agriculture, the timber trade, and the need for fuel wood. Mining destroyed the environment of several islands. The biggest copper mine was located until 1988 in Papua, and phosphate mining is linked to Japanese agriculture and the livestock economies of Australia and New Zealand. All of these processes were facilitated by colonial presences: Australia and New Zealand acquired phosphate under the British power umbrella, and the United States supported the planters and cattle ranchers in Hawaii.

The same forces from Cook's time are present in the twentieth century, but with significant differences: first, population growth and tourism are creating corresponding increments in environmental pressures; and military requirements are having impacts stemming from United States, British, and French nuclear programs. In "The American Pacific: Where the West was also Won," Arthur P. Dudden also places China at the center of analysis. Since 1700 the North American colonists imported Chinese products and, after the American Revolution, merchants from the East Coast arrived in Canton. Shortly thereafter, American ships crossed the Pacific and American expansion accelerated. American whalers and seal hunters reached the South American coast and Antarctica by 1800. In 1854 Commodore Matthew Perry imposed a commercial treaty on the isolationist Tokugawas. These entrepreneurial activities were accompanied by territorial gains, and California joined the Union in 1850, followed by Oregon in 1859, while Alaska was purchased from the Russians in 1867. Hawaii was annexed in 1898, following acquisition of the Philippines after the defeat of Spain in the same year. For the United States, "China's proximity to Manila was the primary attraction the Philippine Islands had to offer."

Behind this chain of events was a political vision of a western commercial empire delineated by William Henry Seward. According to Seward, the contest for world pre-eminence would be in Asia after the commercial unification of both hemispheres. But shortly after the Philippine acquisition, European powers divided China into spheres of influence. In response, US Secretary of State John Hay circulated the "Open Door" notes, which required a policy of open trade, territorial integrity and independence for China. This political framework was the underlying ideology propelling United States actions in East Asia. Underneath such proclamations was the economic struggle for the Chinese market. European wars and revolutions excluded European powers from the East Asia competition, which "by 1919 after the First World War and the Russian Revolution, came to mean [US] competition almost exclusively against Japan over China."

Negotiations in the early 1940s proved fruitless and, after Pearl Harbor, the United States and Japan fought over China. The Japanese "Fifteen Years War" to dominate China was lost, and hegemony in the Pacific region passed to the United States. The fall of Saigon in 1975 "marked [for a brief period of time] the tidal retreat of the American imperial frontier from East Asia and the western Pacific, the end of the epoch of westward destiny." Developments today must be seen in the context of a continuing struggle over the market potential of China.

SELECTED ECONOMIC ISSUES

In "The French Presence in the Pacific Ocean and California (1700–1850)," Annick Foucrier outlines the origins of the French appearance in Pacific waters. Toward the end of the sixteenth century French ships were trading in South American ports, but it was in the early eighteenth century that French navigators began to explore the Pacific. Jean François de Laperouse was a prominent visitor to California, and official expeditions to the same territory followed during the nineteenth century. French whaling ships had already visited Californian shores for repair and rest, but the American West was not the center of the French strategy. The Pacific Islands became focal points of French interests. A French admiral took possession over the Marquesas islands in 1842 and a protectorate was established over Tahiti.

France maintained territories in North America until the end of the eighteenth century, and the sale of Louisiana in 1803 terminated the concept of a French American Empire. French consuls maintained a presence in California, although the major countries there at the end of the eighteenth century were Spain, Russia and the British. The Spanish missions of Alta California were a response to the Russian settlements north of San Francisco. The competition finished when California became Mexican in 1821 after Mexican independence; California became American by the Treaty of Guadalupe Hidalgo in 1848. Prior to the Treaty of Guadalupe Hildalgo, France was given the opportunity to occupy an enclave on the California coast. In 1841 it rejected Sutter's offer to acquire Bodega Bay, which he then sold to the Russians. French captains engaged in the South Pacific paid little attention to such possibilities.

Pacific Rim banking history has been badly neglected in the literature, but in " 'Eastwards of the Cape of Good Hope': British Overseas Banking on the Pacific Rim, 1830–70," Frank H.H. King outlines the main features of Pacific Rim banking during the period 1830–70. British and British imperial institutions developed such a domination that no effective international rivalry appeared prior to 1870. Non-British merchants and others patronized and even became directors of British overseas banks: "Such disparate territories as Australia, China, British Columbia, Chile, California, Japan, the Philippines, and the Straits Settlements – virtually covering the Pacific Rim – were served by British overseas banks characterized by common regulatory origins."

The organizational development of British overseas banks requires study separate from English banks because overseas banking policy was controlled by the Treasury, governments of the various territories, and the Foreign Office, leading to a differentiation in form and jurisdiction among other things.

Operating banks in multiple jurisdictions automatically created problems involving diverse and not necessarily compatible regulatory requirements. Promoters of joint-stock banks wanted one or more of the following privileges: limited liability, the right of note issue, and acceptance of those notes by colonial treasuries. Regulators established rules, the Colonial Banking Regulations (CBR), as a guide accepting banks under a variety of institutional scenarios, and one "particular feature of the CBR was that a chartered bank should publish its accounts so that the public could judge for itself." Banks established under the CBR were totally controlled in terms of note-issuing capabilities, making such notes safer for the general public; banks established in the UK but operating overseas, on the other hand, were not restricted in their overseas note issues (although these entailed unlimited liability). Economic historians have argued that British governments were able to put the latest theories into practice via the CBR, while intractable domestic interests blocked such moves domestically. Except in the case of banknotes, however, the Treasury acted mostly as a "gate-keeper" and made little use of its authority once a bank had been chartered.

Until the late 1840s, British policy intended uniformity, as accounts had to be kept in pound/shilling/pence units, and the CBR requirements obtained. But then responsible legislatures developed in the territories, limited liability became general, and British banking moved into currency areas beyond Imperial control, introducing the issue of currency-exchange risk. Because banks valued government business and/or note issue privileges, even after banking regulations changed in 1862 the "Treasury, which was beginning to question its ability to regulate an Empire-wide banking system, found itself still responsible for chartered banks." While Treasury policy precluded global banking, Frank King concludes that British banking made unique contributions to Pacific Rim commerce in the middle of the nineteenth century.

Economic dynamism in Asia has been of great interest in recent years and in "The Reconstruction of Hong Kong Nineteenth-Century Trade Pacific Statistics: The Emergence of Asian Dynamism," A.J.H. Latham examines the trade activities of Hong Kong from 1877 to the First World War. During those years, Hong Kong's major role was as a redistribution center for Asian goods into China's domestic market. Most merchandise arrived from Chinese ports in transit to other Chinese ports, but some originated elsewhere, like rice from French Indo-China and Siam and opium from India. Besides China, Hong Kong was an important exporter to Singapore and the Straits settlements; much of this merchandise went to Chinese immigrant communities in the Malaysian Peninsula, Java, Sumatra and elsewhere in Asia.

Hong Kong played an important role as distributor of rice from Bangkok and French Indo-China. The main purchaser was again China, but rice also was shipped to Japan, Hawaii, and even California. The imports of rice in great quantities raise the question of a possible crisis in the production of foodstuffs in China; that is, some speculate that rice imports were required because of a collapse in Chinese supplies of food. Latham offers a revisionist argument with the opposite conclusion. He maintains that vigorous economic growth existed in China at this time. Rice was a preferred grain among a range of inferior grains and foods, and can be considered a luxury item. Increments in income generated by a robust Chinese economy allowed: "The reciprocal gain between the agricultural sector and nascent industrial sector which is a necessary process of industrialization [to begin]." Where others see crisis within China, Latham sees boom.

A commercial revolution in China occurred during the eleventh and twelfth centuries, and during the fifteenth century large fleets of junks reached Africa and the Middle East. The lack of subsequent trade developments along European lines, however, has prompted scholars to blame interference by the Chinese state for the failure of China to modernize during modern times. In "Chinese Views of the Money Supply and Foreign Trade, 1400–1850," R. Bin Wong argues that the historical facts do not coincide with this conventional hypothesis.

Chinese merchants established a powerful presence in South-East and North-East Asia during the sixteenth and seventeenth centuries, and along the tribute system a trade network between south China and South-East Asia flourished. A significant indicator of the importance of foreign trade is the prodigious quantities of silver arriving in China. This importation of silver formed the basis of commercial expansion; it also permitted the gradual commutation of land taxes into payments in silver. In other words, both the domestic market and the state itself had become dependent upon foreign trade.

As long as silver flowed into the economy, there was little concern among government officials. During periods of silver scarcity or silver exports, however, officials reacted with great consternation. Such was the case during the transition to the Qing Empire in the mid-seventeenth century, and also during the late nineteenth century when great quantities of silver were exported in exchange for opium. The deflation period of the seventeenth century produced an economic crisis. Proposals for dealing with the lack of silver included expansion of copper coin production and the reintroduction of paper money. When foreign trade resumed, silver imports increased and the price deflation disappeared. During the eighteenth century China's population more than doubled, implying a considerable expansion of the domestic economy and therefore of foreign trade. Again, inflows of silver rose accordingly.

Chinese officials were certainly aware of the crucial role played by international commerce, yet their priorities were different from those of Europeans. To the mercantile states of Europe, trade activity was essential for accumulating profits with which to compete with the other European powers. Merchants and the European states worked together. Merchant companies and new banking institutions were means through which to accumulate capital, and their mercantilist approach was uniquely European. But Chinese economic policy dedicated state support to the domestic economy. The government took care of water projects and food supplies in case of a catastrophe. Foreign trade and merchant activity were of secondary importance and, with the exception of silver scarcities, Chinese officials did not concern themselves much with commercial exchange.

It is not so easy to assess public policies in Europe towards China during this period. Despite attempts to retain them, European mercantilist states lost their silver supplies into international circuits which eventually ended in China, despite the Chinese lack of a theoretical interest in foreign trade. But the absence did not prevent the emergence of extremely successful Chinese commercial networks in Asia during the early modern period. The use of military force, not stronger economic policy, was the key to the trading victories by Europeans over late imperial agrarian China.

In "The Development of the Coal Mining Industry in Taiwan During the Japanese Colonial Occupation, 1895–1945," Tsu-yu Chen explains that after the First World War a strong Japanese market stimulated Taiwan's coal mining industry. Still, Taiwan exported even larger quantities of coal to southern China, South-east Asia, and Hong Kong. The transportation and marketing of coal was in the hands of the Mitsui *zaibatsu*; indeed, the Taiwanese coal industry was integrated with Japanese and Manchurian coal production.

A depression at the end of the war was followed in 1921 by a recovery stimulated partly by sales to steamships. The Jinan incident led to a Chinese ban on Japanese products, and this affected the export of Taiwanese coal to Southern China. Production declined rapidly on the eve of the world depression. To make matters worse, coal from Fushun entered the market after the Japanese conquered Manchuria in 1931, thus aggravating an already battered industry. However, in spite of Sino-Japanese tensions, the Taiyang Mining Co. was able to convince Japanese authorities to give priority to Taiwanese coal imports. Accelerating domestic industry, accompanied by improvements in transportation and mining technology, increased the demand for coal, and a reorganization of production by the Taiwanese Coal Mining Industry Association made Taiwanese coal competitive in the export market. This centralized policy coincided with the continuous increase in heavy industry in Japan, a thriving shipping industry, and expanded domestic industrialization. The Sino-Japanese war further increased the demand for coal, resulting in bigger exports to Japan and other Asian markets. This growth was interrupted by the Second World War.

In "Trade, Institutions, and Law: The Experience of Mexican California," Karen Clay examines the organization of trade in California under the Mexican government during secularization of the missions between 1830 and 1846. The year 1830 is significant because from that date there was distribution of land from the missions in the form of grants, which increased the income of many individuals and also the number of merchants.

British and American merchants, acting as intermediaries between wholesalers and retail customers of Europeans and European-Indians along the coast, are the focus of this study. Interaction with Native Americans appears to have been minimal. The traders' function was to exchange goods from Boston, South America and Mexico for local hides, tallow, furs, lumber and horns. The prosperity of market activity is reflected in records of duties collected in Monterey.

Credit was a crucial feature of trade in California, facilitating the exchange of goods. The use of such financial instruments indicates the existence of "private-order institutions" with rules that "individuals adhere together with punishments imposed by community members for violating these norms." California merchants confronted the complexities of trade along the coast, in a cost-reducing manner, by employing one another as agents. Agents collected debts, conducted business in distant places and established partnerships to purchase merchandise abroad. All of these functions were subject to the possibility of fraud, but such problems were kept in check by a private-order institution, "the merchant coalition." Letters and personal visits kept the coalition informed. Reputation prevented fraud and also was an incentive to resolve disagreements peacefully. It seems that disputes were resolved without need of arbitration, and few merchants were expelled from the coalition. This close-knit information network required exclusion of non-Anglo-American merchants from the coalition, since they could not be trusted. The coalition acted in a favorable environment provided by the merchants' knowledge of common and commercial law. The vast influx of goods, investment opportunities, and additional merchants after the Gold Rush led to dissolution of the coalition.

David J. St. Clair's "California Quicksilver in the Pacific Rim Economy, 1850–90" provides an excellent example of the dangers of focusing on "local" aspects of history while ignoring the global context in which "local events" were often linked over large distances. St. Clair focuses on mercury, one of the first and most important metals mined in Californian history.

By the early nineteenth century the Huancavelica mine in Peru was exhausted and mercury production was restricted to Almaden and Idria, since 1835 owned by the Rothschilds. By 1845 the New Almaden mercury mine was discovered close to San Jose in the Santa Cruz mountains, but full production did not begin until 1850. Between 1850 and 1900 New Almaden's mercury production represented half of world output, surpassing the combined production of the mines of Almaden and Idria. By the 1870s California produced two-thirds of the world's output, thereby breaking the Rothschild cartel monopoly. After 1890 the New Almaden mine suffered protracted decline.

Traditionally, historians have attributed development of the New Almaden mercury mine to stimulation from the rushes for California gold and Nevada silver. Close examination of export data, however, reveals a completely different picture. Over 57 per cent of New Almaden production went to Pacific markets beyond California, Nevada and New York. China was the biggest market, followed by Mexico and South America. New Almaden output had a world-wide impact on the price of mercury, of course, and silver production, including that in Nevada, was positively affected by the low mercury price because of its use in the patio process. Gold processing used much less mercury and therefore was affected less. The real story, however, is that Californian mercury was the raw material for Chinese vermilion, used to dye Chinese textiles marketed throughout the world. Due to elastic demand for mercury in the vermilion industry, price competition explains "why the struggle between the Rothschilds and California quicksilver producers was primarily waged in China." Low prices allowed the New Almaden mine to control the Chinese market until 1884.

The history of the New Almaden mine indicates the crucial importance of economies along the Pacific Rim in terms of developing mining in California. Until 1884 Pacific countries were the main importers of Californian mercury, most important among which was the Chinese vermilion.

According to Douglas Daigle's "Environmental Impacts of the Pacific Rim Timber Trade," the Pacific Basin contains the majority of the earth's forests, and two-thirds of the timber trade occurs around the Rim. Taking into consideration the importance of the forests in the regulation of global climate, the future of Pacific Basin forests is crucial for the well-being of the planet.

Tropical forests in the Rim have been particularly affected since the Second World War. Japan has been the main protagonist in Pacific timber trade for years and "still imports 90 percent of the wood shipped in the Pacific Rim." The Philippines, Indonesia and Malaysia were severely impacted by this trade, with negative consequences for native forests, tribal peoples and endangered species. Replacement of native forests by plantations does not compensate for the losses of natural habitats and biodiversity.

Temperate forests are currently the most intensely harvested in the world. The Pacific Northwest provided the United States with huge quantities of plywood and softwood lumber for decades, far surpassing the "sustained yield" potential of private and public lands. Consequently, the timber industry has moved to the southeast of the United States to such an extent that by "1986, the southeastern US supplied 47 percent of the nation's timber harvest, compared to 25 percent in the Pacific northwest."

Chile joined the Pacific Rim timber market, cutting down forests and converting them to monoculture plantations. Canada's temperate and boreal forests also became part of the global market, aided by government support in the form of infrastructure and tax exemptions. Temperate forests have not been impacted to the same extent as tropical ones, but large tracts have been converted into tree farms with the consequent loss of forest quality.

The boreal forests of Siberia and the Russian Far East are the most extensive forests on the planet. The main threat to these areas comes from the Russian domestic industry, but China is increasingly interested in Siberian forests. At the current rate of timber consumption "China will have harvested all of its remaining productive forests within a decade." Taking into consideration Chinese demand, in conjunction with East Asian and European markets, continued exploitation of Siberian forests is highly likely. Since these boreal areas are believed to be important in the regulation of climate, "widespread depletion of the northern taiga forests could accelerate the process of global warming."

Globalization of the timber trade is reflected in the Pacific market. Chips and pulp dominate demand now, rather than logs. In addition, changing transportation technology has caused a shift from land routes to ocean shipping. Substitutability of timber products now permits use of different species of trees, which explains the movement of the industry from tropical to boreal forests. On the whole, the prognosis for the future of the Pacific Rim timber trade is poor due to "the irreplaceable loss of biodiversity and ecosystems, harmful impacts on local and regional economies, and [questions about] how the timber industry can become sustainable."

CONCLUSION

In its current usage, the concept "Pacific Rim" geographically embraces mainland Asia, Japan and the United States. Australia and New Zealand are afterthoughts, while archipelagos between the coasts and Latin American countries are ignored altogether. The Rim does not seem to possess a common chronology prior to the Second World War.

In order to understand the complex dynamics of the present, it is imperative that the evolution of Pacific Rim structures be studied beyond the narrow limitations imposed by popular misconception. The aim is to establish a new field of research in Pacific Rim History in which historical relations among societies of the Pacific are studied from an interdisciplinary perspective and without exclusions in terms of space or time.

Substantial and sustained trade has spanned the Pacific since the founding of Manila in 1571. A vast demand for silver in China provoked the Acapulco–Manila Galleon trade, and it lasted for centuries. All of the world's dynamism did not emanate from Europe during the "Age of Expansion." The Asian economy, sporting cities five and ten times the size of the largest in Western Europe, was far larger than that of Europe in the sixteenth and seventeenth centuries. Japanese historian Takeshi Hamashita has proposed that tribute–trade relations with China must be considered a pivotal force in any conceptual framework for studying Asian history.[6] Certainly in early-modern times it was Chinese demand for silver which motivated the birth of both Pacific Rim trade and world trade.

As soon as the Pacific became integrated, China began to exercise a powerful pull on the societies of the entire region. The studies of this volume demonstrate that the Chinese market was a powerful attractor for Pacific products: silver from America, coal from Taiwan, rice from South-East Asia, mercury from California, skins, *bêche-de-mer*, and sandalwood from the Pacific archipelagos, timber from Siberia, to name a few of the products studied by the authors. China's relationship with various societies of the Rim is the most prominent intellectual theme unifying this collection of essays. Although much was learned at the 1994 California History Institute conference on the Pacific Rim, we know that most of the work remains to be done.

NOTES

1 See Flynn and Giraldez (1994, 1995) for discussion of the origin of Pacific Rim trade in 1571.

2 Corroboration of smuggled-trade volumes is difficult, of course, because official documents (by definition) do not record smuggled goods. The Manila trade offers an unusual opportunity, however, because it essentially involved a straight swap of American silver against Chinese silks. Flynn and Giraldez (1996) have investigated the value of Chinese silk flowing via Manila to Acapulco. Since silk was swapped directly for silver, export values must have been similar to import values. Interestingly, the secondary literature also suggests silk exports at 2 million pesos per year, the same volume as Chuan's estimate of total silver flows in the opposite direction. Two million pesos of silk could only have entered Acapulco annually if 2 million pesos of silver were also exported.

3 For perspective, Artur Attman (1986) estimates that a minimum of 6 million pesos of silver flowed to Asia via European ports during the seventeenth century. Thus, silver shipments aboard the Manila Galleons amounted to less than one-third of the amount flowing to China via Europe. Still, the Pacific's 2 million peso trade was gigantic and crucial when viewed from a global perspective.

4 Atwell (1977, 1982) has long maintained that American silver significantly impacted China's economy. Goldstone (1991), von Glahn (1996), and others have vigorously criticized Atwell's argument, but Flynn and Giráldez (1995) claim that many points in this dispute can be reconciled when viewed from a fresh perspective.

5 In 1703 Mexico City built permanent facilities for the Parian shopping center (Zaide, 1979, p. 490).

6 Takeshi Hamashita (1994) "The Tribute Trade System and Modern Asia," in *Japanese Industrialization and the Asian Economy,'* A.J.H. Latham and Heita Kawakatsu eds, p. 92.

BIBLIOGRAPHY

Attman, Artur (1986) *American Bullion in the European World Trade, 1600–1800*, Uppsala: Almqvist & Wicksell Tryckeri.

Atwell, William S. (1977) "Notes on silver, foreign trade, and the late Ming economy," *Ch'ing-shih wen-t'i*, 3: 1–33.

—— (1982) "International bullion flows and the Chinese economy circa 1530–1650," *Past and Present*, 95: 68–90.

Blair, E.H. and Robertson, J.A. (1903–9) *The Philippine Islands*, 55 vols, Cleveland, O.: Arthur H. Clarke.

Borah, W. (1954) *Early Colonial Trade and Navigation between Mexico and Peru*, Berkeley and Los Angeles, Calif.: University of California Press.

Chaunu, Pierre (1960) *Les Philippines et le Pacifique des Iberiques (XVIe, XVIIe, XVIIIe, siècles)*, Paris: SEVPEN.

Chuan, Han-Sheng (1969) "The inflow of American silver into China from the late Ming to the mid-Ch'ing Period," *Journal of the Institute of Chinese Studies of the Chinese University of Hong Kong*, 2: 61–75.

Fairbank, John K. (1992) *China: A New History*, Cambridge, Mass.: Harvard University Press.

Flynn, Dennis O. and Arturo Giraldez (1994) "China and the Manila Galleons," in *Japanese Industrialization and the Asian Economy*, eds A.J.H. Latham and H. Kawakatsu, London: Routledge.

—— (1995) "Born with a 'Silver Spoon': The Origin of World Trade in 1571," *Journal of World History*, 6 (2): 201–221.

—— (1996) "Silk for silver: Manila–Macao trade in the 17th Century," *Philippine Studies*, 44: 52–68.

Goldstone, Jack (1991) *Revolution and Rebellion in the Early Modern World*, Berkeley, Calif.: University of California Press.

Schurz, Lyle W. (1959) *The Manila Galleon*, New York: E.P. Dutton.

Takeshi Hamashita (1994) "The Tribute Trade System and Modern Asia," in *Japanese Industrialization and the Asian Economy*, eds A.J.H. Latham and Heita Kawakatsu, London and New York: Routledge.

von Glahn, Richard (1996) *Fountain of Fortune: Money and Monetary Policy in China, 1000–1700*, Berkeley, Calif.: University of California Press.

Zaide, Gregorio F. (1979) *The Pageant of Philippines History, Political, Economic and Socio-Cultural*, Manila: Philippine Education Company.

Part I

OVERVIEWS OF THE PACIFIC RIM

2

NO EMPTY OCEAN

Trade and interaction across the Pacific Ocean to the middle of the eighteenth century

Paul D'Arcy

The Pacific Ocean is a vast body of water. It covers an area greater than all of the land in the world combined: 9,200 miles separate Bering Strait in the north from Antarctica in the south. The Pacific Ocean is 10,400 miles wide at the equator, and over 12,000 miles wide at its widest point, from Singapore to Panama. In places it is devoid of islands for thousands of miles (Thomas 1963: 7–38; Cameron 1987: 24). Writer Ian Cameron typifies the attitudes of the modern inhabitants of the Pacific Rim when he reflects that, 'Nowhere else on Earth are the distances so vast, the sense of loneliness and isolation so aching' (Cameron 1987: 24).

Few have attempted to construct an image of the Pacific Ocean as a coherent entity in the way that Fernand Braudel has for the Mediterranean, or K.N. Chaudhuri has for the Indian Ocean (Braudel 1972–3; Chaudhuri 1985). To Braudel the whole Mediterranean 'shared a common destiny, a heavy one indeed, with identical problems and general trends if not identical consequences' (Braudel 1972–3: I, 14). For Chaudhuri, long distance trade, the monsoon climatic system, and broadly similar historical forces created a degree of cohesion amongst the four great civilizations that spanned the region. In the Irano-Arabic, Hindu, Indonesian and Chinese worlds 'the idea of a common geographical space defined by the exchange of ideas and material objects was quite strong, not only in the minds of merchants but also in those of political rulers and ordinary people' (Chaudhuri 1985: 21).

No such coherence has ever been attributed to the vastly more expansive world encompassed by the Pacific Ocean. The few Pacific-wide histories that have been attempted focus on the region's integration into a wider global economy which is seen as beginning when Europeans began to move into the Pacific. The modern concept of a Pacific community is essentially based on the modern economic relationship between East Asia and North America. It is a relationship with little legacy of pre-existing cultural or historical ties, and one that has only been made possible by communications and transport revolutions in the last two centuries.[1]

Prior to this phase the Pacific is generally viewed as a prohibitive void rather than an avenue for movement. Pre-European Pacific peoples are usually considered to have conducted localized interactions only, with a resultant consciousness that was at best regional rather than Pan-Pacific (Dirlik 1992: 64). This chapter will explore the scale and nature of exchanges between Pacific peoples in, and across, the Pacific (as opposed to around its margins) prior to the establishment of a sustained European presence in the Pacific from the late 1700s onwards. Only by establishing what existed beforehand can the impact of the Pacific's incorporation into a global trading system be fully comprehended.

The task at hand is complicated by the fact that most of the cultures concerned were oral cultures in this era rather than keepers of written records. Those that did record events on paper or stone rarely mention activities in the Pacific Ocean. Alternative sources do exist, but they tend not to produce the mass of detail that historians with recourse to literate cultures enjoy, or endure, as the case may be.

The fundamental problem faced by those investigating cultural interactions between non-literate societies is in assessing whether cultural similarities are the result of independent invention or diffusion between groups.[2] Resemblances may arise independently due to like needs appearing in areas with similar resource bases. The dating of artefacts may provide clues in searching for the diffusion of traits between areas. The probability of diffusion is greater if a trait appears suddenly in the archaeological record of one area without any obvious precedents like clear stylistic sequences, and at a time after the trait's appearance in the record of the assumed donor area.

The archaeological record is usually fragmentary, both in its temporal progression and in its representativeness of a culture in its totality. Non-perishable items may be found, but the host of invisible influences that shape their creation are seldom apparent. Artefacts can be described, but their function and cultural significance cannot unless recourse is made to ethnographic analogy from other, more fully recorded times. It is debatable whether consistency of function and beliefs can be assumed between different times any more than it can between distinct contemporaneous cultures.[3] Stylistic comparisons alone, devoid of meaning within a cultural complex, are shaky foundations upon which to base analysis. In his spirited defense of the idea of the independent invention of Pre-Columbian American cultural achievements, Nigel Davies points out that the Peruvian pottery from 800 BC is almost identical to Magbetu pottery made in Africa in the 1930s (Davies 1979: 14–15). At the very least a whole, linked complex of similar traits should be considered. Traits not shared can be significant. Similar pottery styles carry much less weight when one culture shows evidence of the use of the potter's wheel and the other does not (Davies 1979: 14).

The distribution of linguistic traits and botanic specimens are more solid foundations upon which to base cultural connections. It is unknown for the same plant species to originate in more than one place. Genetic investigation and radiocarbon dating allow origins to be established. If the species concerned cannot be transferred between its areas of distribution by non-human agency such as seeds eaten and excreted by birds, then human travel is implied. Large bodies of ocean form major barriers to many species of flora (and fauna) because of their reproductive vectors' limited tolerance to moisture and salinity (Davies 1979: 60–61). It is significant that the flora and fauna of the Pacific Islands diminishes noticeably the further east one goes as distances from continental land masses increase and gaps between neighbouring islands also increase (Oliver 1989: 10–13). Similar languages do not arise separately either. A group of related languages has one common source of origin. Speakers of related languages therefore have a historical connection which can be plotted by combining geographical location with language evolution through studying relationships between languages.[4]

In the absence of linguistic or botanical evidence for diffusion there is greater need to show that the peoples concerned were able to move between the areas involved when the diffusion of traits is suggested. For the Pacific Ocean this requires information on the historical evolution of maritime technology and skills, as well as on environmental factors affecting seafaring such as winds and ocean currents. Prehistoric sea cultures rarely left detailed accounts of their maritime skills and few prehistoric maritime vessels have been recovered from the sites of their last resting places. Most discussion of prehistoric voyaging in the Pacific is therefore based on analogies drawn from historical observations of early literate observers of Pacific cultures of the sea or on ethnographic data collected this century from cultures which still had knowledge of traditional maritime skills.[5] Some insights have been obtained by linguistic recreations of early proto-languages of current linguistic groups. Such information on maritime cultures is more useful when combined with analysis of environmental constraints on voyaging. Computer simulations of winds and ocean currents allow researchers to distinguish what was feasible and what was not at any given level of voyaging capability.[6] This can then be compared with the archaeological record to contrast what was possible and what appears to have actually happened.

The Pacific Ocean can be envisaged as two distinct zones that owe their features to the movement of the various tectonic plates that make up the earth's crust in this part of the globe. Where the lighter oceanic plates collide with the heavier continental plates of the Pacific Rim the earth's crust is ruptured by great fractures and the molten magma underneath this crust extrudes violently in dramatic volcanic activity; or the earth's crust is thrust upward as continental plates ride over the lighter oceanic plates. The result is a host of volcanic islands and atolls formed from the coral remains of living organisms that establish themselves in shallow waters atop subsided volcanos. About 80 per cent of the world's islands lie within the area bounded by Tokyo, Jakarta and Pitcairn Island. Outside of this area and the Pacific Rim the plates on the Pacific's seabed tend to drift apart rather than collide, so that the underlying magma oozes through the crust with much less pressure behind it. Gentle basins and ridges that do not break the ocean's surface are the result, creating a huge area of 'empty' ocean (Cameron 1987: 19–24; Oliver 1989: 1–6; Thomas 1963: 11).

A number of wind systems affect the Pacific Ocean. In the more open eastern two-thirds a series of zones cross the ocean from east to west, each with its own distinct pattern of surface winds. North of about latitude 25° North and south of about 27° South strong westerlies blow almost continuously all year round. Between these two belts are two belts of trade winds. In the Northern Hemisphere these blow from the northeast, while those south of the equator blow from the southeast. Their strength diminishes in the western third of the Pacific Ocean. Pacific trade winds are not continuous but do blow in every month of the year. They are at their most consistent between May and September. The remainder of the year is characterized by winds from the west as well as trade winds. Large areas of doldrums lie between the two trade-wind belts as far west as the Solomon Islands. The doldrums are noted for their light, variable winds and calms as well as squalls, heavy showers and thunderstorms (Oliver 1989: 8–9; Irwin 1992: 11–13; Muller and Oberlander 1978: 122–124).

The western third of the Pacific is dominated by monsoon and typhoon weather patterns arising from the periodic heating and cooling of the Asian land mass. The monsoon winds blow from the northwest away from Asia in the Northern Hemisphere winter, and from the southeast towards Asia in the Northern Hemisphere summer. Typhoons or hurricanes occur throughout much of the western tropical Pacific. Their associated high winds and torrential rains cause much devastation to islands in their path. In the Southern Hemisphere they generally coincide with the summer monsoon from November to March, typically forming at about 8° South and tracking west and then south. In the Northern Hemisphere they originate between 7° and 20° North around the Philippines in August through to October and move north towards Japan (Oliver 1984: 8–9; Irwin 1992: 11–12; Braden 1976: 75–89).

Two vast closed loops of ocean currents, or gyres, dominate the Pacific Ocean. The one north of the equator flows clockwise, while the other south of the equator flows anti-clockwise. The currents on the western side of these gyres increase in intensity as they flow to higher latitudes (i.e. away from the equator). This intensification is most noticeable in the Kuroshio Current in the Northwest Pacific where the current attains speeds of around 250 centimetres a second. These currents are deflected in places by intervening islands, particularly the southern, westward-moving flow. Between these two gyres is the Equatorial Countercurrent which flows eastward from the Caroline Islands across to Panama. Its width and position on a north–south axis varies during the year because of the seasonal inclination of the earth. This current attains speeds of only 50 centimetres per second. In the far north the Bering Strait bottleneck means that the North Pacific Ocean basin and the Arctic Ocean basin have their own separate, circulating currents rather one united system. The vast Southern Ocean surrounding Antarctica presents no such obstructions so that the largest surface flow in the world, the West Wind Drift, can flow eastward around the whole of the Antarctic continent (Oliver 1989: 7; Irwin 1992: 11–12; Braden 1976: 77; Muller and Oberlander 1978: 144–145; Anikouchine and Sternberg 1973: 96–98).

The Pacific Ocean is not a notably treacherous body of water upon which to travel. Experience and skill are needed to read its signs, but its wind and current patterns are constant enough to be relied upon, while sporadic and seasonal wind shifts ensure the possibility of voyaging in most directions for those incapable of sailing into the wind, and willing to wait for their desired conditions. There are many accounts of drift voyages both eastward and westward in the Pacific. The sun and stars are seldom obscured for more than 3 days at a time so that bearings can be maintained by those skilled in the art of celestial navigation.[7]

After years of debate it is now generally agreed that the part of the Pacific studded with islands was settled by peoples who came from Island South-East Asia. Their initial movement into the western margins of Oceania has been radiocarbon-dated to around 50,000 years ago during the Pleistocene era, when cooler global temperatures locked up much of the earth's water in huge ice sheets and glaciers. As a result the sea-level was considerably lower than it is today and islands were therefore larger and sea passages between land narrower than they are today (Thomas 1963: 10; Oliver 1989: 3–4; Irwin 1992: 124–125; Gibbons and Clunie 1986: 58–82; Bellwood 1987: 106–108). These same conditions created a land bridge across the Bering Strait. By the time that the warming of global temperatures created conditions close to today's sea-levels around 10,000 years ago there had been 30,000 years of movement across the Bering landbridge into the Americas, and humans had spread throughout much of the New World (Davies 1979: 243–244; Zegura 1985: 1–18). In the South-West Pacific human settlement had spread to Australia, New Guinea and some of New Guinea's more accessible offshore neighbouring islands in Island Melanesia. (Irwin 1992: 3, 18–30, 215; Howe 1984: 9–10, Campbell 1989: 31–33).

The remainder of Oceania seems to have been colonized in a 2,000-year period beginning around 3,500 years ago by what appears to have been a relatively coherent culture that is associated with the distribution of the Austronesian family of languages, a highly developed maritime culture based on outrigger sailing canoes and a distinct style of pottery known as lapita ware. There is a direct correlation between the distribution of outrigger canoes and Austronesian languages, while terms associated with outrigger canoes and sails appear in reconstructions of the Proto-Austronesian language. Lapita ware is found throughout Island Melanesia and Western Polynesia, with a high level of stylistic consistency throughout.[8] Archaeologist Patrick Kirch has suggested that this consistency reflects long-distance exchanges which would have served as a social mechanism encouraging exploration and colonization, secure in the knowledge that continued links with parent communities were a lifeline in case of adversity in newly discovered environments.[9] Spectrographic analysis enabling the identification of specific sources of obsidian, a volcanic rock much valued for sharp cutting tools, shows that obsidian from Talasea in New Britain was distributed through much of the Lapita culture area (Bellwood 1978: 247). Talasea obsidian has also been found at the site of Bukit Tengkorak on Borneo dated to the first millennium BC (Bellwood and Koon 1989: 613–622). Lapita culture exchanges were not necessarily via long distance voyaging. They may have passed through a series of shorter transfers down the line between neighboring communities as was the pattern in later prehistory for much of Island Melanesia.

Oceania is usually divided into three regions: Melanesia, Polynesia and Micronesia. This scheme is a European creation based largely on European perceptions. While differences in physical appearance and cultural practices between these regions are nowhere near as clean-cut as some have implied, differences do exist.[10] This has posed a problem for scholars of Oceania, particularly since mounting archaeological evidence suggests that the colonization of Oceania went from Island South-East Asia into Melanesia and on into Polynesia and Eastern Micronesia, while Western Micronesia seems to have been settled directly from Island South-East Asia.[11]

The archaeological record no longer allows for differences between Melanesians and Polynesians to be explained in terms of Polynesians passing rapidly through Melanesia as a discrete wave of people who had little interaction with Melanesians. Nor can the *main* source of Polynesia's colonizers be said to have bypassed Melanesia and come through Micronesia, the North Pacific or from South America, as some suggested earlier this century without the hindsight of today's archaeological record.[12] It is now generally regarded that today's Polynesians developed their distinctive culture and appearance in Polynesia. Even with Polynesia's relatively late settlement there was time for these distinctions to develop culturally and genetically, given that the initial colonizers would have formed a relatively small gene pool which would have brought out certain traits given the population's relative isolation from that time onwards (Houghton 1991: 167–196).

Outsiders still marvel at Oceanic peoples' mastery of their ocean environment. Until recently some still maintained that the Pacific Islands were settled as a result of unplanned or unwanted voyages brought about by an incomplete mastery of the skills needed to navigate and sail in open ocean out of sight of land.[13] In the last three decades a wealth of research has largely demolished this myth. Computer simulations of wind patterns and ocean currents show that canoes could not have reached all the islands that have evidence of pre-European settlement merely by drifting at the mercy of these winds and currents.[14] Ethnographic and historical research into Oceanic navigational skills and maritime technology, including reconstructed voyages using traditional skills and technology have greatly enhanced the impression of Oceanic peoples' abilities at sea.[15]

The most recent and most sophisticated work in this vein has been by archaeologist Geoffrey Irwin (Irwin 1992). A keen yachtsman himself, Irwin has argued convincingly that Oceania was settled by a deliberate strategy of sailing *into* prevailing south east trade winds. Navigational skills and maritime technology improved as early mariners moved into the Pacific. It was a gradual learning process. As Irwin notes:

> Without a doubt, it is safest to sail first in the direction that is normally upwind because one can expect the fastest trip back. The hard way is really the easy or safe way and this simple paradox is one of the keys to explaining the trajectory of human settlement. Practically every radiocarbon date in the remote Pacific supports the view that colonization went first against the prevailing winds and only then across and down them.
>
> (Irwin 1992: 7–8)

Historical records from the first Europeans to encounter Pacific Island cultures show that inter-island voyaging existed, but on a reduced scale from that of the past. Long-distance voyaging was still apparent in central Eastern Polynesia centred on the Society Islands, Western Polynesia and Fiji, and in much of Micronesia (Irwin 1992: 213–214; Finney 1979: 349–350; Lewis 1977: 29). Modern, academic writings portray external contacts as being of limited significance in the historical development of individual island societies after their initial colonization. Pre-European cultural development is usually seen to be driven by the interaction of a number of internal processes: the adaptation of the founding culture to a new environment, population growth on a limited land area, environmental change (both natural and human-induced), and cultural emphasis on competition for status channelled into warfare or the intensification of production for redistribution to forge social and political obligation.[16] The possibility of new arrivals introducing cultural innovations is not dismissed, but it is almost always considered of secondary importance to internal processes. Anthropologist Douglas Oliver's summation of his view of Tahitian prehistory is typical:

> The picture I perceive . . . is of numerous landings on the Society Islands throughout a millennium or more, from other archipelagoes near and far, and ranging in size from a lone and near-dead survivor in a drifting canoe to a modest-sized fleet. Most newcomers would have added some new ideas and objects to the local cultural inventory, and during the earlier centuries some of the larger-scale immigrations were probably near revolutionary in their influence. But as time passed and the local population made settlements on all islands of the archipelago, subsequent new arrivals, (say after about A.D. 1200), even large-scale ones, could not have been large enough, or culturally 'superior' enough, to have effected radical changes in the technological and social patterns that had by then become fairly well consolidated.
>
> (Oliver 1984: 1122)

Only recently have scholars begun to question this outlook. Irwin is critical of the tendency to focus studies on single island groups, or even on single islands, that this approach engenders. He writes that, 'communities were commonly connected in a wider social world of moving items and ideas, and were mutually if differentially exposed to changing circumstances' (Irwin 1992: 204).

Voyaging should not be seen as declining steadily from the days of initial exploration and colonization. It is more likely that it waxed and waned according to circumstances. Climatic variation may have influenced this process. A phenomena known as El Niño–Southern Oscillation occurs periodically in the South Pacific Ocean. It is characterized by a slackening of trade winds, increased westerly winds, and changes to ocean currents, with warm equatorial water extending down the South American coast (Irwin 1992: 89). During the little climatic Optimum (AD 750–1250) average temperatures warmed, trade winds became more mild, and there were more frequent and persistent westerly wind shifts (Irwin 1992: 89; Finney 1979: 349). Later the Little Ice Age (AD 1400–1850) resulted in stronger trade winds, more storms and decreased westerlies (Irwin 1992: 89). While the Pacific historian Oscar Spate believes that the Little Ice Age led to a decline in voyaging (Spate 1988: 30), anthropologist Ben Finney notes that in this era voyaging actually increased in some areas, notably Western Polynesia (Finney 1979: 349). Irwin is also unwilling to concede that climatic variation was detrimental to voyaging. He notes that the colonization of Oceania required coping with a number of weather systems in two hemispheres. Why should climatic variation in time be any more of a problem than climatic variation in space? Seafarers must be prepared for changeable weather conditions in any situation (Irwin 1992: 89–90).

Historian Ian Campbell does not emphasize climatic factors, but notes that archaeology, linguistics and oral traditions all suggest that the period from *c.* AD 1100 to 1500 was one of significant upheaval and inter-island movement in much of Oceania (Campbell 1989: 36). Long-distance trade networks along the southern coast of Papua seem to have been disrupted and reformulated in this era, judging from sharp discontinuities in pottery traditions followed by a later spreading of new pottery styles (Bellwood 1978: 269–270). Upheavals in Vanuatu are suggested by the end of Mangaasi pottery ware just before the appearance of stylistically very similar Vuda ware in Fiji, which seems distinct from previous Fijian pottery. Oral traditions from Vanuatu refer to inroads from peoples to the south around this time (Howe 1984: 30–31; Bellwood 1978: 265, 269–70). In Island Melanesia in general there is a trend towards a diminishing range for trade networks which, nevertheless, display historical continuity (Lewthwaite 1967: 62–63; Bellwood 1978: 102–104). Small, outlying islands in Melanesia seem to have been settled from Western Polynesia in this time, forming Polynesian enclaves – the so-called Polynesian outliers (Howe 1984: 15–16; Lewthwaite 1967: 63; Lewis 1977: 17, 30; Irwin 1992: 183–189). Significant changes also occur in Hawaiian and New Zealand Maori society in this era. These changes are often attributed, in part at least, to visiting voyagers from 'Kahiki' in oral traditions. Cultural similarities strongly suggest Tahiti as 'Kahiki', although many academics dismiss the idea of such contacts, preferring to attribute changes in the prehistoric record to internal evolution rather than a revolution from without.[17] (The case for Tahitian–Hawaiian links will be discussed in more detail later in this chapter.) No single, immediately apparent explanation exists to account for the events of this period just related. They may not be influenced by any common phenomena, but rather may be a series of unconnected events. Phenomena of greater significance may not be apparent in the sample of evidence archaeology has unearthed.

There is more solid evidence for the widespread influence of an external trait in the 1600s and 1700s. European records show that a new sail technology made its appearance at this time.[18] These new 'fore-and-aft' sails were more suited to sailing into the wind than existing Oceanic sails and soon became popular. The sails were almost identical to the lateen sails which Europeans had borrowed from the Arab world a few centuries earlier. It probably came into Oceania through Micronesia from Arab-influenced designs in use in South-East Asia. Spanish records show that this new sail was widespread in Micronesia when it was first noticed in Western Polynesia. The sail seems to have been introduced into Fiji from Kiribati, and from there to Samoa and Tonga. For much of their history Tonga, Samoa and Fiji have had sustained interactions. By the time European visits became regular in Eastern Polynesia in the late 1700s this new sail had reached Rakahanga, Tahiti, Ra'iatea, and the Tuamotus. Europeans noted that these new sails were relatively rare in Eastern Polynesia, possibly suggesting that they had not long been introduced into the region.

The distribution of the 'fore-and-aft' sail probably proceeded via a series of interactions between neighbouring peoples. But this should not be taken as fact. Recently Robert Langdon has presented linguistic and botanical evidence to suggest Indonesian influence from Sulawesi to Rotuma and Futuna in Western Polynesia sometime after the Lapita era. In particular, several words relating to bark cloth manufacture are almost identical in Rotuman and the Toradja language of Sulawesi. The bark cloth used in Rotuma was from the paper mulberry tree, a species found in Polynesia and South-East Asia, but not Melanesia in the pre-European era (Langdon 1989: 164–192).

The 'fore-and-aft' sail does not have historical precedents in Polynesia. Its appearance in Eastern Polynesia was therefore probably the result of diffusion from Western Polynesia rather than independent invention. But Eastern Polynesian traditions and cultural traits strongly suggest that the region was relatively (but not totally) isolated from Western Polynesia during prehistory.[19] Tahitian voyaging range seems to have diminished in the last few centuries before sustained European contact. The Raiatean navigator/priest Tupaia revealed knowledge to Captain Cook's expedition of islands that were then beyond the sailing range of Tahitians. A map made of Tupaia's known world included Fiji and every major island group in Polynesia except New Zealand, Rapanui (Easter Island) and Hawaii. It is unclear how much of this information had been recently confirmed first hand by Tahitians as opposed to handed down orally from past generations.[20]

A similar picture is presented for Eastern Micronesia. The Marshallese and Kiribati ranged throughout their own, extensive atoll archipelagos, but had limited interaction with neighbouring island groups, and little firm knowledge of groups beyond their immediate neighbors at European contact (Lewthwaite 1967: 77–78). The skilled seafarers of the Caroline Islands sailed throughout their own vast archipelago as well as to the high islands of Western Micronesia and the atoll chains of the Marshall Islands and Kiribati (Lewthwaite 1967: 76–77; Lewis 1977: 37). The most coherent of all the long-distance inter-island networks was the Yapese Empire, a tributary and exchange system that linked much of the Eastern Carolines to Yap, a high island in Western Micronesia.[21] Given its proximity to South-East Asia and the dynamic seafaring cultures that plied the waters of Eastern Indonesia and the Philippines, it is not surprising to find South-East Asian traits common in Western Micronesia. Local traditions suggest a long history of contacts and mixing with other Micronesians, Melanesians, Filipinos, and possibly even Taiwanese and Japanese (Lewthwaite 1967: 75; Howe 1984: 12; Lewis 1977: 17).

Oceania was a veritable 'sea of islands'.[22] Moving east into the Pacific, explorers and colonizers continued to be rewarded by island upon island on which to settle. This must have been a powerful incentive to develop maritime skills and push on.[23] No such incentive existed to entice the inhabitants of the North Pacific or the Pacific Coastline of the Americas.

Obviously the vast open expanses of the northern and eastern Pacific offer much less evidence of pre-European voyaging than the archaeologically and ethnographically rich islands of Oceania. Nevertheless there is strong evidence of some form of diffusion of traits from East Asia to the Americas, and from the Americas to Polynesia. In 1994 a newspaper reported on genetic research being carried out at Emory University that shows part of the DNA of American Indians is the same as that of aboriginal peoples in Asia, Polynesia and Melanesia.[24]

Modern writings on voyaging across the empty parts of the Pacific still focus on where winds and currents would have deposited voyagers. Much is made of historical drift voyages across the Pacific. Less is made of East Asian, and particularly Southern Chinese, maritime skills and technology. Given the implications of Irwin's work, and the impressive achievements of the Chinese elsewhere on the high seas, perhaps emphasis should be placed on why the Chinese chose to focus on other seas rather than the 'Eastern Ocean' instead of questioning their ability to master conditions in the Pacific.[25]

Being blown on to leeward shores and trapped there by winds is the mariner's worst fear. With proficiency in celestial navigation, and adequately provisioned, a long voyage out of sight of land is no more difficult than a short voyage.[26]

Reports in Shih Chi, the earliest of the Chinese official dynastic histories, mention voyages setting out into the east from China.[27] The Shih Chi was finished in the first century BC, and the voyages concerned occurred in the third century BC when official expeditions were sent in search of plants that could enhance longevity. The most detailed account is of a large, well-equipped expedition said to number in the thousands, led by one Hsu Fu who, it is implied, found land. Most Chinese scholars opt for Japan as Hsu Fu's final destination. A later text written in AD 629 describes a monk's observations of a land that lay east of Japan called Fu-Sang. There is also an account of a ship being blown far out into the Pacific from Fukien in Southern China and reaching another land. But otherwise there is little mention of the Eastern Ocean in the volumes of Chinese records collected over the centuries. The Chinese were aware of the Kuroshio current, but merely write of it flowing out into the unknown ocean which was envisaged as 'a boundless place'.[28] The historical post-European record of Chinese and Japanese fishermen reaching the coast of North America suggests that unofficial and unintended voyages could have spanned the Pacific in earlier times also.

A number of modern scholars have noted cultural similarities between Chinese and Meso-American cultures. In particular, there seems to be a strong correlation between the Shang Dynasty (1700 BC onwards) and Olmec civilizations (1200 BC onwards) in terms of settlement patterns, writing, calendar usage, esteem for jade, feline deities, and the worship of mountains.[29] However, often these proposed similarities are tenuous in their generality. All traits could have conceivably developed independently. Certainly both civilizations have clear progressions towards higher forms of civilization in their archaeological records. Furthermore, Chinese items which one would expect to be adopted in such a broad range of similarities such as rice, millet and the ubiquitous rat are absent in Meso-America's pre-Columbian record.[30]

A stronger case can be made for links between East Asia and coastal Equador/Northern Peru. Equadorian Valdivia ware dating to around 3000 BC bears a remarkable resemblance to Middle Jomon ware from southern Kyushu which dates to around the same time. It is a tenuous link, particularly if one accepts Nigel Davies's argument that there is no evidence for maritime skills or technology capable of such a voyage at such an early date in Japan.[31] Since Davies's book was published Langdon has made a more water tight argument for a Japanese–Equadorian prehistoric link. It is the presence of *Gallus inauris*, a distinctive chicken that lays blue-shelled eggs, in South America but not North America, and in Japan but nowhere else in East Asia. South American terms for this chicken divide into two distinct groups whose linguistic boundary is central Equador. Central American terms for this chicken recorded by early Spanish observers suggest Japanese linguistic links: *totori* and *tototl*, as examples, compared to the Japanese words *totori*, *jidori*, and *undori*. Langdon also notes that the gourd originates in the Old World and is found in middens from Northern Peru dating to the second millennium BC.[32]

Japanese traits need not have come directly from Japan. Coastal Equador is also linked to Asia by the presence of sailing rafts steered by inserted dagger boards. Such craft are found only in South China, Taiwan, Vietnam, Equador and Peru at European contact. Their earliest known use is in China in the fifth century BC. Equadorian sailing rafts used sails, the only incidence of sail usage on the Pacific coast of pre-Columbian America. The Equadorian sail closely resembled the lateen sail that made such an impact in late oceanic prehistory. But the lack of dagger-board sailing rafts in Polynesia suggests other sources for South American and Oceanic lateen sails rather than direct contact between the two areas.[33]

Evidence of links between Polynesia and South America does exist, however. Langdon's investigation of the distribution of *Gallus inaurus* extended into Polynesia. Early European writings on Easter Island show that there were two types of chicken on the island. One was a large chicken found in most of Polynesia and known by the Polynesian word 'moa'. The other was *Gallus inaurus* which the locals called *huahua*, and words similar to names for the fowl south of Equador (Langdon 1989: 178). Easter Island also contained a number of plants that originated in the Americas: the sweet potato, pineapple, soapberry, capsicum, manioc, 26–chromosome cotton, and the lagenaria species of gourd (Langdon 1988: 334; Spate 1988: 7–8; Davies 1979: 63).

Of these species the sweet potato has excited the most debate because of its distribution. The Spanish are known to have introduced it from the Americas into Europe, the Philippines, Guam and Malaysia. It spread from its South-East Asian entry points to China, Japan and Melanesia. But the early Spanish explorers of Oceania, Mendana and Quiros, make no mention of it in the islands they visited in the late 1500s and early 1600s: the Marquesas, Solomon Islands and Vanuatu. Yet the first westerners to land at the margins of Polynesia in the 1700s describe the sweet potato as being a very important crop in Hawaii, Easter Island and New Zealand.[34] The great variety of sweet potato in Oceania, its presence in Proto-Polynesian language reconstructions, and its successful adaptation to New Zealand's temperate climate by the 1700s all suggest that it was in Polynesia well before the Spanish arrived (O'Brien 1972: 348, 350, 353).

It is conceivable that the sweet potato was introduced into Polynesia by birds, as its means of propagation is a small hard seed that could have been carried in a bird's gut (O'Brien 1972: 354). On the other hand, both Polynesians and the South American sailing raft culture had the ability to reach each other's area.[35] There are vague Marquesan and Peruvian traditions of voyages to lands in the direction of the other's area (Lewthwaite 1967: 86; Lewis 1977: 54–55; Howe 1984: 17; Finney 1979: 347; Davies 1979: 198–199, 208–212, 217–218). But there is little linguistic or cultural evidence to suggest the significant influence of one culture on the other.

Most of the evidence connecting areas that have been mentioned could have resulted from sporadic contacts, and perhaps even solitary vessels. The record suggests local adaptation of external items but not necessarily the cultural values that were connected with them. Regular and sustained interaction beyond localized areas after the Lapita era is only clearly apparent in the Fiji, Samoa, Tonga triangle, the Society Islands–Tuamotu area, and the Yapese Empire. Elsewhere inter-island contacts waxed and waned for reasons largely unknown to modern researchers. Surviving traditions generally support Oliver's vision of periodic external contacts causing less and less radical changes to the cultural development of islands as time progressed and local patterns and trajectories of development became established.

The exchange of goods between Oceanic peoples should not be viewed as 'trade' in the western capitalist sense of a transfer of goods or services, or equivalent monetary units in what was essentially an economic transaction. Although demand for goods scarce in the recipient's locality spurred some exchanges, much more than an economic exchange was involved. As Kerry Howe notes in reference to the Kula ring of southern Papua, such

> an institutionalised exchange of goods was more than just a simple matter of economic supply and demand, having a wider range of social and political (as well as economic) features. The trading was usually associated with some form of sociopolitical obligation or expression and was as much a means in itself as a way to some narrow economic goal.
>
> (Howe 1984: 57–58)

Power was based as much on sacred status through association with the power of the gods and the spirit realm as it was on coercive force. Material wealth was used to gain influence through its redistribution to create social obligation and followers. Material wealth was measured in agricultural produce and relatively scarce decorative manufactures to which great symbolic meaning was usually attached.[36] New items coming into the island world from across the beach were thus not necessarily assessed for their worth in purely functional economic terms.

The fleeting contacts of Europeans with Pacific populations prior to the real take-off of European commerce in the Pacific in the late 1700s seem to conform to Oliver's vision on the limitations of external influences. As with non-western outsiders before them, these Europeans lacked the power to impose their ways upon local populations. Rather, local populations borrowed items and ideas selectively from outsiders, and adapted them to suit local cultural priorities and local circumstances. A comparison of Hawaiian accounts of the impact of Tahitian and Spanish contacts supports this hypothesis. It also illustrates the methodological difficulties inherent in studying events from a pre-literate era. Above all, it emphasizes the need for an anthropologically informed approach to understanding trade and other cultural interactions in the Pacific.

The standard interpretation of Hawaiian prehistory is best presented in P.V. Kirch's masterful 1985 work *Feathered Gods and Fishhooks* (Kirch 1985). Kirch sees status rivalry between chiefs and a rapidly expanding population as the major driving forces behind Hawaii's sociopolitical evolution. These forces become particularly apparent in Kirch's second phase of Hawaiian prehistory. Defined by Kirch as the Expansion Period, the era from AD 1100–1650 appears to have been one of major population expansion as the archipelago's population is hypothesized to have grown to number several hundred thousand. This theory is based on the evidence of major agricultural intensification on settled areas and the expansion of settlement – even into agriculturally marginal, arid zones. Kirch believes this population take-off gave rise to a number of major technological, social and political changes in this period (Kirch 1985: 304–305).

Whereas the two previous periods had seen settlements generally arranged in small nucleated clusters of dwellings in ecologically favourable sites, now a pattern of dispersed residence developed. Small household clusters began to occur in the interior of windward valleys in addition to existing coastal clusters along windward and leeward coastlines. Not surprisingly the growth of the population is associated with the extension and intensification of all aspects of production. The first clear evidence of irrigation agriculture occurs in this period in well-watered valleys, while vast upland field systems were developed where soils and rain permitted, most notably on the leeward slopes of Kona and Kohala on the Big Island. Fishponds seem to have also been developed in this period (Kirch 1985: 303).

Radical changes in social and political organization are hypothesized, with the basic structure witnessed in 1778 by Cook evolving in this period. Artefacts used as symbols of chiefly rank at contact became common in this period, suggesting to many that rank differentiation began to solidify. Settlement expansion is seen as a key factor in the breakdown of kin group organization and its replacement with territorial affiliations and class-based social organization. Robert Hommon has suggested that as all the land best suited to agriculture came into use it became necessary to define territorial boundaries more precisely. Bounded land units known as *ahupua'a* may have begun to develop at this time. Dispersed settlement patterns may have cut down kin group identity beyond the household, while the general economic self-sufficiency of most *ahupua'a*, and increasing population may have reduced the need for exchanges of food and marriage partners between *ahupua'a* (Kirch 1985: 55–68; Hommon 1976: 230–231).

Land reforms may have set in train processes that led to an increase in chiefly power relative to commoners, but it appears to have been warfare that consolidated this power. Competition for arable land could well have precipitated inter-group warfare. Hawaiian traditions note the beginnings of antagonism between chiefs in leeward and windward areas of Hawaii island. While the windward areas were based on long-established, stable economics, those to leeward seem to have been rapidly growing, but unstable because of their reliance in part on unpredictable yields from marginal, drought-prone and possibly over-used lands (Hommon 1987: 67; Kirch 1985: 306; Kamakau 1961: 62). The greater effort required to break-in and maintain drier lands may have served to enhance chiefly power in leeward areas by providing a need for coordinated supervision above the lineage level. Marginal and fluctuating surpluses may have pressured rulers to seek to enhance their logistical base through conquest rather than risk commoner dissent by drawing too heavily on production not normally earmarked for the support of chiefly retinues. Whatever the case, on the Big Island at least there is a noticeable increase in the prominence of leeward chiefs relative to those from windward areas from the time that the island's first unifier, 'Umi-a-liloa, moved his main residence from Waipi'o in windward Hamakua to Honaunau in leeward Kona (Kirch 1985: 307; Hommon

1987: 67, Hommon 1976: 285–286; Handy and Handy 1972: 533–535; Malo 1951: 258).

There is one group of Hawaiian traditions that Kirch does not incorporate into his model of sociopolitical evolution in Hawai'i. A number of traditions refer to the arrival of small groups of foreigners in this period.[37] One relates that a couple of white men had arrived in Maui around the middle of the seventeenth century. The rest relate to the Big Island (i.e. Hawai'i).

According to one tradition, a solitary man arrived at Kohala on the Big Island during the reign of the *mo'i* Kahoukapu.[38] He is remembered as Paao. Paao became an influential figure, and the two idols he brought with him were incorporated into the Hawaiian pantheon. The reference to idols led the missionary William Ellis to speculate that Paao may have been a Roman Catholic priest. Paao's son, Opiri, is said to have acted as an interpreter for a small group of white men who landed somewhere on the Kona coast after Paao's death. This group lived in the mountains and were treated with great respect by the Hawaiians. After a stay of an unspecified duration, these foreigners left the islands. Another tradition refers to the arrival of a group of foreigners at Kealakekua Bay, also in the reign of Kahoukapu, then resident at Kaawaloa on the northern side of the bay. The foreigners were well received. They were made chiefs and given local wives. In return, they proved to be good warriors and became very influential on the Big Island. Similar versions to these last two traditions occur in *Ka Mooolelo Hawaii*. In these versions, however, the events are dated to the reign of the *mo'i* Kealiiokaloa, the son of 'Umi-a-liloa. The most specific account refers to the shipwreck of a foreign vessel just off Keei at the southern end of Kealakekua Bay. A foreigner name Kukunaloa and his sister swam ashore and were married into the local community.

In 1975 Robert Langdon suggested that these foreigners may have been from Spanish vessels lost *en route* on the Manila–Acapulco passage that operated from the 1560s onwards. Vessels were lost without trace on this passage in 1574, 1576, 1578, 1586, 1693, and 1705 (Langdon 1975: 271–272). The Hawaiian islands lie in the vicinity of the latitudes used by the Spanish, and these dates tie in well with Kirch's dates for sociopolitical upheaval, and for estimates of the dates for the reigns of 'Umi-a-liloa and his immediate successors.

The observation of iron implements, distinctive crested helmets and capes, and lighter-skinned people amongst the Hawaiian population by members of Cook's expedition in 1778, have all been cited as possible evidence of previous Spanish contact. Critics have pointed out that iron may have arrived on driftwood, the helmets and capes are more classical than Spanish in style, and that lighter skin could be accounted for by the avoidance of gruelling outdoor work by the fairer-skinned chiefly class.[39] Such criticisms are possibilities, but they do not disprove the Spanish thesis.

Harder to explain is the discovery of a burial casket containing a piece of iron, embedded in a wooden handle, and a length of woven cloth. The contents pre-date Cook's era, and analysis of the cloth suggests that it is exceptionally close to the weave used on seventeenth-century European sail cloth. Such a weave is quite distinct from any Hawaiian fabric. The casket reputedly contains the remains of either 'Umi-a-liloa, or his great grandson Lono-i-ka-makahiki, the nephew of the Kealiiokaloa in the above traditions (Langdon 1975: 278–279).

Given the possible implications of Spanish contact upon Hawaiian socio-political evolution, the lack of even a passing reference to this subject by most prehistorians is somewhat puzzling. How might Spanish contact in the late 1500s or the period 1693–1705 have influenced Hawaiian history? The association of foreigners with *mo'i* after 'Umi-a-liloa implies that attempts to unify the Big Island did not owe their origins to external influences. The martial prowess of the foreigners, and any iron weaponry they possessed, probably only conferred a temporary advantage, judging by the inability of the windward and leeward chiefly lines to secure lasting control of the Big Island prior to the 1790s. It is tempting to see the influence of Spanish pike drill in the Hawaiian tactic of massed columns of warriors armed with *polulu*, Hawaiian hardwood pikes up to 20 feet in length.[40] Certainly massed pike formations were not used anywhere else in Oceania. If such a tactical innovation did occur, it did not confer a decisive advantage according to subsequent Hawaiian traditions. Military effectiveness could only be decisive if it was followed up by an enduring means of consolidation. The decentralized nature of Hawaiian chiefdoms up until the early 1800s, and logistical problems, imposed powerful constraints upon attempts at unified rule. If military success could not be consolidated politically, the victors' tactics could be learnt and copied by their enemies.

Paao and his 'gods' may have provided a potential unifying force to transcend local gods and local loyalties. The Hawaiian religious festival known as the Makahiki, and its associated regalia, has a strong resemblance to the Spanish festival of Morriones. 'Morriones' means an open, vizorless helmet, a reference to the helmets worn by actors portraying Roman soldiers in the Morriones festivals' passion plays. According to Langdon the Hawaiian word for helmet is '*Mahiole*', a word that is structurally non-Polynesian and sounds very similar to how Hawaiians would pronounce Marriones. Eighteenth-century Hawaiian helmets certainly resemble those used in Spanish passion plays (Langdon 1987: 371–379).

It may also be significant that the foreigner named in Ka Mooolelo Hawaii traditions was called Kukunalua (Ku-kunaloa?). In his war god form Ku was a major Hawaiian deity. Ku begins to figure prominently in Hawaiian traditions around this time. However, the reference to Paao's gods being incorporated into the Hawaiian pantheon may mean that

Spanish beliefs modified Hawaiian concepts of already existing gods, rather than introducing new ones.

There are passages in Hawaiian traditions about a priest also known as Paao (Pa'ao) arriving in Hawaii at a much earlier time from 'Kahiki' which was located somewhere south of Hawaii. Paao's arrival is not the only reference to contacts with Kahiki. A number of two-way voyages are implied within these references. Paao is mentioned in four different points in the Hawaiian traditions aside from those referred to above in connection with possible Spanish influence. These four references span *c.* fifteen generations, the last one dated to around two generations after 'Umi-a-liloa. What this suggests is that Paao founded a priestly order and that its high priests adopted the name of their founder. Most modern scholars date the arrival of the original Paao to the twelfth or thirteenth century AD. Paao is said to have significantly altered Hawaiian religious practices by introducing human sacrifice, and the *luakini*, a temple of human sacrifice.[41]

The association of Tahiti with the Kahiki of the legends is supported by a variety of evidence. Tahitian and Hawaiian fishhook forms, adze forms, and gaming stones all show notable similarities, and Hawaiian *luakini* temples resemble Tahitian *marae* (temple) forms. More compelling is the fact that Hawaiian and Tahitian have the highest percentage of shared words of any two groups in Eastern Polynesia, among them words that Tahitians and Hawaiians share uniquely. These unique words relate to aspects of worship in temples and lunar calendar terms.[42]

The Pacific world was not one of isolated island worlds that were suddenly opened up by the arrival of European and American explorers and traders. Inter-island voyaging may have waxed and waned through time, but it never died out. Influences from across the sea were a feature of most coastal peoples' histories. The experience of Hawaii recounted above suggests that external ideas and items were adopted selectively to suit local cultural priorities and local circumstances. Such culturally specific historical trajectories suggest that a more anthropologically informed approach is of value in understanding trade and other cultural interactions in the Pacific, including the region's eventual incorporation into a global, capitalist trading system.

NOTES

1 For an overview of this concept see Dirlik (1992).
2 For discussions of this issue as they relate specifically to trans-Pacific contacts see Meggers (1975: 20, 22); Davies (1979: 9 ff.); Jett (1971: 5–53); and Tolstoy (1974: 124–144).
3 On the problems of archaeological interpretation from ethnographic analogy see Heider (1967: 52–64); Trigger (1978); and Meggers (1975: 18).
4 Davies (1979: 11). For more detail see Clark (1979: 249–270).

5 For overviews on this research see Irwin (1992: 3, 217–219); Finney (1979: 335–343); Lewis (1977: 31); and Howe (1984: 21–22).

6 The two major computer simulations are those of Irwin (1992), discussed in his ch. 8, 'Voyaging by Computer', 135–171, and Levison *et al.* (1973).

7 G.R. Lewthwaite (1967: 66). On drift voyages in the North Pacific see Lewis (1977: 49–50) and Jetts (1971: 14–15, 17), while for Oceania see Parsonson (1963: 11–63).

8 On the so-called 'Lapita Complex' see Irwin (1992: 6–7, 118–120, 130–132); Howe (1984: 11–12); Campbell (1989: 35–36). For more detail see Green (1979: 27–60); Spriggs (1984: 202–233); and Green (1985: 220–224).

9 Irwin (1992), in discussing this issue on p. 211, refers toVirginia Butler, 'Lapita Fishing Strategies; The Faunal Evidence', p. 104 in Kirch and Hunt (1988).

10 On the three regions as cultural entities see Howe (1984: 44–66), and Campbell (1989: 11–27).

11 For the most up-to-date overview see Irwin (1992: 4–7, 214–216).

12 For the historical evolution of theories on Oceanic origins see Bellwood (1978: 303–311, 362–374); Irwin (1992: 13–16); and Campbell (1989: 28–34).

13 Mostly notable in Sharp (1957).

14 See note 16.

15 Refer to note 5. Lewis (1972), and Gladwin (1970) are particularly impressive. The most famous voyage on a reconstructed canoe was that of the Hokulea between Hawaii and Tahiti, see Finney (1979: 329–341).

16 This scheme is most elegantly argued in Kirch (1984: 71–216). For a concise overview on the evolution of theory in Oceanic prehistory see Kirch (1989: 13–46).

17 For the question of post-colonization contact with central East Polynesia for New Zealand see Irwin (1992: 105–113); Lewis (1977: 26–30); Howe (1984: 40–43); Finney (1979: 348); Lewthwaite (1967: 83–84).

18 Campbell (1988: 37–38) gives a good overview of this. The detailed research appears in Lewis (1978: 52, 54–56), and Parsonson (1975: 7–8). On prehistoric interactions between Fiji, Tonga and Samoa see Howe (1984: 34–37); Lewthwaite (1967: 79–81); Davidson (1978: 383–390); and Kaeppler (1978: 246–252).

19 Bellwood (1978: 308–309). He bases much of this section on Burrows (1938). See also Lewthwaite (1967: 81); Lewis (1977: 20–21).

20 On Tupaia's chart and voyaging in central East Polynesia see Irwin (1992: 176–182); Lewthwaite (1967: 81–83); and Dening (1963: 102–131).

21 On the seafaring cultures of Eastern Indonesia and the Philippines see Lewis (1977: 44–47), and Chaudhuri (1985: 152).

22 The term was coined by Tongan writer Epeil Hau'ofa (1993: 3–4).

23 Irwin (1992: 62), citing Keegan and Diamond (1987: 49–92).

24 *New Zealand Sunday Times*, 30 January 1994, 10. On possible genetic links between the Americas, Oceania and Southern China, see Salzano (1985: 19–29).

25 The standard work on Chinese maritime technology and seafaring abilities is Needham (1971: vol. 4, part 3, 379–699). Few deny the capabilities of Chinese ocean-going junks and the effectiveness of Chinese sail technology to cope with high winds, or to sail close to the wind, e.g. Needham (1971: 141–2, 147, 155, 595–597); Chaudhuri (1985: 155–156). The question is rather when these capabilities can be dated to. Davies (1979: 118–120) cites Needham (1971) to suggest that Chinese junks were not reliable open-ocean vessels until the third century AD. (See Needham's historical overview on pp. 600–605, and in more detail for the earliest times on pp. 440–451.)

26 This point is made by Irwin (1992: 101–102), citing Lewis's (1972: 158, 223) fieldwork with Micronesian navigators as evidence.
27 These various accounts are reproduced in Needham's section on the possibility of Chinese trans-Pacific voyages, (1971: 540–553). For an interesting commentary on this information see Davies (1979: 108–116).
28 On Chinese geographical images of the Pacific see Needham (1971: 548–549); Lewis (1977: 41); Dirlik (1992: 68, n. 17); and Hsieh (1967: 88–90).
29 See Meggers (1975: esp. 23); Davies (1979: 108–116); Needham (1971: 543–547).
30 Davies (1979: 117) offers the most effective case for arguing against Chinese contact with Meso-America.
31 On the coastal Ecuadorian archaeological record Langdon (1989: 176, n. 51) cites Meggers *et al.*, (1965). On the possibility of early Japanese trans-Pacific voyaging see Braden (1976: 76–79, 83–84, 86), and Davies (1979: 69–72).
32 Langdon (1989: 177–178, 192). The reference to gourd remains in the Peruvian archaeological record comes from Langdon (1988: 334).
33 See Doran (1971: 115–138); see also discussions in Lewis (1977: 50–54), Jets (1971: 11), and Needham (1970: 64).
34 For a succinct overview of scholarship on the sweet potato see O'Brien (1972: 342–365, esp. 342, 348, 360). Early European observations on the sweet potato in Oceania are reviewed in Dixon (1932: 40–66, esp. 45). The most comprehensive survey of the issue is probably still Yen (1974).
35 Davies (1979: 211–212). Irwin's (1992: 163–164) computer simulation of voyaging possibilities between Eastern Polynesia and South America also supports this idea.
36 For an overview of traditional power bases and exchange systems in Oceania see Howe (1984: 57–66).
37 The best overview of these various traditions is found in Langdon (1975: 271–280). Spanish contact was generally acknowledged in traditions recorded in the nineteenth century, see Ellis (1969: 392–404, 437–440); *idem* (1917: 295, 330–331); Fornander (1969: vol. 2, 106–107); and Jarves (1843: 89–95). Interestingly, Stokes (1932: 597) believes the outsiders referred to were Japanese, not Spanish. However his evidence is tenuous, being based on perceived stylistic similarities between a few cultural items and the history of Japanese drift voyages in the North Pacific.
38 Jarves (1843: 90), places his arrival specifically at Kohala.
39 For a summary of criticisms of the Spanish contact theses see Langdon (1975: 277–278).
40 Jarves (1843: 94) linked Hawaiian tactics with Spanish drill. Certainly massed pike formations were not used anywhere else in Oceania, and observed Hawaiian tactics did resemble Spanish tactical formations in the sixteenth century – see Montgomery of Alamein (1972: 145–152). However, Hawaiian massed pike tactics were only observed directly by Europeans in the 1790s: see Vancouver (1801: vol. 3, 252–258).
41 For commentaries on Hawaiian traditions referring to post-settlement links with 'Kahiki', see Kirch (1985: 259), and Masse *et al.*, (1991: 46–47).
42 On evidence for Tahiti–Hawaii links see Kirch (1985: 66); Masse *et al.* (1991: 43); Lewthwaite (1967: 85–86). The linguistic connections were made by Emory (1963: 89). Finney (1979: 348), and Irwin (1992: 104–105, 164–167) comment on the feasibility of such links from a navigational point of view.

BIBLIOGRAPHY

Anikouchine A. and Sternberg, R.W. (1973) *The World Ocean. An Introduction to Oceanography*, New Jersey: Prentice-Hall.

Bellwood, P. (1978) *Man's Conquest of the Pacific – The Prehistory of Southeast Asia and Oceania*, Auckland: Collins.

—— (1987) 'The Impact of Sea Level Changes on Pacific Prehistory', *Journal of Pacific History* 22, 2: 106–108.

Bellwood, P. and Koon, P. (1989) 'Lapita Colonists Leave Boats Unburned! The Question of Lapita Links with Southeast Asia', *Antiquity* 63: 613–622.

Braden, W.E. (1976) 'On the Probability of Pre-1778 Japanese Drifts to Hawaii', *Hawaiian Journal of History* 24: 75–89.

Braudel, F. (1972–3) *The Mediterranean and the Mediterranean World in the Age of Philip II*, London: Harper Colophon Books.

Burrows, E.G. (1938) *Western Polynesia: A Study of Cultural Differentiation*, Ethnologiska Studies 7 (reprinted 1978, University Bookshop, Dunedin, New Zealand).

Cameron, I. (1987) *Lost Paradise – The Exploration of the Pacific*, Boston: Salem House.

Campbell, I.C. (1989) *A History of the Pacific Islands*, Christchurch: University of Canterbury Press.

Chaudhuri, K.N. (1985) *Trade and Civilisation in the Indian Ocean – An Economic History from the Rise of Islam to 1750*, Cambridge: Cambridge University Press.

Clark, R. (1979) 'Language' in Jesse D. Jennings (ed.) *The Prehistory of Polynesia*, Canberra: Australian National University Press.

Davidson, J. (1978) 'Western Polynesia and Fiji: The Archaeological Evidence', *Mankind* 11, 3: 383–390.

Davies, N. (1979) *Voyagers to the New World: Fact or Fantasy?*, London: Macmillan.

Dening, G.M. (1963) 'The Geographical Knowledge of the Polynesians and the Nature of Inter-island Contact' in J. Golson (ed.) *Polynesian Navigation*, Wellington: Polynesian Society Memoir 34.

Dirlik, A. (1992) 'The Asia–Pacific idea: Reality and Representation in the Invention of a Regional Structure', *Journal of World History* 3, 1: 55–79.

Dixon, R.B. (1932) 'The Problem of the Sweet Potato in Polynesia', *American Anthropologist* 34: 40–66.

Doran, E. (1971) 'The Sailing Raft as a Great Tradition' in C.L. Riley *et al.* (eds) *Man across the Sea – Problems of Pre-Columbian Contacts*, Austin: University of Texas Press.

Ellis, W. (1917) *A Narrative of a Tour Through Hawaii, or Owhyhee*, Honolulu: Hawaii Gazette Co. Ltd.

—— (1969) *Polynesian Researches*, Tokyo: Charles E. Tuttle Company.

Emory, K.P. (1963) 'East Polynesian Relationships: Settlement Pattern and Time Involved as Indicated by Vocabulary Agreements', *Journal of the Polynesian Society* 72: 78–100.

Finney, B.R. (1979) 'Voyaging' in J.D. Jennings (ed.) *Prehistory of Polynesia*, Canberra: Australian National University Press.

Fornander, A. (1969) *An Account of the Polynesian Race*, Rutland, Vt.: Charles E. Tuttle Company.

Gibbons, J. and Clunie, F. (1986) 'Sea Level Changes and Pacific Prehistory – New Insights into Early Human Settlement of Oceania', *Journal of Pacific History* 24, 2: 58–82.

Gladwin, T. (1970) *East is a Big Bird*, Cambridge, Mass.: Harvard University Press.

Green, R.C. (1979) 'Lapita' in J.D. Jennings (ed.) *The Prehistory of Polynesia*, Canberra: The Australian National University Press.

—— (1985) 'Sprigg's The Lapita Cultural Complex' *Journal of Pacific History*, 20, 4: 220–224.

Handy, E.S.C. and Handy E.G. (1972) *Native Planters of Old Hawaii: Their Life, Lore, and Environments*, Honolulu: Bernice P. Bishop Museum.

Hau'ofa, E. (1993) 'A Sea of Islands: A New Paradigm for the Pacific', *East West Centre Views* 3, 3: 3–4.

Heider, K.G. (1967) 'Archaeological Assumptions and Ethnographical Facts: A Cautionary Tale from New Guinea', *Southwestern Journal of Anthropology* 23: 52–64.

Hommon, R.J. (1976) 'The Formation of Primitive States in Pre-Contact Hawaii', Unpublished Ph.D. Dissertation, University of Arizona.

—— (1987) 'Social Evolution in Ancient Hawaii' in P.V. Kirch (ed.) *Island Societies – Archaeological Approaches to Evolution and Transformation*, Cambridge: Cambridge University Press.

Houghton, P. (1991) 'The Early Human Biology of the Pacific: Some Considerations', *Journal of the Polynesian Society* 100, 2: 167–196.

Howe, K.R. (1984) *Where the Waves Fall: A New South Seas Islands History From First Settlement to Colonial Rule*, Sydney: Allen and Unwin.

Hsieh, C. (1967) 'Geographical Exploration by the Chinese' in H.R. Friis (ed.) *The Pacific Basin – A History of its Geographical Exploration*, New York: American Geographical Society.

Irwin, G. (1992) *The Prehistoric Exploration and Colonisation of the Pacific*, Cambridge: Cambridge University Press

Jarves, J.J. (1843) *History of the Hawaiian or Sandwich Islands*, Boston: Tappan and Dennet.

Jett, S.C. (1971) 'Diffusion Versus Independent Development: The Bases of Controversy' in C.L. Riley *et al.* (eds) *Man Across the Sea – Problems of Pre-Columbian Contacts*, Austin: University of Texas Press.

Kaeppler, A.C. (1978) 'Exchange Patterns in Goods and Spouses: Fiji, Tonga and Samoa', *Mankind* 11, 3: 246–252.

Kamakan, S.M. (1961) *Ruling Chiefs of Hawaii*, Honolulu: Kamehameha Schools Press.

Keegan, W.F. and Diamond, J.M. (1987) 'Colonisation of Islands by Humans: A Biogeographical Perspective' in M. Schiffer (ed.) *Advances in Archaeological Method and Theory* 10: 49–92.

Kirch, P.V. (1984) *The Evolution of the Polynesian Chiefdoms*, Cambridge: Cambridge University Press.

—— (1985) *Feathered Gods and Fishhooks – An Introduction to Hawaiian Archaeology and Prehistory*, Honolulu: University of Hawaii Press.

—— (1989) 'Prehistory' in A. Howard and R. Borofsky (eds) *Developments in Polynesian Ethnology*, Honolulu: University of Hawaii Press.

Kirch, P.V. and Hunt, T.L. (eds) (1988) *Archaeology of the Lapita Cultural Complex: A Critical Review*, Research Report no. 5, Seattle: Thomas Burke Memorial Washington State Museum.

Langdon, R. (1975) *The Lost Caravel*, Sydney: Pacific Publications.

—— (1987) 'Benevolent Invaders Among Hawaii's Aborigines' in D.C. Laycock and W. Winter (eds) *A World of Language: Papers Presented to Professor S.A. Wurm on his 65th Birthday*, Pacific Linguistics.

—— (1988) 'Manioc, A Long Concealed Key to the Enigma of Easter Island', *The Geographical Journal* 154, 3: 324–336.

—— (1989) 'When the Blue-Egg Chickens Came Home to Roost: New Thoughts on the Prehistory of the Domestic Fowl in Asia, America and the Pacific Islands', *Journal of Pacific History* 24, 2: 164–192.

Lessa, W. (1950) 'The Place of Ulithi in the Yap Empire', *Human Organisation* 9, 1: 16–18.

Levison, M., Ward, R.G. and Webb, J.W. (1973) *The Settlement of Polynesia: A Computer Simulation*, Minneapolis: University of Minnesota Press.

Lewis, D. (1972) *We, the Navigators: The Ancient Art of Land Finding in the Pacific*, Canberra: Australian National University Press.

—— (1977) *From Maui to Cook – The Discovery and Settlement of the Pacific*, Sydney: Doubleday.

—— (1978) 'The Pacific Navigators Debt to the Ancient Seafarers of Asia' in N. Gunson (ed.) *The Changing Pacific: Essays in Honour of H.E. Maude*, Melbourne: Oxford University Press.

Lewthwaite, G.R. (1967) 'Geographical Knowledge of the Pacific Peoples' in H.R. Friis (ed.) *The Pacific Basin: A History of Its Geographical Exploration*, New York: American Geographical Society Special Publication no. 38: 57–86.

Malo, D. (1951) *Hawaiian Antiquities* Honolulu: Bernice P. Bishop Museum.

Masse, B. *et al.* (1991) 'Waha'ula Heiau: The Regional and Symbolic Context of Hawaii's Islands "Red Mouth" Temple', *Asian Perspectives* 30, 1: 19–56.

Meggers, B.J. (1975) 'The Transpacific Origin of Mesoamerican Civilisation: A Preliminary Review of the Evidence and Its Theoretical Implications', *American Anthropologist* 77, 1: 1–27.

Meggers, B.J. *et al.* (1965) *Early Formative Period in Coastal Ecuador: The Valdivia and Machalilla Phases*, Washington, DC: Smithsonian Institution Contributions to Anthropology 1.

Montgomery (Field-Marshal Montgomery of Alamein) (1972) *A Concise History of Warfare*, London: Collins.

Muller, R.A. and Oberlander, T.M. (1978) *Physical Geography Today – A Portrait of a Planet*, New York: CRM/Random House.

Needham, J. (1970) *Clerks and Craftsmen in China and the West*, London: Cambridge University Press.

—— (1971) *Science and Civilisation in China*, Cambridge: Cambridge University Press.

O'Brien, P.J. (1972) 'The Sweet Potato: Its Origin and Dispersal', *American Anthropologist* 74: 342–365.

Oliver, D.L. (1984) *Ancient Tahitian Society*, Honolulu: University of Hawaii Press.

—— (1989) *Native Cultures of the Pacific Islands*, Honolulu: University of Hawaii Press.

Parsonson, G.S. (1963) 'The Settlement of Oceania: An Examination of the Accidental Voyage Theory' in J. Golson (ed.) *Polynesian Navigation*, Wellington: Polynesian Society Memoir no. 34: 11–63.

—— (1975) 'The Nautical Revolution in Polynesia' (typescript essay, based on a Macmillan Brown Lecture, 1969), Dunedin: Hocken Library.

Salzano, F.M. (1985) 'The Peopling of the Americas as Viewed from South America' in R. Kirk and E. Szathmary (eds) *Out of Asia – Peopling the Americas and the Pacific*, Canberra: The Journal of Pacific History.

Sharp, A. (1957) *Ancient Voyagers in the Pacific*, Harmondsworth, Middlesex: Penguin.

Spate, O.H.K. (1988) *Paradise Found and Lost (The Pacific since Magellan*, vol. 3), Canberra: Australian National University Press.

Spriggs, M. (1984) 'The Lapita Cultural Complex' *Journal of Pacific History* 19, 4: 202–233.

Stokes, J.F.G. (1932) 'Spaniards and the Sweet Potato in Hawaii and Hawaiian–American Contacts', *American Anthropologist* 34: 594–600.

Thomas, W.L. (1963) 'The Variety of Physical Environments Among Pacific Islands' in F.R. Fosberg (ed.) *Man's Place in the Island Ecosystem*, Honolulu: Bishop Museum Press

Tolstoy, P. (1974) 'Transoceanic Diffusion and Nuclear America' in S. Gorenstein *et al.* (eds) *Prehispanic America*, New York: St Martin's Press.

Trigger, B.G. (1978) *Times and Traditions: Essays in Archaeological Interpretation*, Edinburgh: Edinburgh University Press.

Vancouver, G. (1801) *A Voyage of Discovery to the North Pacific Ocean and Around the World*, London: John Stockdale.

Yen, D.E. (1974) *The Sweet Potato and Oceania*, Honolulu: Bernice P. Bishop Museum Bulletin no. 236.

Zegura, S. (1985) 'The Initial Peopling of the Americas: An Overview' in R. Kirk and E. Szathmary (eds) *Out of Asia – Peopling The Americas and the Pacific*, Canberra: The Journal of Pacific History.

3

COMING FULL CIRCLE

A long-term perspective on the Pacific Rim

Lionel E. Frost

When Ferdinand Marcos became president of the Philippines in 1965, he took over a state which had higher living standards than most Asian countries (George 1992: 89). It seemed to be more likely to achieve lasting economic success than, for example, Korea, which had been damaged severely by the war of 1950–3 and its northern half had fallen under communist rule. Asian manufacturing produced cheap, inferior copies of Western goods; a label indicative of Asian origin was taken to suggest shoddiness. Some writers still doubted whether even Japan would be able to sustain its post-Second World War recovery and achieve continuing economic growth.

But the seemingly unpromising economies of East Asia have since achieved three decades of economic growth. From 1965 to 1990, the economies of what the World Bank calls the Asian 'superstars' – Hong Kong, Indonesia, Japan, Malaysia, Singapore, South Korea, Taiwan, and Thailand – have together grown at an annual rate of over 5 per cent, more than twice as fast as the rest of Asia and three times as fast as Latin America (Anon. 1993a: 29). The Philippines now falls well behind most of the rest of Asia. Japanese growth has continued and its example has spread to other parts of the Asia–Pacific region. The southern parts of the People's Republic of China, where the government has established several Special Economic Zones to draw in capital and technology from Hong Kong and Taiwan and other foreign countries, are currently the site of the biggest economic boom in world history.

There are several possible explanations for East Asia's stellar economic performance and the relative lack of success in Latin America and the Philippines. Was it due to market forces being allowed to operate freely? How much did government have to interfere in the workings of the economy, and what were the appropriate policies needed, to bring about efficient allocation of resources? How was the economy affected by cultural factors – that is, by sets of values which stress the importance of thrift, family loyalty, education, hard work, pride in one's work, and punctuality?

Each of these explanations has its supporters, but the matter is so complex that no simple, monocausal explanation will do. Culture, for instance, has proved to be difficult to define, with scholars from various disciplines tending to assign either a peripheral or central role to it in explanations of economic change. As R.J. Holton writes:

> While some reach for the scalpel to remove this interloper, others are carried away with enthusiasm at the apparent discovery of a holistic explanatory key to the comparative fate of nations and civilizations. Culture has indeed proved one of the hardest issues for social scientists to come to terms with. There remains no agreement how this most slippery of terms should be defined, theorized or operationalized in empirical research. Is culture to be defined in terms of values and beliefs conceived of as somehow exogenous to the economy or polity? Or is it to be identified with an entire way of life, such that we may speak, for example, of economic or political culture? In the former approach, preferred by economists and political scientists, culture tends to become an awkward residual to be grudgingly invoked when rational choice or power-centred explanations turn out to be inadequate. In the latter more anthropological approach, culture, in the form of discrete sets of material and symbolic practices, takes on a more inflated significance as the generic basis of social life, and the source of social difference.
>
> (Holton 1995: 139)

This chapter adopts a position between these two schools of thought. While it will argue that culture is something which is endogenous to economic life, and that changes in the values and preferences of consumers and producers can exert a powerful transforming influence on a society and its production of goods and services, this does not mean that cultural factors are the cause of economic success. We need to be aware of why various societies respond (or fail to respond) readily to economic opportunities, but we also need to consider why these opportunities arise in the first place if a balanced explanation of economic performance is to be formulated.

The chapter looks at three cases from the long-term history of the Pacific Rim and explores how culture and economics have interacted with one another in each. The first explores the rise of market-based activity in China during the Song dynasty and how political factors brought about economic changes which bypassed traditional Chinese values. The second looks at how various Pacific Rim societies responded to European attempts to impose their own culture and economic institutions on the region. The final section examines the economic and political context which has made it possible for Americans to build up large corporations which supply products to a world market. It will argue that while the values of a particular population shape its spending habits and can create economic and environmental problems, these values are shaped in the first place by a vital economic and political setting.

TRADITIONAL VALUES AND THE CREATION OF WEALTH: THE CASE OF SONG CHINA

China is the one big land mass that drains into the Pacific Rim. Its fertile, easily worked loess soil and rivers suitable for irrigation make it naturally suited to agriculture. Ever since the first villages were established along the Yangtze River at least 7,000 years ago, China has accounted for a substantial proportion of the Pacific Rim's, and indeed the world's, population. By AD 1, 86 per cent of the total population of the countries bordering the Pacific, and 31 per cent of the world's population, lived in China. By 1000, the respective figures were 67 per cent and 23 per cent (calculated from data in McEvedy and Jones 1978).

People in the earliest Chinese village communities worked collectively, using methods passed from generation to generation, to open up and farm areas. Population grew and farming areas spread as wild crops became domesticated and agricultural productivity increased through irrigation, fallowing, manuring and the use of iron tools. This reduced the area of wild territory suitable for hunting and when food became scarce farming communities were vulnerable to the incursions of nomad raiding parties. The need for protection encouraged political organization, with the rise of military regimes which collected taxes, in the form of surplus food or labour services, in return for keeping the peace. For most peasants, the routine of everyday life followed time-honoured customary methods. But a command element of economic life came into play when the regime collected taxes after each harvest and during periods when peasant labour was conscripted to build fortifications and serve in the army. These command regimes provided security and created conditions which made it possible for food output to roughly keep pace with population growth, but the high cost of defence against an ever-present threat of invasion from northern barbarian tribes and the taxing of surplus food created disincentives for peasants to increase their productivity.

The periods between China's great dynasties – the Han (206 BC–AD 220), T'ang (AD 618–906), Song (960–1279), and Ming (1368–1644) – were troubled times during which large military expenditures were required. Warlords clashed with each other and divided the Han empire; invaders from the north brought down the T'ang, Song, and Ming dynasties. During the Song dynasty, the need for the regime to obtain resources for self-preservation brought about a major change in the structure of the economy. A standing army of over one million men was assembled and a network of fortified garrison posts built along the northern border to hold back formidable, well-organized raiding parties. In 1127 the capital, Kaifeng, was conquered by Manchurian tribes, called the Jurchen, forcing the Song to retreat southwards, where they ruled until the Mongols captured all of China. The coastal provinces of the southern Song were protected by river barriers and defended by a navy with hundreds of armed fighting ships (see McNeill 1982: 33–43).

To equip and maintain the army and navy of the Song required enormous quantities of iron and steel, raw materials, artisanal products (such as crossbows), and food. To build up its military strength the regime undertook an emergency marketization of the economy. When the Song dynasty was established it immediately began to rebuild the agricultural sector which had been damaged by warfare. Refugees were encouraged to return to the land with an offer of five years' exemption from taxes and labour services (Ma 1971: 12). During the early T'ang period, peasants were allocated plots of land in return for periodic labour service. Taxes were paid in kind. By the late T'ang period, peasants in some regions were permitted to own land, for which they paid rent in cash. The Song accelerated this process of privatization, with private ownership and the payment of taxes in cash becoming a nationwide characteristic (Ma 1971: 18–21; Elvin 1973: 148–9). Because the tax was levied on the value of land, rather than output, and, like rents, had to be paid in cash, it was impossible for self-sufficient peasants to remain debt free. There was now a real incentive for market-minded farmers to work harder and more efficiently: once they had sold their produce and paid their taxes and rents any extra cash could be saved, re-invested, or spent on consumer goods.

The government contributed to the increased volume of agricultural production by building canals and removing obstacles to river navigation. This made it possible for people in different regions to exploit local comparative advantage by becoming specialist producers. For instance, in southeastern coastal areas citrus fruits were grown widely, while different kinds of tea were planted in parts of hilly southern China (Ma 1971: 15).

China's population rose from around 60 million in 1000 to 115 million in 1200 (McEvedy and Jones 1978: 171), but it seems certain that output increased at a faster rate than this. Agriculture was highly productive and benefited from new strains of early-ripening and drought-resistant rice and better techniques of fertilizing. As a result, the amount of labour needed to feed the population fell and this created a problem of surplus rural labour. Farmers who could not sell enough to pay their bills hired out their labour to the better and/or more highly capitalized farmers, or worked as carriers, or manufactured simple goods for sale at home in their spare time, or else migrated to the cities, which were growing very large as the economy became more commercialized. The cities were flooded with workers driven from the countryside by poverty. The marketization of the Chinese economy encouraged people to seek personal gain by operating in niches – according to their skills and resources – as specialist farmers, part-time artisans, or unskilled labourers. Specialization and exchange 'allowed spectacular increases in total production, as all the advantages of specialization that Adam Smith later analyzed so persuasively came into operation' (McNeill 1982: 29).

This was an economic transformation of such power that it was able to brush aside traditional Chinese values about the nobility of rural work and abhorrence of the pursuit of private gain. Classical Confucian philosophy, which all members of the bureaucracy had studied intensively, regarded the accumulation and conspicuous consumption of personal wealth with disdain. Real wealth came from the land, extracted by the toil of honest peasants, whereas in the towns merchants grew rich by what were seen as sharp practices.

> Goodness develops only in the village, evil in the city. The city is the place of commerce and trade. People relate to one another only with the aim of making profits. They are superficial and pretentious. As a result, the city is a sink of iniquities. The village is different. There people are self-reliant and have deep emotional ties with each other.
>
> (quoted by Murphey 1980: 24)

Before the Song period cities were divided into walled districts, or wards. The gates to these wards and to the city walls were locked at night and a dusk to dawn curfew was enforced strictly. Within each ward there were specified market areas where for a few hours each day commercial activity took place under the eye of officials. Officials issued certificates of sale and checked the accuracy of weights and measures. Merchants who breached regulations were flogged. There was a penalty of a beating of eighty strokes for 'any person who dared to profit from price manipulation by buying cheap and selling dear' (Ma 1971: 77).

The logic behind such policies has been an enduring characteristic of Chinese thinking about towns and the countryside. The long quotation in the paragraph above is from an imperial official of the mid-seventeenth century, and the sentiments expressed differ not a whit from those of Mao Zedong.

Yet such was the Song regime's need for resources that it was unwilling to risk imposing restrictions and confiscatory taxes on the burgeoning market sector. The Song 'recognized that indiscriminate resort to such a policy might cost the state dearly by diminishing tax revenue in future years. Officials therefore struggled to reconcile justice with fiscal expediency, and long-range with short-range advantage' (McNeill 1982: 32). In the cities, the walls around the wards were taken down and a blind eye was turned to the 'injustice' of profit-making. Sumptuary laws relating to dress, furniture, and buildings were not enforced and widely ignored (Shiba 1970: 203–4).

Two points may be made here. First, merchants – and other specialist producers throughout the economy – embraced the opportunity to increase their personal wealth in spite of the fact that this contradicted traditional Chinese values. The incentives created by political circumstances proved to be more powerful than time-honoured cultural values.

Second, as merchants became confident enough to spend their profits openly, the result was the emergence of conspicuous consumption on a scale hitherto probably unknown in Chinese history. An eleventh-century high official wrote that:

> control over the merchants has not yet been well established. They enjoy a luxurious way of life, living on dainty foods and delicious rice and meat, owning handsome houses and many carts, adorning their wives and children with pearls and jades, and dressing their slaves in white silk. In the morning they think about how to make a fortune, and in the evening they devise means of fleecing the poor . . . Since this relaxed control over merchants is regarded by the people as a common rule, they despise agricultural pursuits and place high value on an idle living by trade.
>
> (quoted by McNeill 1982: 31)

This was a complaint about the ways in which people in towns were prepared to spend their money. This cultural change, which originated from new incentives and the restructuring of the economy, had a significant economic impact. The tastes and demands of wealthy urbanites created new jobs which made the cities larger and the range of urban occupations wider. In part, Chinese cities grew because poverty 'pushed' people out of rural areas, but there was a substantial 'pull' element as well, as consumer spending created a broad demand for luxury and everyday goods and services.

Big cities were not new in China: the capitals were seats of power with large, well-paid bureaucracies and this elite created much work for merchants, clerks, artisans, labourers, builders, and a range of service workers. Marketization of the economy changed the character of these cities. While Chang'an, capital of the T'ang dynasty, had perhaps a million inhabitants within its walls and another million without (Tyrwitt 1968–9: 30; Wright 1967: 143–9), it was austere and dead after dark because of its curfew and ward system. Kiafeng, the Song capital, had a similar number of inhabitants, but was a much livelier place, jam-packed with shops, taverns, and restaurants which faced the street and were open all hours.

The great cities of China, and the other towns in its urban network, were places of consumption (shaped by wealth and the development of new cultural values about its creation and enjoyment) as well as production. Their basic needs of food and shelter, and the frivolity and waste of luxury, further helped to commercialize what had been a largely peasant economy. In the big cities, privileged officials and rich merchants started new fads and fashions, which as a contemporary noted, 'all other places look up to, follow, and imitate' (quoted by Ma 1971: 141–2). Conspicuous consumption affected the values and spending habits of all levels of Chinese society. 'Things are discarded when they are not yet worn out, and those who follow the old fashions are sneered at by people. [The] poor are ashamed of being inferior [and thus] imitate the rich by being showy' (quoted by Ma 1971: 141–2).

William McNeill has written that once China's economy became marketized the result was that 'a powerful wind of change began to blow across the southern seas that connected the Far East with India and the Middle East'. There was 'an intensified flow of goods and movement of persons responding to mainly market opportunities'. For McNeill, 'China's rapid evolution towards market-regulated behaviour on either side of the year 1000 tipped a critical balance in world history' (McNeill 1982: 24–5). China's growth and structural change provided a clear illustration of what rulers could achieve by allowing people to pursue opportunities for personal gain instead of merely issuing commands. By encouraging trade and private wealth creation, rulers could then impose taxes and use the revenue for defence or expansion. The process by which this lesson was learnt by people in other parts of the world remains unclear. Did merchants who did long-distance business with Asia convince rulers that such an approach would be to their mutual advantage? Or did these changes occur independently in a number of places? What is clear is that rulers in Europe were, in contrast, able to consolidate and hold their territories if they provided merchants with the protection and infrastructure they needed. They had to be able to tax this trade to buy the latest weapons and pay professional soldiers. Because Europe's political system was competitive and multicentred, merchants were able to demand fair treatment, and even a share of political power, if they were to continue doing business in a particular state.

But in China, where political power was more centralized, the command sector of the economy was never out of control. Rulers and officials remained free to behave in ways which would make life difficult and unprofitable for merchants. The Mongol Yuan dynasty enjoyed good relations with traders, which led to a reaction to this under the succeeding Ming dynasty. Overseas exploration and shipping was stopped by the emperor in 1430. The Ming and Qing dynasties were lethargic states which provided little in the way of infrastructure or law and order to protect and encourage merchants and specialist farmers (Jones 1990). China's failure to repeat its economic performance under the Song meant that the economy became less urbanized and more peasant-based. Elvin (1973: 177–8) suggests that in 1900 China was less urbanized than it had been in 1300. Agricultural output increased because the farming system was replicated as settlement spread to the south, but per capita output was probably stagnant. The Chinese tended to embrace traditional conservative values but this was a symptom, not a cause, of economic stagnation. There were less opportunities for would-be capitalists because of the way society was organized politically.

EUROPE AND THE PACIFIC RIM

With the rise of the economies of Mediterranean Europe, and later Northwest Europe, the centre of gravity of world economic life shifted away from China. In 1480, China abandoned plans to restart the impressive overseas voyages of exploration which had been led by Admiral Cheng Ho, and in the following decade Europeans discovered sea routes to Asia and the Americas. The Chinese economy did not cease to grow during the Ming period, but it certainly failed to return to the heights of the Song era. In the sixteenth and seventeenth centuries, China was the world's most important buyer of silver, from mines in Japan and Spanish America, and was the centrepiece of the first system of global trade (Flynn and Giraldez 1995). Nevertheless, it was Europe's system of states which provided the infrastructure and incentives needed to foster the growth of an autonomous, prosperous market sector. In 1500, Europe was a peripheral economic power: it had only three of the world's twenty largest cities (the rest were in Asia, the Middle East, or Africa). By the nineteenth century, a world economy had emerged which was centred on an increasingly urbanized and industrialized Europe. Thirteen of the world's twenty largest cities in 1850 were in Europe, or across the Atlantic Ocean in areas which had been colonized by Europeans (Jones *et al.*, 1993: 137).

Thus when Europeans arrived in the Pacific region in search of raw materials, markets, and investment opportunities, several cultures in different stages of economic development were brought into contact with one another. Europeans, whose societies had made a full transition to a market system, interacted or clashed with societies where the transition to market-based behaviour had been made only partly (as in Asia) or not at all (as in North America and Australia). People who had been free to exploit and privatize resources in the pursuit of profit entered worlds where such behaviour had been restricted by command structures, or was a completely foreign concept.

European capitalism influenced every part of the non-capitalist world with which it came in contact. But the impact of European power on the various Pacific cultures varied widely: for some societies the arrival of Europeans proved to be a disaster, while others were able to adjust to the new situation and in the long run benefit from involvement in the world economy. In some parts of the Pacific Rim the influence of global capitalism created societies which were stable and prosperous, while other parts of the region remained squalid and underdeveloped. This section explores the reasons for this divergence and why it has largely persisted to this day.

There were two types of colonies established by Europeans, which may be called colonies of settlement and colonies of sojourn. The former were settled by people who wished to build a permanent home, while the latter were places where Europeans were interested in settling only briefly, making their fortune by exploiting the local resources and/or population and then returning home to spend it. The purpose for which a colony was settled created economic and political characteristics which tended to be enduring, as the effects of initial choices and circumstances proved difficult to shake off. The continuing prosperity of settlement colonies in the American West, Australia, and New Zealand, and the lingering poverty and instability of former colonies of sojourn in Central and South America, are classic cases of what economic historians call path dependency.

In the colonies of settlement, the transformation of what seemed to Europeans to be a wilderness into a capitalist society took place very rapidly. The gold rushes brought in investments and swarms of people, galvanizing the economies of the Pacific slope and southeastern Australia. As William Robbins (1994: 12) writes of the American experience, 'this was market capitalism at the moment of its most expansive growth'. Railroads across the North American continent and into the Australian interior then opened up vast areas of land suitable for pastoralism, grazing, or farming. 'Juvenile cities', as Mark Twain called them, soon emerged. San Francisco and Melbourne grew so large, so quickly, that they amazed European visitors (Frost 1991). By the end of the nineteenth century, Australians and New Zealanders were probably the richest people in the world (Butlin 1965: 8).

There were several reasons why the settler colonies were able to grow into such successful capitalist societies. First, the indigenous population was suppressed and dispossessed fairly easily. The values of the nomadic, customary indigenous peoples and those of the sedentary, capitalistic invaders clashed while land was crucial to the economic well-being of both groups; Native Americans and Australian Aborigines used the land intermittently and in co-operation with other members of the tribe, moving on when food supplies were exhausted, but white settlers saw the frontier as a giant piece of real estate. They needed the land to be privatized to maximize the rate of return on their investment. They wanted to be able to buy land, develop and exploit its productive potential, and then sell it for a profit. To white settlers, the indigenous peoples and their way of life contradicted everything they understood by 'progress':

> [Indigenous peoples] did not till the soil, they knew nothing of metals and had no animal husbandry. In fact they were so innocent of the mainsprings of European culture that they were despised as ignorant

> savages. People who felt mastery over the earth were bound to treat them as irrelevant and expendable.
>
> (Bate 1978: 1)

The result was an unequal confrontation between the two cultures. Superior firearms and the spread of lethal European diseases meant that the indigenous peoples were rarely able to offer much resistance to white settlers.

Second, the world economy was at this time growing rapidly and Europe and the eastern United States were able to transfer surplus profits and labour which the newly settled regions needed. By investing in and developing new areas of settlement, the industrial regions of the world economy were able to obtain food and raw materials for their towns and factories. In the new societies, resources were fairly easy to exploit and the primary sector was efficient. Wealth from the land enabled the new societies to attract investment and migrants, and pay for imports of industrial goods and capital equipment.

Third, the government sector of the settlement colonies contributed strongly and effectively to economic growth. The political system was decentralized and a dense network of state (or provincial or colonial) and local governments competed with one another to attract investors and settlers. The new societies were short of capital and labour and distant from potential markets. They needed transport improvements, and in some cases irrigation works, if their resources were to be made productive. The state made sure that the needed infrastructure was provided by subsidizing private companies which built canals and railroads (in Australia the state built railroads itself). As the private sector thrived there was an increase in economic activity which was to the advantage of the public sector because of increased tax revenues. This symbiotic partnership between the public and private sector was called 'mixed enterprise' in North America and 'colonial (or state) socialism' in Australia (Hughes 1977; Frost 1992).

It was the contribution of city governments to the building of canals and railroads, beginning with the construction of the Erie Canal, linking New York's Hudson River with Lake Erie in 1825, which pushed settlement inwards from the Atlantic seaboard by providing settlers with cheaper access to markets. In the American West the federal government became increasingly active through its policies towards transcontinental railroads, the Homestead Act, and the building of dams. Because voters in individual towns were usually willing to support public spending which promised to boost general prosperity (Los Angeles, for instance, dug an artificial harbour and paid a subsidy to the Southern Pacific railroad in return for inclusion on its transcontinental route), migrants usually had a wide choice of places where they could put their money and skills to productive use.

Fourth, there was scope in these societies for individuals to make a contribution to technological change and improvements in organization.

Farmers had a businesslike attitude to their piece of dirt and wanted to make it as productive as possible. They were not peasants. The various levels of government helped in ways outlined above, but still technical problems remained, such as finding ways to deal with the effects of unpredictable weather, depletion of soil fertility, and plant diseases. Farming communities coped by co-operating during periods of misfortune, helping out neighbours who became sick, for instance (Neugebauer 1991: 119). These societies had high levels of literacy and could develop and share ideas through local and specialist farming newspapers and formal agricultural societies. Farmers could discuss problems when they came to town to sell their produce, buy supplies, or to socialize or worship. It was a setting in which innovative and thoughtful farmers could experiment, and knowledge of their discoveries could be disseminated to other farmers.

Such a setting was lacking in the colonies of sojourn. The native population was swept aside brutally, and plantations and mines which supplied food and resources for overseas markets were soon established. But the transience of these places discouraged the establishment of dense government structures and community institutions needed for economic development. The structure of government was highly centralized and most instructions came from Madrid. Local government was virtually non-existent and functioned mainly to protect the elite. Little investment was made in public goods. Most of the wealth which was created in these colonies went back to Spain, either as taxation or when the elite went home. Land was usually tied up in large holdings, and slavery and other forms of forced labour were common. Thus began a tradition of excessively centralized government which was difficult to change. After the colonies became independent of Spain, long periods of anarchic conflict followed and when new nation-states emerged the tendency to centralized politics reasserted itself. Regimes won and retained power – not by investing productively in infrastructure and human capital but through violence and corruption (Jones *et al.* 1993: 51–5).

While Europeans were able to sweep through the Americas, in Asia (and Africa) they were kept in check for a long time by lack of a swift means of overland transport and by tropical diseases. Europeans enjoyed considerable superiority at sea, especially in gunnery, but their movement inland was restricted. 'In 1800, after three centuries of lurking offshore, Europeans could only claim a few footholds in Asia and Africa, mainly harbors and islands' (Headrick 1988: 5). This situation changed during the nineteenth century. Europeans developed new technology which improved their speed of movement inland (steamships, riverboats, and railroads) and their firepower (improved firearms, and the submarine cable, which provided fast transfer of military information). New medicines, notably quinine, reduced the impact of tropical disease (Headrick 1981). Furthermore, as Europe industrialized, increased demand for tropical products such as tin, rubber, palm oil, sugar, coffee, tea, and cocoa created greater incentives for Europeans to do business with Asia.

What led to an increase in British involvement in China during the nineteenth century was the fact that the Chinese let British goods into their own market in only limited amounts. The Qing dynasty was an isolationist one, and as the Emperor told Lord Macartney, the British emissary who arrived in 1799, China had no need for inferior barbarian products. The government allowed foreign merchants to do business in only one city – Canton (Guangzhou) – where trade was supervised by Chinese officials. As a result, British industrialists and merchants were largely denied access to a market which at the start of the nineteenth century accounted for over one-third of the world's population. Furthermore, because Britain was such a substantial importer of Chinese products – tea in particular, and also porcelain and silk – it built up a substantial trade deficit with China.

British businessmen changed this situation by shamefully selling drugs (opium, grown in British India) to the Chinese. By bribing Chinese officials, the British were able to land opium and sell it to Chinese merchants at a large profit. This was a disaster for China. Millions of Chinese became drug addicts and the government was powerless to stop the evil trade. When the government confiscated and destroyed stocks of opium in Canton and boycotted British ships, the British government resorted to force to protect its commercial interests. At the end of the Opium Wars (1839–42) Britain was given six Chinese ports where it could trade with complete freedom. In these 'treaty ports' British, not Chinese, laws applied. Britain's success in breaking open the Chinese market encouraged the French, Germans, Americans, and Russians to do the same, and eventually around one hundred treaty ports were opened. By the early twentieth century, China had also lost control of Taiwan and Korea to Japan.

Before the First World War, competition between Europe's imperialist powers saw virtually the whole of the Pacific region carved up into separate colonial preserves. The arrival of an American fleet under Commodore Matthew Perry in 1853 brought a demand that Japan, which had been largely isolated from the rest of the world under the Tokugawa Shogunate, open itself to world trade. At first the Tokugawa regime resisted, adopting a slogan of 'expel the barbarian' (George 1992: 30). But it was soon realized that pursuing such a stance would risk the kind of humiliation which China had suffered after the Opium Wars. Japan agreed to open up and what resulted was a remarkable period of successful modernization. Japan was able to build up its economic strength quickly and remain independent of the colonial powers. Many of the changes which took place were political in origin: the overthrow of the Tokugawa and the Meiji Restoration in 1868 provided a decisive policy shift towards openness to foreign ideas and technology. Infrastructure and communications were improved. The government paid for pilot plants in textiles, shipping, and railways, and then sold them off to the private sector (Jones *et al.* 1993: 101–5). Unlike China, Japan had a more solid economic base upon which to build an industrial society. During the Tokugawa era substantial economic development had occurred. Trade within Japan had encouraged the creation of a merchant class. The quality of human capital was very high (Hanley 1983).

Japan's long period of virtual isolation from the rest of the world, and its racial homogeneity, created a unique culture which values hard work and loyalty to other Japanese (Christopher 1984). As a result, the Japanese have their own way of doing business, and their capacity for work and concern for national well-being are surely positive influences on economic performance. But the decision to open Japan up to foreign influence was a political one which could have gone the other way (as it did in China), as was the decision of the Americans to occupy and rebuild Japan, rather than cripple it, after the Second World War.

There was a similar opening up to the West in Siam (Thailand), where no resistance to foreigners was attempted. During the reign of Mongkut (King Rama IV) and his son Chulalongkorn (King Rama V) from 1851 to 1910, commercial treaties were negotiated with the British, on terms favourable to the latter. Mongkut 'could see clearly that if China had failed to maintain its isolation against European pressure, Siam must come to terms with threats from external forces and begin to accommodate itself to the new world in which Asian traditionalism appeared outworn and inefficient' (George 1992: 36). This openness allowed Siam to remain independent, and, like the Japanese, keep its traditional culture. Siam's experience contrasted with that of its neighbours, Burma and Indo-China, which fell under the rule of Britain and France respectively. The rest of Southeast Asia became colonial possessions as well.

If Japan and Siam were able to derive economic benefit by restructuring their economies to accommodate Western demands for free trade, what became of the Asian societies which tried to repel the foreigners but instead found themselves under colonial domination? This was culturally humiliating and had negative political consequences, but in an economic sense 'the effect of the Europeans' presence can be seen in retrospect as a giant transfer of technology' (Jones *et al.* 1993: 118). Britain in particular had more technology to transfer to its colonies that Spain did, and its colonial governments were less parasitic. In Southeast Asia, European-operated plantations and mines encouraged substantial growth of primary production, and 'between 1883 and 1913, the growth of per capita GNP, especially in Indochina, may have been as fast as in many industrial countries' (Jones *et al.* 1993: 118).

Nevertheless, Daniel Headrick (1988) has argued convincingly that such imperialism *widened* the gap between industrial Europe and its supply regions in the tropics. The latter economies were efficient producers of food and raw materials and did grow before the First World War, but with scientific research European manufacturing became more efficient and this affected the world demand for primary production. After the First World War, substitutes were developed for tropical products such as palm oil and silk, and overproduction of commodities saw prices slump. European investment had created a series of colonies which overspecialized in primary production, and in the post-colonial period policies were needed to enable economic diversification to take place. It was not until the next major boom in the world economy after the Second World War that, with the assistance of American aid, some governments in Asia were able to bring in such policies.

THE VITAL SETTING

A case can be made that the two most influential Americans of the twentieth century are Henry Ford and Walt Disney. From humble beginnings, both built American business empires based on new methods of production and organization which came to exert an influence which was global, as well as national. They were but two of many people who helped to bring about the prosperity of the American Century. Nevertheless, Jonathan Hughes (1986) includes Ford among his 'Vital Few' – people who made a distinct contribution to the creation of an economic powerhouse.

Ford took a luxury product and by developing methods of mass production reduced its price and made it accessible to ordinary workers. His Model T cost $950 in 1910, but by 1924 its price had been slashed to $290. In the meantime, average wages and disposable incomes had risen substantially. Owning an automobile was widely seen as a symbol of success; Ford's achievement was to put that accomplishment within reach of people of only modest incomes. By 1927, America produced 85 per cent of the world's automobiles and every second car on earth was a Ford (Jackson 1985: 160–2). As to Disney, beginning in the late 1920s, he built a huge corporation which provided a range of products which included cartoons, feature-length animation, live action films and documentaries, television shows, and theme parks.

> At the founder's death in 1966, Disney creations and Disney consumer merchandise had flooded much of the globe. From Chile to China, tens of millions of people who had never heard of Franklin D. Roosevelt or William Faulkner or Martin Luther King, Jr., could identify Mickey Mouse or Donald Duck in an instant.
>
> (Watts 1995: 84)

Cheap automobiles transformed America's economic and cultural life, especially in the period of rising affluence following the Second World War.

By then, the mobility which cars made possible, and their affordability for even blue-collar workers, had changed the way Americans lived and worked by allowing houses and jobs to be spread far and wide across metropolitan areas. It changed the way people relaxed, socialized, shopped, studied, and courted (see Jackson 1985: 246–71; Garreau 1991; Bailey 1988). Americans were far more likely to have a car to drive than their counterparts in Europe: in 1930, there was one automobile for every five Americans; in the UK the figure was forty-two people for every car. The UK did not reach the mark of five people for every car until 1970; by that time, there was one automobile for every two Americans (Jackson 1985: 163). No other country in the world embraced the automobile as early and as fully as did the USA.

Disney's products, like Ford's Model T, were designed to be accessible to average, rather than affluent, consumers. Their huge popularity meant that the values they were imbued with – the virtues of hard work and family and community stability, which Disney saw as being typically American – were appreciated by a wide audience which extended outside the USA. Steven Watts (1995: 107) writes that Disney's post-war films 'legislated a kind of cultural Marshall Plan. They nourished a genial cultural imperialism that magically overran the rest of the globe with the values, expectations, and goods of a prosperous middle-class United States.' Disneyland, the theme park which is a monument to those values, has proved to be an enormously influential piece of urban design. 'Those concerned with the layout, architecture, and construction of the built urban environment have taken Disneyland as a model for such projects as shopping malls, public and private buildings, sports stadiums, and historic preservation efforts' (Findlay 1992: 53).

In the economic success of these two corporate empires, one can detect the dominating influence of the personal characteristics and values of the founders: Ford's desire to find cost-effective solutions to technical and organizational problems, and Disney's nostalgia, imagination, and creativity. Yet the experience of Ford and Disney also confirms two basic truths about the relationship between values and economics. First, Ford and Disney needed commercial success to be able to develop their ideas to their full potential, and this depended on the wider economic and political framework within which they operated. Second, wherever societies experienced economic growth and were open to outside influences, new consumerist values and expectations were diffused rapidly. Local cultures were modified and in the process changes were brought about in the nature of demand as consumer preferences were altered.

Ford and Disney were both from rural backgrounds (Disney was born in Chicago, but spent his boyhood on a Missouri farm), but only by moving to big cities were they able to make a living out of following their boyhood interests. There they found the pool of skilled and unskilled workers and distribution networks they needed to produce in a cost-effective way. When Ford arrived in Detroit in 1879, at the age of 16, the city was beginning to boom as a heavy industrial centre. In the 1920s, when Disney built his first Los Angeles studio, the city and the Hollywood film industry was growing at an astonishing pace. People who invested in and worked in Detroit and Los Angeles, and indeed in every major American city, were the beneficiaries of earlier periods of boosterism and economic development. Such towns were large and prosperous because in the past public provision of basic infrastructure had been successful and this encouraged private investment and the building up of economies of scale, agglomeration, and location. Cheap oil and Federal highway building were to the advantage of Ford and other car manufacturers. Economic growth in general created a mass domestic market for consumer durables and leisure services and products. Ford and Disney deserved their success and made their own personal contribution to it (on economic grounds, few businesspeople would have persisted as Disney did with such 'follies' as a feature-length cartoon and a hugely expensive themed amusement park), but it could not have been achieved without an economic setting which saw America evolve into a consumer-oriented society.

Economic reform and growth in Asia has generated disposable incomes which people may choose to spend on consumer goods. In China, for instance, rising incomes and expectations have led to strong consumer spending on durables such as televisions, and on brand-name products such as clothing and sporting equipment. But the product most in demand is the automobile. The number of cars in East Asia is currently doubling every five years, and in China alone the potential market for automobiles is enormous (Anon. 1993b: 67; Xian 1994). The spending patterns of well-off households are being shaped by the idea that owning a car constitutes a tangible expression of success. Earlier this century, such values were largely confined to the Western world, and to the United States in particular, but now they have spread rapidly through Asia. These values will exert a profound influence on Asian cities. Already some are bulldozing their old buildings, widening streets, and making plans to reduce bicycle ownership, in the hope that this will solve problems of traffic congestion by making more room for cars. These are political decisions, shaped by culture (what the public values and expects) and economics (what it can afford); these decisions will in turn have a lasting economic and environmental impact. In cities all around the Pacific Rim – from Los Angeles to Mexico City to Sydney to Bangkok – the limitations of such an approach are obvious. Building more roads encourages urban sprawl, which is expensive. Greater road capacity also encourages people to drive, which ensures that the problem of traffic congestion and pollution recurs (see Frost 1995).

CONCLUSION

In each of the three case studies examined in this chapter, economic success depended on the existence of a partnership between cultures which embraced opportunities for the creation and spending of personal wealth and the political structures which created those opportunities. The appropriate setting for economic development was where a symbiotic relationship existed between productive government behaviour and the market sector. The behaviour of the market sector was shaped by people's attitudes and values, but this could only be translated into economic prosperity if governments effectively provided appropriate infrastructure and incentives. As Akio Morita (1987: 130), Head of the Sony Corporation, has written: 'No theory or plan or government policy will make a business a success; that can only be done by people.' Businesses need people who can read the market and make appropriate choices, but there are certain things which only governments can do and which they need to do well if business life is to flourish.

BIBLIOGRAPHY

Abbott, C. (1994) 'The Federal Presence', in C.A. Milner II, C.A. O'Connor and M.A. Sandweiss (eds) *The Oxford History of the American West*, New York: Oxford University Press.

Anon. (1993a) 'Economic Miracle or Myth?', *The Economist*, v. 328, n. 7380, 2 October: 29–30.

—— (1993b) 'Pollution in Asia: Pay Now, Save Later', *The Economist*, v. 329, n. 7841, 11 December: 67.

Bailey, B.L. (1988) *From Front Porch to Back Seat: Courtship in Twentieth-century America*, Baltimore: Johns Hopkins University Press.

Bate, W. (1978) *Lucky City: The First Generation at Ballarat*, Carlton: Melbourne University Press.

Butlin, N.G. (1965) 'Long-run Trends in Australian *Per Capita* Consumption', in K.J. Hancock (ed.) *The National Income and Social Welfare*, Melbourne: Cheshire.

Christopher, R.C. (1984) *The Japanese Mind: The Goliath Explained*, London: Pan Books.

Elvin, M. (1973) *The Pattern of the Chinese Past: A Social and Economic Interpretation*, Stanford: Stanford University Press.

Findlay, J.M. (1992) *Magic Lands: Western Cityscapes and American Culture After 1940*, Berkeley and Los Angeles: University of California Press.

Flynn, D.O. and Giraldez, A. (1995) 'Born with a 'Silver Spoon': The Origin of World Trade in 1571', *Journal of World History*, v. 6, n. 2: 201–21.

Frost, L. (1991) *The New Urban Frontier: Urbanisation and City-building in Australasia and the American West*, Sydney: New South Wales University Press.

—— (1992) 'Government and Economic Development: The Case of Irrigation in Victoria', *Australian Economic History Review*, v. 32, n. 1: 47–65.

—— (1995) 'The City on the Global Frontier', *Journal of the West*, 34: 42–8.

Garreau, J. (1991) *Edge City: Life on the New Frontier*, New York: Doubleday.

George, R.L. (1992) *The East–West Pendulum*, New York: Woodhead Faulkner.

Hanley, S.B. (1983) 'A High Standard of Living in Nineteenth-century Japan: Fact or Fantasy?', *Journal of Economic History*, v. 43, n. 1: 183–92.
Headrick, D.R. (1981) *The Tools of Empire: Technology and European Imperialism in the Nineteenth Century*, New York: Oxford University Press.
—— (1988) *The Tentacles of Progress: Technology Transfer in the Age of Imperialism, 1850–1940*, New York: Oxford University Press.
Holton, R.J. (1995) 'Review of J. Melling and J. Barry (eds) *Culture in History: Production, Consumption and Values in Historical Perspective* (1992)', *Urban History*, v. 22, n. 1: 139–40.
Hughes, J.R.T. (1977) *The Governmental Habit: Economic Controls from Colonial Times to the Present*, New York: Basic Books.
—— (1986) *The Vital Few: The Entrepreneur and American Economic Progress*, New York: Oxford University Press.
Jackson, K.T. (1985) *Crabgrass Frontier: The Suburbanization of the United States*, New York: Oxford University Press.
Jones, E., Frost, L. and White, C. (1993) *Coming Full Circle: An Economic History of the Pacific Rim*, Boulder: Westview Press.
Jones, E.L. (1990) 'The Real Question About China: Why was the Song Economic Achievement Not Repeated?', *Australian Economic History Review*, v. 30, n. 2: 5–22.
Ma, J.C. (1971) *Commercial Development and Urban Change in Sung China (960–1279)*, Ann Arbor: Department of Geography, University of Michigan.
McEvedy, C. and Jones, R. (1978) *Atlas of World Population History*, Harmondsworth: Penguin.
McNeill, W.H. (1982) *The Pursuit of Power: Technology, Armed Force, and Society Since A.D. 1000*, Oxford: Basil Blackwell.
Morita, A., with Reingold, E.M. and Shimomura, M. (1987) *Made in Japan: Akio Morita and Sony*, London: Collins.
Murphey, R. (1980) *The Fading of the Maoist Vision: City and Country in China's Development*, New York: Methuen.
Neugebauer, J.M. (1991) *Plains Farmer: The Diary of William G. DeLoach, 1914–1964*, College Station: Texas A&M University Press.
Robbins, W.G. (1994) *Colony and Empire: The Capitalist Transformation of the American West*, Lawrence: University Press of Kansas.
Shiba, Y. (1970) *Commerce and Society in Sung China*, Ann Arbor: Center for Chinese Studies, University of Michigan.
Tyrwitt, J. (1968–9) 'The City of Ch'ang-an: Capital of the T'ang Dynasty of China', *Town Planning Review*, v. 39, n. 1: 21–37.
Watts, S. (1995) 'Walt Disney: Art and Politics in the American Century', *Journal of American History*, v. 82, n. 1: 84–110.
Wright, A.F. (1967) 'Changan', in A. Toynbee (ed.) *Cities of Destiny*, London: Thames and Hudson.
Xian, L. (1994) 'The National Dream: 'A Car, Just a Car, Not Too Fancy . . . '', *China Today*, April: 36–43.

4

PERIPHERALIZING THE CENTER

An historical overview of Pacific Island micro-states

David A. Chappell

The recent growth of export-driven Asian economies has inspired visions of a coming "Pacific Century." Historian Paul Kennedy has predicted that East Asia will be a future core of world power (Kennedy, 1987: chapter 8). Others describe this prospect as "coming full circle," since China was once before a locus of global economic activity (Jones *et al.* 1993). Yet this optimistic image of the Pacific basin as a booming, integrated economy has been questioned by some scholars.[1] In fact, when viewed from the Island micro-states at its geographic center, the region shows far more incoherence, limitations and inequities than might be expected. Like survivors in the eye of a hurricane, the small, insular societies surrounded by today's Pacific Rim "dynamism" have developed strategies that enable them to preserve some traditions while selecting what they want from the outside. In doing so, they offer alternative models for "peripheries" in an interdependent world.[2]

Before Ferdinand Magellan named and crossed the Pacific in the years 1520–21, the ocean basin was segmented into sub-regions by what might be called an equilibrium of disinterest. For thousands of years, sheer distance made the ocean more of a barrier than a crossroads for Pacific Rim peoples. There is no solid evidence of transformative contact between Native American and Pacific Island people, despite Thor Heyerdahl's *Kon Tiki* voyage in 1947.[3] The seafaring Indians of Northwest America apparently believed that the ocean had a foggy limit beyond which no human could survive (Hilbert, 1986: 77). The ancient Chinese believed that there was a deadly whirlpool in the center of the Pacific, and the first emperor's expedition in quest of the drug of immortality never returned (Needham, 1971: 548–53). The westerly *kuroshio* current may well have brought wayward vessels from Japan to the Americas, but assessments of the impact of these voyages remain purely speculative (Plummer 1985). East Asian seafarers traded, for the most part, with each other, and the only route into the central Pacific was controlled by a network of Malay middlemen between insular South-East Asia and the Papuans of Melanesia (Hughes, 1977: 13–22).

It was along this southwestern "corridor" that various Austronesian-speaking peoples began voyaging eastward about five thousand years ago. Using only the stars and wave patterns as guides, their navigators sailed to archipelagos of the inner Pacific, sometimes as far as two thousand miles across open sea. These ancient migrations might potentially have bridged the geographic discontinuities of the Pacific, but because they were multi-generational, and the landfalls were so scattered over the largest ocean in the world, the old equilibrium of disinterest persisted. Over time, new linguistic and cultural diversities emerged among the Island peoples in the center of the Pacific. Their vast, self-contained maritime world hovered just out of reach of the better-known Rim civilizations. Perhaps, in some unrecorded encounter, Incas and Polynesians exchanged the sweet potato for the coconut (Buck, 1959: 322).

In many cases, the descendants of these first settlers continued to maintain contact with other Islanders, thereby escaping total isolation. This process of inter-island communication led to regular exchanges of prestige goods and scarce resources, sometimes for social insurance. Every year, for example, a dozen atolls in Micronesia sent canoes 1,000 miles westward to the larger island of Yap, where they exchanged gifts to ensure a safety net in case of natural disaster (Alkire, 1978: 122–4). Another circuit linked eastern New Guinea with offshore islands in the Kula ring (Malinowski, 1961). Samoa, Tonga and Fiji, at the core of ancient Polynesia, built alliances among chiefly elites by exchanging finely woven mats, ceremonial cloth, tattooing, spouses, and timber for canoes (Kaeppler, 1978: 11–13, 246–52). There were also innovators, such as Pa'ao, a priest who, according to oral tradition, sailed 2,000 miles from Tahiti to Hawai'i to introduce a new political hierarchy and sacrificial worship of a war god (Beckwith, 1970: 363–73).

Yet relative to the outer Pacific Rim, the Islands of the inner Pacific were generally cut off, technologically, epidemiologically and culturally. For example, no Pacific Island people used metal tools or writing until Europeans arrived.[4] Moreover, their populations proved as vulnerable to introduced Eurasian diseases as were Native Americans. The rate of depopulation after foreign contact would reach 90 per cent on islands like Guam and Hawai'i.[5] Inner Pacific peoples were accustomed to visits from strangers, but Europeans did not obey their rules of property, and old legends in some cases confused the hosts. James Cook, for example, arrived in Hawai'i during the annual festival in honor of Lono, a god who had left and vowed to return. Like Cortez in Mexico, Cook enjoyed special hospitality at first, but unlike Cortez he died on the beach, after overstaying his welcome and fighting over property (Sahlins 1981).

In the sixteenth century, Spain initiated European contact with Pacific Islanders, and for 200 years treasure galleons provided the region with its first regular transoceanic shipping route. In 1521, Magellan's round-the-world expedition touched at Guam in Micronesia. Not only was Magellan the first known navigator to cross the Pacific, but his expedition did so without encountering other human beings for three months. After sailing 10,000 miles from Cape Horn, his sailors were so starved that they soon fought over property with the Chamorros of Guam. Magellan labeled Guam the Island of Thieves and went on to the Philippines, where he was killed in another battle. More Spanish expeditions crossed the Pacific where they fought unsuccessfully with Portugal over control of the Indonesian Spice Islands, and searched in vain for King Solomon's legendary gold mines. In 1565, the Spanish succeeded in establishing a colony at Manila, which opened the markets of Asia to Mexican Silver (Hezel 1983).

The annual Manila-to-Acapulco treasure galleons almost made the Pacific a coherent region, but most Spanish encounters with inner Pacific Islanders were fleeting and violent. While passing through the Marquesas in 1595, Spanish gunmen shot and killed 200 native canoers, often for recreation (Markham, 1904: 137–56). Even after 1668, when Guam became a formal Spanish colony, most Pacific Islands remained unknown to outsiders, except for occasional pirate ships. This neglect ended when England and France signed the Treaty of Paris in 1763: their naval vessels then began to explore the Pacific Islands more systematically. In 1767, Tahiti became the first major provisioning station in the South Pacific because the native people quickly learned to pacify and manipulate foreign ships. After discovering the dangers of European firepower, Tahitian leaders sent out their women to barter sex for iron nails (Pearson, 1969: 199–217). The myth of South Seas hospitality derives, therefore, from a deliberate strategy to acquire foreign goods, a practice that the modern tourist industry perpetuates.

It was Cook's explorations that inspired more intensive economic penetration of the region. His three expeditions discovered the value of Northwest American furs in Canton, the abundance of whales and seals, and the availability of provisions in the Islands. A process of transformation then began, which increasingly tied Pacific Islanders to the world economy. In the 1780s, Anglo-American traders bought furs from Indians in Northwest America and, on their way to Canton, stopped for provisions in Hawai'i. There they sold guns to ambitious chiefs. Such interaction helped King Kamehameha to unite the Hawaiian Islands for the first time. The China market also induced tradeships to buy sandalwood and *bêche-de-mer* from Islanders, thereby incorporating more natives into export production (Howe 1984). Ship captains soon began to complain about the bargaining skills of some Islanders, calling them "Jews of the South Seas." (Jarman 1838: 117-18). Whalers and sealers not only bought supplies but hired thousands of indigenous sailors for their crews. By the 1840s, perhaps one-fifth of the seamen on American whaleships were Pacific Islanders. Three thousand Hawaiians a year shipped out, 500 of whom worked in Northwest America for fur companies; they also worked as boatmen in the California cowhide trade and as '49ers during the gold rush (Chappell 1991).

Island demographies changed as alien diseases killed thousands of natives while foreign immigration increased. Beachcombers, traders, missionaries and consuls took up residence in the Islands, introducing new ideas and creating new wants. Commercial plantations multiplied during a world cotton shortage caused by the American Civil War; after the 1860s, sugar, copra and coffee replaced cotton growing. Land was available wherever local chiefs bought firearms for wars and needed to pay off their debts. As thousands of Asians arrived in places like Hawai'i and Fiji to work on sugar plantations, Islanders who had once been able to manipulate outsiders increasingly came under the rule of colonial powers. This loss of sovereignty was complete by 1900 (Campbell, 1989: chapter 10).

Colonialism removed control over political decision-making from most Pacific Islanders. Britain and its two surrogates, Australia and New Zealand, acquired over a dozen colonies, while Germany, France and the United States ruled another dozen. The First World War transferred German Micronesia to Japan, which introduced so many Japanese and Okinawan sugar plantation workers that the immigrants soon outnumbered the natives (Peattie, 1988: chapters 4–6). The Second World War exposed Pacific Islanders to more physical destruction – and imported cargo – than they had ever imagined. Not only did common soldiers from the United States and Australia treat Islanders more equally than the colonialists had, but Islanders realized that there was far greater material wealth in the outer world than they had been led to believe (White and Lindstrom 1989). The strategic competitions of the Cold War subjected Pacific Islanders to a peculiar mixture of radiation from nuclear testing and development aid from ambitious superpowers (Firth 1987). Colonialism thus left Pacific Islanders with an ambivalent legacy of marginalization and rising expectations. Their dilemma was that, apart from mineral-rich Melanesia, most Islands were a periphery without valuable resources to barter for modernization.

In fact, half the micro-states in the Pacific Islands are still political dependencies of some outside power (Larmour 1983; Robie 1989). When decolonization began after 1945, only those Pacific Island countries ruled by Britain or its surrogates became fully independent. No American or French Pacific territory has completely separated from its colonial ruler because, unlike Britain, the United States and France continue to see important roles for themselves in the region. In 1947, the United States acquired Micronesia as a "strategic" Trust Territory from Japan, and it wants ongoing military options there. France wants to retain control of its nuclear testing facilities in the Tuamotus and strategic mineral deposits in New Caledonia. Hawai'i depends on American military spending and on money from five million tourists a year for nearly all its needs; of every three shipping containers that come to the state, two return empty to the mainland (Beechert, 1991: 174). Even politically sovereign nations like Western Samoa or Tonga depend primarily on foreign aid and labor out-migration for income.

To-day, what most inner Pacific Islands have to offer the outside world are tourist fantasies, strategic bases, and migrant labor. They appear to be totally dependent on outside monies to support a modern living standard (Connell 1991). Yet this very inequity forces them into a role that allows them to preserve their own distinctive identity. Futurist James Dator has argued that they are already living in the twenty-first century because they know how to acquire and use modern technology even if they don't produce it (Dator, 1985). Indeed, their strategies, precarious as they may seem, represent the cutting edge of global interdependence.

One innovation is a partial form of sovereignty known as Free Association, which as a legal concept dates back only to 1960 (Roff 1991). This new international status, proposed by the United Nations as an alternative to independence or incorporation, is without precedent.[6] In 1965, the Cook Islands chose this option and became Freely Associated with New Zealand; nearby Niue followed suit in 1974. Both Island countries are internally self-governing, but their people are citizens of New Zealand. In fact, over two-thirds of them have now emigrated to Auckland, which has become, in effect, the largest "Polynesian" city in the world. In 1983 a Compact of Free Association was negotiated between the United States and the Marshall Islands and the Federated States of Micronesia (later expanded by the inclusion of Belau (Palau)) states; they are self-governing and have joined the United Nations, but the United States retains important military powers in exchange for millions of dollars in aid (Firth 1989).

An even more widespread strategy for modernization is what political economists have called MIRAB (Bertram and Watters, 1985: 497–519). This acronym stands for migration, remittance, aid and bureaucracy. Many resource-poor Pacific Island countries today export people, as students or workers, who then send home money to their families. One-third of Tonga's national income derives from this source. Altogether, 500,000 Islanders have migrated to industrial cores around the Pacific Rim – mainly the United States, Australia and New Zealand – so that there are more Samoans in Los Angeles today than in Pago Pago (McCall and Connell 1993). In addition, industrial powers donate aid money for development, which usually pays the salaries of local government officials. Tonga relies on such aid for over 90 per cent of its state revenues. Yet Tonga also retains its traditional monarchy, and no foreigner is allowed to own land in Tonga. Foreign powers are willing to give aid to Tonga and other South Pacific nations in order to keep them friendly and to nurture markets for their own exports. Even in Micronesia, most of the millions donated by the American government return to US banks through purchases of American products. Pacific Islanders, who have a long tradition of reciprocal exchange systems, regard international aid not as charity but as a redistribution of world income from countries that consume more than their fair share of global resources (Sevele, 1985: 71–77).

Other options for the peripheralized center of the Pacific exist. One is charging foreign ships for the use of their 200-mile Exclusive Economic Zones – a United Nations concept that significantly enlarges Pacific Islands on the map. For example, the South Pacific Forum (to which sixteen self-governing states belong) has concluded a lucrative regional fishing agreement with the American Tuna Association. Off-shore banking and tax havens are being developed in several Pacific Island countries, and non-residential passports are even being sold to potentially stateless people like Hong Kong Chinese. Inner Pacific micro-states have thus demonstrated an enterprising attitude toward the regional economy, despite their disadvantages. Tourism is a growing industry in the Islands, some of which are looking to Hawaii as a model, and there is increasing investment from Japan and other Asian countries, as well as from the European Community (Fairbairn *et al.* 1991).

Some Island governments have tried to imitate the Pacific Rim model of labor-intensive manufacturing to achieve economic take-off. In Fiji and Saipan, for example, tax-free incentives have given rise to garment industries; wages remain very low and access to markets can be threatened by changes in trade agreements.[7] Melanesia, especially Papua New Guinea and New Caledonia, has valuable minerals to export, such as gold, copper and nickel, so there is little outmigration (Howard, 1991: 7; McCall and Connell, 1993). In fact, New Caledonia is a magnet for Polynesian migrants from other French Territories.

Henry Kissinger once said of Micronesia, "There are only 90,000 people out there – who gives a damn?" (McHenry, 1975: 98). The obvious answer is, the Islanders do. They survive in the "Pacific Century" by keeping one foot in the world economy and another in the Islands, where they send remittances and perhaps come home to retire after a career overseas. In 1778, a Hawaiian is said to have seen the iron on Captain Cook's ship and announced, "I'll go and gather that treasure because that's how I make my living, merely by scooping up whatever I can" (Kahananui 1984: 167–8). Epeli Hau'ofa, a Tongan sociologist, has argued that modern outmigration from the Pacific Islands is the continuation of an ancient dynamic, that of voyaging to seek new lands and opportunities. Rather then viewing Oceania as poor dots scattered across a vast region, he preferes to see it as a holistic circuit he calls "our sea of islands," where people "are flying back and forth across national boundaries . . . far above and completely undaunted by the deadly discourses below . . . cultivating their ever-growing universe in their own ways, which is as it should be, for therein lies their independence" (Hau'ofa 1994: 160). Where others see dependency or interdependence, he reads independence, since families at the grassroots level are pursuing their own strategies regardless of analysis based on "national" boundaries. In other words, Hau'ofa suggests that Pacific Islanders are reversing core and periphery by extending their ancient frontiers to the Pacific Rim. As a Samoan states, there are now many shades of Samoa, from Pago Pago to Los Angeles, and every segment of this global community needs each other to survive in the modern world: "We are no longer a people united as one race, but more like a people searching . . . "[8] It is still possible to survive on an outer island by fishing or farming, but many Islanders have become urbanized, and returning to the subsistance life-style would not be easy. Increasingly, families are sending migrants overseas to work, even at low-paying jobs where they encounter discrimination, lay-offs or deportation during economic slumps. But Pacific Islanders have a heritage of voyaging. Today, their "transnational corporations of kin" (Bertram and Watters 1985) are building diasporic societies whose cores and peripheries meet at the airport.

NOTES

1 Dirlik (1992) regards the "Asia–Pacific" region as a Euro-American concept, and Palat (1992) suggests that the subcontracting system at the base of East Asian "dynamism" is exploitative and indicative of new global, not regional, hierarchies of finance–power.

2 Wallerstein (1974–89) has argued that after 1500 a capitalist European power "core" won increasing control over the world economy, reducing such areas as the Pacific to the lowest rungs of a global hierarchy. Once-self-sufficient regions became "peripheralized" as raw material producers dependent on foreign manufactures.

3 Compare Heyerdahl (1952) with Kirch (1989).

4 The sole example of "writing" comes from Easter Island, but there is debate about its meaning and date. See Kirch (1989: 273–74).

5 The degree of depopulation is a controversial topic. Compare, for example, Stannard (1989) with Dye (1994).

6 It could, however, be compared with the nineteenth-century notion of a "protectorate." Tonga, for example, preserved its monarchy intact this way, while conceding its foreign affairs to Britain. See Campbell (1992).

7 The most important trade agreement is the South Pacific Regional Trade and Economic Cooperation Agreement (SPARTECA), which grants special access for South Pacific Forum countries to the Australian and New Zealand markets. Forum exporters also benefit from the Lomé Convention with the EC. See Fairbairn *et al* (1991).

8 Author interview with Vaipuna Kaulave in Pago Pago, June 1995.

BIBLIOGRAPHY

Alkire, W. (1978) *Coral Islanders*, Arlington Heights, IL. AHM Publishing.

Beckwith, M. (1970) *Hawaiian Mythology*, Honolulu: University of Hawaii Press.

Beechert, E. (1991) *Honolulu: Crossroads of the Pacific*, Columbia: University of South Caroline Press.

Bertram, I.G. and Watters, R.F. (1985) "The Concept of the Mirab Economy in Small South Pacific Countries" *Pacific Viewpoint*, 26, 2: 497–519.

Buck, P. (1959) *Vikings of the Pacific*, Chicago: University of Chicago Press.

Campbell, I.C. (1989) *A History of the Pacific Islands*, Berkeley: University of California Press.

—— (1992) *Island Kingdom: Tonga, Ancient and Modern*, Christchurch, NZ: University of Canterbury.

Chappell, D.A. (1991) "Beyond the Beach: Periplean Frontiers of Pacific Islanders aboard Euroamerican Ships 1767–1887", Ph.D. dissertation, University of Hawaii.

Connell, J. (1991) "Island Microstates: The Mirage of Development," *Contemporary Pacific* 3, 2: 251–87.

Dator, James (1985) *The Pacific Islands Region in the Twenty-First Century*, Honolulu: Center for Pacific Island Studies.

Dirlik, Arif (1992) 'The Asia–Pacific Idea: Reality and Representation in the Invention of a Regional Structure" *Journal of World History*, 3, 1: 55–79.

Dye, T. (1994) "Population Trends in Hawai'i Before 1778," *Hawaiian Journal of History* 28: 1–20.

Fairbairn, T., Morrison, C., Baker, R. and Groves, S. (1991) *The Pacific Islands: Politics, Economics and International Relations*, Honolulu: University of Hawaii.

Firth, S. (1987) *Nuclear Playground*, Honolulu: University of Hawaii.

—— (1989) "Sovereignty and Independence in the Contemporary Pacific," *Contemporary Pacific* 1, 1: 75–96.

Hau'ofa, E. (1994) "Our Sea of Islands," *Contemporary Pacific* 6, 1: 148–61.

Heyerdahl, T. (1952) *American Indians in the Pacific: The Theory Behind the Kon Tiki Expedition*, London: Allen and Unwin.

Hezel, F.X. (1983) *The First Taint of Civilization*, Honolulu: University of Hawaii Press.

Hilbert, V. (1986) *Haboo, Native American Stories from Puget Sound*, Seattle: University of Washington Press.

Howard, M. (1991) *Mining, Politics and Development in the South Pacific*, Boulder: Westview Press.

Howe, K.R. (1984) *Where the Waves Fall*, Honolulu: University of Hawaii.

Hughes, I. (1977) *New Guinea Stone Age Trade*, Canberra: The Australian National University.

Jarman, R. (1838) *Journal of a Voyage to the South Seas in the 'Japan'*, London: Longman

Jones, E., Frost, L., and White, C. (1993) *Coming Full Circle: An Economic History of the Pacific Rim*, Boulder: Westview Press.

Kaeppler, A.C. (1978) "Exchange Patterns in Goods and Spouses: Fiji, Tonga, Samoa," *Mankind* 11, 3: 246–52.

Kahananui, D. (ed.) (1984) *Ka Mooolelo Hawai'i*, Honolulu: University of Hawaii Press.

Kennedy, P. (1987) *The Rise and Fall of the Great Powers*, New York: Vintage.

Kirch, P. (1989) *The Evolution of the Polynesian Chiefdoms*, Cambridge: Cambridge University Press.

Larmour, P. (1983) "The Decolonization of the Pacific," in R. Crocombe (ed.), *Foreign Forces in Pacific Politics*, Suva: University of the South Pacific, 1–23.
McCall, G. and Connell, J. (eds) (1993) *A World Perspective on Pacific Islander Migration: Australia, New Zealand and the USA*, Kensington: University of New South Wales.
McHenry, D. (1975) *Micronesia: Trust Betrayed*, Washington, DC: Carnegie Foundation.
Malinowski, B. (1961) *Argonauts of the Western Pacific*, New York: Dutton.
Markham, C. (ed.) (1904) *The Voyages of Pedro Fernandez de Quiros, 1595–1606*, London: Hakluyt, Vol. I.
Needham, J. (1971) *Science and Civilisation in China*, Cambridge: Cambridge University Press, Vol. 4, Part III.
Palat, R.A. (1992) "The Myth of an Impending Pacific Century", Paper presented at the Department of Sociology Seminar, University of Auckland, New Zealand, November 23
Pearson, W.H. (1969) "European Intimidation and the Myth of Tahiti," *Journal of Pacific History*, 4: 199–217.
Peattie, M. (1988) *Nan'yo: The Rise and Fall of the Japanese in Micronesia*, Honolulu: University of Hawaii Press.
Plummer, K. (1985) *The Shogun's Reluctant Ambassadors: Sea Drifters*, Tokyo: Tuttle.
Robie, D. (1989) *Blood on Their Banner: Nationalist Struggles in the South Pacific*, London: Zed Books
Roff, S. (1991) *Overreaching in Paradise: United States Policy in Palau since 1945*, Juneau: Denali Press.
Sahlins, M. (1981) *Historical Metaphors and Mythical Realities*, Ann Arbor: University of Michigan.
Sevele, F. (1985) "Aid to the Pacific Reviewed," in Cooper, Antony *et al.* (eds.), *Class and Culture in the South Pacific*, Suva: University of the South Pacific.
Stannard, D. (1989) *Before the Horror: The Population of Hawai'i on the Eve of Western Contact*, Honolulu: University of Hawaii Press.
Wallerstein, I. (1974–89) *The Modern World System*, San Diego: Academic Press, 3 volumes.
White, G. and Lindstrom, L. (eds.) (1989) *The Pacific Theater*, Honolulu: University of Hawaii Press.

5

FROM MAGELLAN TO MITI: PACIFIC RIM ECONOMIES AND PACIFIC ISLAND ECOLOGIES: SINCE 1521

John McNeill

Late in 1520 Ferdinand Magellan left the Chilean coast with three ships. After ninety-nine days at sea they made land at Guam. A month's sailing brought them to the Philippines, where Magellan soon met his death. While probably not the first mariner to cross the Ocean, nonetheless Magellan's voyage inaugurated a new era for the Pacific, pioneering the connections between the Americas and Asia that would solidify after the establishment of the Manila Galleons in 1565 and the foundation of Manila in 1571 (Flynn and Giraldez 1995).

While this volume as a whole seeks to explore the consequences and meaning of the development of a Pacific Rim, this chapter focuses on what lay inside the Rim: the oceanic islands of the Pacific. In particular, it explores the environmental changes that took place in the island Pacific after 1521. It seeks to explain those changes, highlighting the role of connections between island ecosystems and the coalescing Rim economy.[1]

BEFORE MAGELLAN

When people first arrived in the Pacific they came to islands long isolated from the continental main theaters of (terrestrial) evolution. Plants and animals had evolved in splendid isolation. Consequently island ecosystems were vulnerable to rapid change: they were, in the language of ecologists, highly labile. Indeed, archeological evidence suggests that when humans first arrived they provoked rapid and significant environmental change. They burned off vegetation, depleted reef and lagoon species, and caused the extinction of many flightless birds.[2] Eventually many societies learned how to mitigate their impact. But they never ceased to change their island environments, and, where population pressure built up, they often continued to degrade them. Anything else would be surprising, and inconsistent with human experience.

Nonetheless, greater environmental changes lay ahead. Melanesians, Micronesians, and Polynesians have occupied their homes for anywhere from 40,000 (Solomon Islands) to 1,000 years (New Zealand). Over these centuries islanders traded only sporadically with one another, and not at all with the Rim. Consequently, one major driving force behind environmental change, the impact of long-distance trade, had no bearing upon Oceania before Magellan. Another agent of ecological change, biological invasion by alien species, affected oceanic islands soon after initial settlement, but thereafter vanished. In both the commercial and the ecological sense, oceanic islands remained isolated from the broader currents of the Pacific Rim and the world. In the sixteenth century that would begin to change. Henceforth distant demand from large societies around the Rim, and in some cases from beyond, would increasingly shape production, economic life, and environmental change on hundreds of Pacific islands. And with increasingly regular contact came wave after wave of biological invasion. These processes of incorporation, initiated by Magellan, accelerated with the voyages (1768–79) of James Cook. Although Magellan and Cook were Europeans, and it was for the most part Europeans who knit the farther reaches of the Rim together after 1521, the long-distance trade that drove much of Oceania's environmental change derived from Chinese demand. European and American merchants served as middlemen between Chinese markets and Pacific island ecosystems. The biological invasions derived from all over the world.

THE MAGELLAN EXCHANGE THAT NEVER WAS

When Columbus's trans-Atlantic voyages united the ecosystems of the New World and the Old, a dramatic biological exchange ensued, with enduring and momentous consequences for many parts of the world. The islands of the Atlantic felt the greatest ecological changes of all (Crosby 1972). No such result followed upon Magellan's trans-Pacific voyage.

Japanese, Chinese, Malay and other mariners had sailed the western Pacific for centuries before Magellan. From 1520 to 1760 Spanish, Dutch, French, and British sailors joined them, trading around the Pacific Rim. In the 1760s two circumnavigators, Byron and Bougainville, traversed the Pacific. Perhaps 450 European ships had crossed the Pacific between 1521 and 1769, but their impact on the oceanic islands – like the impact of Columbus's predecessors on the Americas – was minimal. The Spanish Manila Galleons (1565–1815), probably the most durable shipping line in world history, accounted for the vast majority of the 450. After 1668 the galleons usually paused, like Magellan, in Guam.

The Spanish presence there inevitably led to ecological changes. Spanish Jesuits inaugurated a mission (1668), and in converting the population to Christianity communicated to them influenza and smallpox, which (combined with egregious violence on the part of Spanish soldiers) soon reduced the population by about 90 percent. The mission also imported (intentionally or otherwise) many American plants and animals, and more came with the galleons. By 1914 20–21 percent of Guam's flora were American species, mostly from Mexico and Brazil (Merrill 1954: 230–7).

Elsewhere in the Pacific, Europeans had sighted perhaps a hundred of the islands east of New Guinea, but had landed only at about thirty. No mariners dallied outside of Guam except for Mendaña and Quiros in 1595. They stopped for nine weeks at a small island in the Solomons, and in the Marquesas tried (and failed) to grow maize.[3] Thus there was no great and sudden "Magellan Exchange" across the Pacific, let alone one involving the islands.

A modest Magellan Exchange took place between the American continents and the Philippine Islands. Many American plants were transported westward across the Ocean, including maize, potato, and cassava. Very few went the other way. Most exotic Philippine weeds were introduced from Mexico and Brazil, but not via Acapulco and the Manila Galleons. Rather, they came along the Portuguese routes from Brazil to Goa to the East Indies. The only oceanic island affected by the biotic exchange was Guam, the way station to the Philippines.[4]

A second exception to the rule of ecological stability before Cook's arrival is the uninhabited Juan Fernández Islands off the Chilean shore, in the eastern Pacific. Spanish mariners introduced alien species and effected a biotic revolution there between 1574 and 1750 (Wester 1991).[5] In this respect these islands parallel the Madeiras of the eastern Atlantic, uninhabited before the fifteenth century, and profoundly altered by species (and fire) brought by Portuguese mariners. But in general the ecological isolation of Oceania endured until Cook.

Cook made the difference because he always knew where he was. Armed with chronometers, Cook and his contemporaries could describe any location with precision, and return to it directly if desired. European exploration of the Pacific became more a matter of science and less a dangerous venture. In this lay great peril for the island populations.

THE AGE OF COOK, 1769–1880

The 1760s were to the Pacific what the 1490s were to Atlantic America. Europeans brought new tools to the Pacific, a new "portmanteau biota," and new economic principles and possibilities, all of which eventually combined to create radical disruptions to biotic communities, not least human ones.[6] The greatest disruption brought on by the arrival of European mariners in the late eighteenth century was human depopulation.[7] The general picture is as grim as Guam's. Over a few generations, many island populations declined by 90–95 percent (the Marquesas), meaning that the Pacific's encounter with the Eurasian disease pool was roughly as lethal as that of the Americas.[8] Declines of 2–3 percent per annum persisted over decades in many cases, due in part to high sterility (from sexually transmitted diseases) but more to heightened mortality. As in the Americas, populations stabilized 120–150 years after initial contact (roughly 1880–1920 in the Pacific), and then grew. Most islands (but not the Marquesas) have more people today than ever before.

Taking the Pacific as a whole, diseases surely did the most damage, but the islands also lost people through enslavement, blackbirding (as forced labor recruitment was known), and labor migration. Many island men joined whaling ships in the early nineteenth century and never came home again. Far more migrated to the economic hot spots around the Rim and the plantations developing in certain archipelagos such as Fiji and Hawaii. Peruvian slavers took 3,500 Polynesians (mostly Easter Islanders) to work Peru's coastal guano and sugar in the years 1862–3. By 1866 almost all were dead. About 100,000 men left Melanesia to work the canefields of Queensland and Fiji between 1860 and 1900. About one-third of them never returned. Another 16,000 islanders, mostly Melanesians, went to the plantations of French Polynesia, New Caledonia, and German Samoa (Campbell 1989: 110–15). The depopulation occasioned by labor exodus from Melanesia reached about half a percent per year at its height, accounting for about a quarter or a fifth of Melanesia's general demographic decline (Rallu 1990: 336).

Labor migration on this scale not only directly lowered population in many places, it promoted the circulation of diseases around the Pacific, contributing to higher death rates. Epidemics following up the slave raids on Easter Island from 1862–3 nearly exterminated the remaining population. Returning labor migrants often brought deadly infectious diseases home with them, notably tuberculosis, influenza, and pneumonia.[9] Labor migration presumably increased traffic of a variety of other organisms as well – food crops, weeds, small animals, insect pests – and contributed to the ecological homogenization of the islands.

The labor demands of dynamic zones of the Pacific Rim helped depopulate the oceanic islands and shuffle their biotic decks. At the same time, however, the labor demands of plantation islands brought people to the islands from the Rim – and beyond. The sugar zones of Fiji and Hawaii in particular occasioned large immigrations from India (to Fiji) and from China and Japan (to Hawaii). These mass movements must also have introduced new species to these islands.

The human demographic catastrophe of the oceanic islands indirectly affected other creatures on land and at sea. Depopulation destabilized anthropogenic landscapes and opened niche space for other species. At sea, it probably permitted reef and lagoon life to recover where human pressures had depleted it. But on land the population collapse led to consequences more complex than a simple return to more 'natural' conditions. Population decline and land abandonment opened the way for forest recovery – a massive fallowing. In Fiji, for example, the bush reclaimed land from villages abandoned around 1860 (Brookfield and Overton 1988: 91). If agricultural area diminished in proportion to population, then perhaps 90 percent of cultivated land fell out of use. In 1840 cultivation on Tonga appeared "entirely neglected" to an American navigator (Wilkes [1845] 1970: III, 32). Where horticulture had relied on terraces or irrigation (Hawaii, for example), labor shortage brought these to ruin, promoting soil erosion. On many islands grazing animals checked recolonization by forest. Their introduction was part of a Noah's Ark of alien species introductions to the Pacific after the 1760s, some intentional but many accidental. The effect of this invading swarm was first to destabilize island ecosystems, then to further their homogenization.

Grazing animals found the abandoned lands provided better forage than tall forest. So the ecological vacuum created by drastic human depopulation helped goats, cattle and pigs to colonize widely. Their numbers grew exponentially in the absence of predators, and perhaps initially of diseases. In one documented instance, in the Galapagos, three goats released in 1959 became 20,000 goats by 1971 (Nunn 1990: 133). Whalers often stranded goats on Pacific islands so as to ensure a ready food supply in event of need, hoping for and often achieving caprine population explosions of similar proportions. Cattle, introduced to Hawaii in 1793, became a pest by 1845, eating and trampling crops. Teeth and hooves were enemies new to Pacific plants, many of which could not survive the cattles and goats' attentions and became extinct or much reduced in extent (Kirch and Sahlins 1992: II, 169–70).[10] This spelled opportunity for alien weeds able to co-exist with grazing animals. Hawaii acquired 111 new plant species between Cook's arrival and 1838, and has almost 5,000 alien plants today. Some, like Brazil's guava and Central American clidemia are pernicious weeds that thrive on the disturbed conditions humankind and grazing animals have created.[11]

Other alien species triggered far-reaching effects too. Hawaii acquired mosquitoes for the first time in 1826, and the *aedes aegypti* in 1892, providing suitable vectors for the transmission of new tropical diseases (Laird 1984). New rodents, particularly the brown rat and the Norway rat, upset every island's ecology. Imported in their millions and breeding prodigiously, their populations exploded to the detriment of birds, the Polynesian rat, crops, and some wild plants (Druett 1983: 213).[12] Rats' devotion to certain seeds even affected the species composition of Hawaiian forests (Cuddihy and Stone 1990: 68–70). In many cases, rats may have been the single most consequential alien intruder, and ought to be considered the shock troops of ecological imperialism in the Pacific. The bird life of New Zealand and Hawaii, already reduced in its variety since the arrival of Polynesians, suffered further depredations with the new rat species. The powerful effect of rats on unprepared bird life is especially clear in the case of Lord Howe Island, because it had no human population until the eighteenth century. Once, the island had fifteen or sixteen land birds, of which three became extinct between 1788 and 1870 under the impact of European sailors and settlers. There were no further extinctions until 1918, when *Rattus rattus* first set foot on Lord Howe Island and began to feast on birds' eggs. Five further extinctions followed in short order, and then a second era of stability ensued (Hindwood 1940).[13]

Where exotic species flourished and became pests, interested parties often deliberately imported yet another alien to check the pests. Frequently the hired assassins ignored their missions and attacked more vulnerable native species. In New Zealand, introductions of cats, stoats, weasels, and ferrets, intended to control the runaway rat populations, led to further decay of native bird numbers (King 1984). The mongoose, introduced in 1873 to control rats in Fiji's canefields, turned its attentions to the local birds instead, extinguishing seven native species (Mitchell 1989: 208–9).[14] Biological pest control in fragile ecosystems invites unpredictable results.

Throughout the Pacific new connections to the Rim brought new crops, generally to the benefit of human populations. One valley on Oahu (Anahulu) acquired watermelon, corn, tobacco (perhaps not beneficial), cabbage, beans, oranges, limes, lemons, guava, cucumber, squash, red peppers, coffee and rice, all between 1821 and 1846. Many of these aliens ran wild and colonized on their own, replacing native species in the gashes left behind by human depopulation (Kirch and Sahlins 1992: II, 169). The Maori of New Zealand acquired the potato in the late eighteenth century, which improved their food supply in what were to be difficult times ahead.

All told, the arrival of Europeans, with their 'portmanteau biota' and their frequent connections to the Rim, was a disaster for lowland organisms and soils in the Pacific islands. Native species suffered extinction, and many more found their domains reduced under the onslaught of the invaders. Highlands, however, felt far less impact.[15]

All this disturbance, extinction, and replacement was done by ecological teamwork with one invader clearing the path for the next. Microbes, by killing so many people, paved the way for livestock, which in turned paved the way for new weeds. The process resembles the ecological imperialism outlined by Crosby (1986), except that outside of New Zealand it did not involve, nor did it require, considerable European settlement. Occasional visits and the extreme vulnerability of island biotas sufficed.

The Pacific islands – and Pacific waters, too – were also vulnerable to ecological change that came not through the shock troops and other allies of European intruders, but through the economic activity of Europeans themselves (and Euroamericans and Japanese). The explorations of Cook were followed by exploitations of Pacific resources on a grander scale than anything seen hitherto. Most of this involved connections to China.

In 1784 Britain reduced its tea duty to 12 percent, bringing tea from the palace to the cottage and bringing the world to Canton. Except for whaling, all the nineteenth-century pillaging of the Pacific – for sandalwood, sealskins, *bêche-de-mer* (known as sea slugs or sea cucumbers to connoisseurs, as Holothuroidea to marine biologists), in some cases even timber – was done for the Chinese market. European, American, and Australian merchants organized the exchange, in which Pacific island products were acquired for Western manufactures, then exchanged for Chinese silk and tea. From the 1790s to 1850 a world-girdling "triangular trade" linked the Pacific island economies and ecosystems to Europe, North America, and China, with the most powerful consequences for the smallest and least integrated. New Englanders played a prominent role. But China's exports were the prize that energized the whole system (Spate 1979–88: III, 264–96; Dodge 1965).

The marine creatures of island lagoons attracted commercial attention in the nineteenth century. Sea slugs or sea cucumbers enjoyed a strong market in China, where they found their way into countless soups. Fiji and other islands produced sea slugs in quantity, especially between 1828 and 1850, temporarily depleting lagoons (Ward 1972). Truk, in the Carolines, produced half a million tons of sea slugs annually around 1900. Whatever the impact on lagoons, it did not last. The trade withered away and sea slugs are abundant today in Fiji and Truk. But the trade also affected vegetation. Drying the sea slugs, an operation that involved keeping fires burning day and night, consumed "enormous amounts of timber" in Fiji. Even productive palm groves were cut to supply the drying houses (Campbell 1989: 65–6).[16]

Sandalwood (*Santalum*), a genus of aromatic tree, was once common throughout the high islands of the tropical Pacific (as well as in South and South-East Asia). Pacific Islanders had used it for various purposes, and had burned it off to clear land. But the Chinese market, long fed from India, turned to Pacific sources of supply in the nineteenth century. Sandalwood, used for ornamental chests, boxes and furniture, and together with its fragrant oil, for Chinese incense, perfumes, and medicines, attracted traders aware of its value in Canton. They went first to Fiji (1804–16), then to the Marquesas (1815–20), and to Hawaii where an efficient royal monopoly expedited depletion (1811–31), and lastly to Melanesia, especially the New Hebrides (1841–65). In Hawaii kings and chiefs put several thousand commoners to work cutting sandalwood. They burned dry forests to make the precious timber easy to find by its scent (only its heartwood was valuable so charred trunks were acceptable). In the heyday of the Hawaiian trade, 1–2 million kilograms of heartwood went to China every year, eventually reducing the supply by about 90 percent. Only the poorest and remotest specimens remained. Hawaiian royalty, attached to the goods that sandalwood could buy, even tried to exploit stands in the New Hebrides, outfitting two ships for Vanuatu in 1829. Shipwreck and scurvy put an end to that expedition. Everywhere sandalwood disappeared widely and quickly, and in most places scarcely returned: the China connection of 150 years ago made an enduring impact on the species composition of Pacific vegetation.[17]

Other Pacific island trees became the target of timber merchants, especially in Hawaii. In the late nineteenth century, roads, draft animals, and metal tools gave rise to a Hawaiian logging industry, which focused on *koa*. A native acacia that makes a fine cabinet or furniture wood, some Hawaiian *koa* went for railroad ties in the western United States (Cuddihy and Stone 1990: 45–7).

Smaller trades in the nineteenth century had less extensive ecological impacts. The pig and pork trade from Tahiti to Sydney (1793–1825) provoked a boom in Tahitian hogs, with deleterious consequences for Tahitian vegetation. The tortoiseshell trade (actually Hawkesbill turtle) led to a sharp depletion in turtle numbers. Pearls, pearl shell, coral moss, and birds' nests were traded to China from the Society Islands and elsewhere. Mother of pearl oyster (*Pinctada margaritifera*), especially sought for buttons, found a strong market after 1802. About 150,000 metric tonnes were extracted from the oyster beds of the Society Islands. Here and in the Cook Islands, the only sizeable oyster banks in the Pacific, supplies declined after 1820 and the trade declined into obscurity.[18]

REFLECTIONS ON THE AGE OF COOK

Throughout the nineteenth century, commerce that meant little to China, the United States or Europe had powerful effects on the Pacific islands. This was true politically: much disruption followed upon the development of new wealth and the arrival of new weapons, such as guns. It was true economically, as many islanders for the first time found themselves linked to long-distance trade networks about which they generally had little information and therefore could not often use to their advantage. It was also true ecologically.

There are two major reasons why nineteenth-century commerce proved so ecologically disruptive; perhaps two sides of the same coin. First is the ecological condition of the islands at the beginning of the Age of Cook. Their long isolation from other ecosystems had made them vulnerable: Pacific island birds were not equipped to compete for niche space with rats, cats, and mongooses. Pacific islander immune systems could not recognize tuberculosis and smallpox. Pacific plants had not adapted to an environment of fire. This accounts for the spectacular impact of exotic introductions, especially mammals and micro-organisms.

Beyond the direct ecological effects of isolation, there are cultural ones that carried environmental consequences. The cultural configurations of island societies (some more than others) contributed to their vulnerability to ecological (and other) disruptions. Where firm hierarchy prevailed, as in Fiji and Hawaii, the extractive trades of the nineteenth century recommended themselves to chiefs and kings who saw profit in them. They organized the necessary labor, sold the desired products, and participated in the ecological depletion of their islands. Some no doubt felt they needed to, as guns were now required for their survival and guns came only from the traders. Others did so simply for the satisfaction of possessing exotic goods, useful or not. European and American traders operated in the Pacific at great financial and personal risk; they wanted to make money fast, had no stake in preserving any resource, and behaved accordingly. Island politics often encouraged islanders to do the same. Pacific island politics and ecology interacted in unfortunate ways when confronted with new commercial opportunities, a story with many parallels around the world.

Beyond this, the constraints island societies had devised against resource depletion often disintegrated with the cultural transformations of the nineteenth century. Christianity has no taboos on resource use, but rather on abortion and infanticide. It is a continental ideology, not an island one. Mission education (and its public successors) neglected local ecological knowledge, so that in the course of the nineteenth and twentieth centuries each successive generation understood less and less of the cycles of nature. The price mechanism and the doctrine of individual advancement contributed to the corrosion of traditional restraints on overexploitation. What had been in many cases a moderately well-regulated commons became, for reasons of chaotic culture change, a poorly regulated, or utterly unregulated commons. The forests, pastures, lagoons and reefs of the Pacific suffered tragedies of the commons.[19]

The rapid and widespread environmental change in the early Age of Cook derived momentum from two main driving forces: one essentially ecological, the other economic. The ecological driving force was the sudden uniting after Cook of inherently labile Pacific ecosystems with those of the wider world. The economic driving force was that of concentrated demand: dispersed markets containing millions of people became united suddenly to small zones of supply in the Pacific. The demand for sandalwood, hogs, pearl, and sea slugs focused the consumer demand of millions in China and Australia with a laser-like intensity upon Fiji, Hawaii, and Tahiti.

Taking the bird's-eye view of evolutionary biology, the entire Age of Cook, from 1769 to 1880, appears as a point of punctuation in the punctuated equilibrium of Pacific evolution. But from the lesser heights of history, one can see an era of accelerated change from about 1790 to 1850, followed by a slackening in the rate of change, from about 1850 to 1880.

The important exotic species (mammals and micro-organisms) had arrived at the start of the century, and while their disruptive effects would continue their greatest impact came early in their Pacific careers when their populations burgeoned. The rate of human depopulation slowed and in most islands stopped before the end of the nineteenth century. These slackenings were mild, indistinct, and impossible to demonstrate satisfactorily given the overlapping complexities of population biology among dozens of introduced and native species. Much clearer is the slackening derived from the decline of the China market.

Whale oil aside, the major products hunted and gathered for export from the Pacific after 1780 went to China. But by 1850 Chinese tea could be had without going to the trouble of hunting down the last stands of sandalwood. Opium provided the key that unlocked Chinese trade. As the British East India Company converted tracts of Bengal to opium production, China's commercial horizons shifted and the Pacific trade lapsed into insignificance. At the same time, the great Taiping Rebellion (1850–64) convulsed China, reducing its appetite for, among others, Pacific specialty goods. And, after a few decades, pearl, sandalwood, and sea slugs grew scarce: the China trade had skimmed off the cream of readily exploitable resources. Until commercial production replaced commercial hunting and gathering, the ecological change of the Age of Cook would abate.

STEAMSHIPS AND PLANTATIONS, 1880 TO THE PRESENT

With the development of plantation agriculture and regular transport and communication networks, organized within the context of colonial economies, environmental change accelerated once again. Toward the end of the nineteenth century European and American interest in the Pacific heightened, as it had in the 1760s, primarily for geopolitical reasons. Reputable great powers required a presence in the Pacific. Keeping colonies and coaling stations supplied in turn required regular shipping, which Europeans now established for the first time. Steamships shortened travelling time, allowing certain organisms a better chance of surviving transit from one place to another in the wide Pacific. The Panama Canal, completed in 1914, sharply lowered the costs of sailing between the Atlantic and Pacific, easing transport between the Pacific islands and the economic powers of the day. The effect of more extensive and more regular transport, made possible by steamships, was to link the Pacific more firmly to the Rim and the wider world, which naturally had its ecological repercussions. The links grew tighter still during the Second World War, when the movement of men and goods around the Pacific briefly accelerated still further. Air travel during the war, and civilian air travel after 1950, reduced formidable distances, and permitted the introduction of alien organisms that did not ordinarily travel well. As in 1769–1850, advances in human transport produced considerable ecological change, almost all of it unintended and unforeseen.[20]

Most of the consequential exotic intrusions into the Pacific occurred before the 1880s. Naturally, some of the species involved had yet to make their way everywhere they could, so their colonizations and consequences continued to ripple throughout the Pacific. Cats in the Cook Islands, introduced in the nineteenth century, exterminated indigenous birds throughout the twentieth. But countless new species also joined the Pacific ark: Hawaii, which acquired a new species every 100,000 years in prehuman times, now acquires twenty invertebrates alone every year, mostly by airplane.[21] This account will be confined to the histories of the treesnake of Guam (*Boiga irregularis*), and the giant African snail (*Achatina fulica*), biological invaders transported by the tides of war and trade.

B. irregularis is native to Melanesia. It did not exist on Guam when American forces arrived there in 1944. But when salvaged war equipment from Melanesia was routed through Guam it probably carried snakes, which disembarked. Up to 1960 their numbers remained modest. But by 1970 the snake had colonized most of the island. In the 1970s people began to notice that the native birds of Guam were fast disappearing. Eventually a graduate student named Julie Savidge identified the culprit as *B. irregularis*. It climbs trees and devours chicks and fledglings in one gulp. Guam's avifauna had no experience of such a predator and lacked any defenses. Bats and lizards too almost disappeared, while the snake's population densities in some places reached 100 per hectare.[22] The snake also likes to climb on electrical wires and has caused hundreds of power outages. Its history is a classic case of population explosion among an introduced predator. Even without another war, *B. irregularis* is likely to spread to other islands, with much the same consequences.[23]

The giant African snail is native to the East African coast.[24] It was deliberately introduced to Mauritius and Réunion early in the nineteenth century so French planters could enjoy outsized *escargots* in their soups. The snail is a superb stowaway, capable of attaching itself to materials of almost any sort. It soon spread throughout the Indian Ocean – it was in India itself by 1847 – and entered the South Pacific via Indonesia and the Philippines by 1930 at the latest. Before the Second World War it was well ensconced in Papua New Guinea, Micronesia, and Hawaii. It reached Guam during the war. It is now very widely distributed throughout the tropical Pacific, where it is a major crop pest, afflicting cocoa, rubber, banana, sweet potato, cassava, yams, breadfruit, and papaya among other victims.

Numerous other crop pests infiltrated the Pacific after 1880, including rabbits, insects, and diseases.[25] Most pests spread during the golden age of Pacific shipping, from 1914 to 1965, when 2–3 vessels sailed weekly along the main shipping routes.

One factor that helped crop pests to spread was the creation of plantation agriculture, with its monocrop production patterns and emphasis on exports. This improved the prospects of both travel and sustenance for the Rhinoceros beetle, the coconut beetle and others that delight in coconut groves, sugar-cane fields and the like.

Plantation agriculture appeared in the middle of the nineteenth century, and developed extensively toward the end of it. Steamships, colonialism, and, in cases such as Fiji, imported indentured labor helped. Plantations invariably mean large-scale environmental change. Broad expanses must be cleared for crops, and generally forest land is preferred, certainly for sugar. In the Pacific, suitable lowland forest had often already been cleared, so plantations made do with swidden fields where virgin forest no longer existed. The fuelwood requirements of sugar boiling contributed greatly to forest clearance in Fiji and Hawaii, as they had in Brazil and the Caribbean. In Hawaii sugar took off in the 1890s and eventually covered 100,000 ha (1970s). Pineapple, introduced early in the nineteenth century, covered up to 30,000 ha at its peak in the 1950s. Bananas and coffee accounted for smaller areas. Land clearing for commercial crops has been the main cause of plant extinctions in twentieth-century Hawaii, where about 10 percent of the native flora is gone and another 50 percent is endangered (Cuddihy and Stone 1990: 41–4, 104).

Smaller-scale plantation agriculture developed in the Society Islands after 1860, at first emphasizing cotton in response to shortages arising from the American Civil War. In the 1920s the Japanese converted Saipan, Tinian and Rota (recently acquired from Germany) into "one vast cane plantation."[26] Most small islands, in so far as they developed plantation agriculture, produced only copra, which in the days of regular inter-island shipping found ready markets.

Ranching, which might be considered plantation pastoralism, also contributed to vegetation change in the twentieth-century Pacific. Cattle suppress forest regrowth and favor the success of introduced grasses. So did repeated burning: ranching (and plantation agriculture) intensified the fire regime of much of Hawaii, promoting fire-resistant (mostly African) grasses.[27] In Hawaii commercial ranching dates from the middle of the nineteenth century, but expanded quickly only in the twentieth century. By 1960, half of the archipelago's area was turned over to beef cattle, the proportion declining to a quarter by 1990. A large chunk of forest conversion in Hawaii is a result of the beef export trade.[28] Even remote Easter Island felt the touch of commercial ranching. Sheep first arrived in 1864 at a time when the human population verged on extinction. Commercial sheep ranching began in 1870; cattle ranching followed. Sheep-raising formed the backbone of the island economy for over a century and endured until the 1980s (cattle are still raised there). Ruminants (owned and controlled by Chileans) have in effect selected the modern vegetation of Easter Island.

Forest clearance in the twentieth century has affected all the high islands in the Pacific. In some cases plantation agriculture (see above) played the dominant role, in other cases subsistence agriculture, driven by population expansion (see below) has done so. In the Solomons, and elsewhere in Melanesia, the richest forests in the tropical Pacific have attracted timber traders, lately for the Japanese market. As throughout the tropics, since 1970 timber harvesting has combined with agricultural expansion to reduce forest cover in the Solomons, Fiji, and Samoa, bringing on erosion problems, habitat loss, and some extinctions (Mitchell 1989; Brookland and Overton 1988; Routley and Routley 1977; Nunn 1990: 132).

Extractive activities have changed more than the vegetation in the Pacific. In New Caledonia and the Solomons mining has changed the face of land directly in recent decades. Until 1988 the biggest copper mine in the world operated on Bougainville in Papua New Guinea's Solomons province. It spewed forth 150,000 tons of waste rock and tailings per day in the 1970s. Its slurry killed all life in the Jaba River, altered the river's bed and its delta (Nunn 1990: 133; Gilles 1977). Phosphate mining on Makatea (French Polynesia) destroyed much of the island's surface between 1910 and 1960 in the interest of agricultural productivity in Japan, New Zealand, and the United States. Japanese phosphate mining did much the same in Palau after 1914 (Newbury 1972b; Purcell 1976: 190). But nowhere has mining affected the environment as dramatically as on Nauru and Banaba (formerly Ocean Island).

On these two atolls, millennia of visiting seabirds have left deep fossil guano deposits, the richest in the world and almost pure phosphate. In 1900 and for a long time previously, the phosphate was covered over by topsoil and forest. Mining began in 1905. About 100 million tons have been extracted, of which two-thirds went to Australia, more than a quarter to New Zealand, and the balance to Britain, Malaysia and Japan. Like Makatea's phosphate, Nauru's and Banaba's have bolstered agriculture in Rim countries. The population of Banaba has not done well out of this, having had its island mined out by 1979. Nauruans are more fortunate. None of them need work. They renegotiated the lease after independence in 1968, and have since become both the least populated (c. 5,000) state in the world and the richest, with a per capita income greater than Saudi Arabia's or Switzerland's. Nauruans have invested their proceeds, so that they will be *rentiers* when the phosphate runs out, as they expect it will before the turn of the century. But there is little surface left of their island: on four-fifths of Nauru miners have extracted the guano to a depth of 6 or 7 meters, leaving empty pits amid limestone pillars to show where the land surface once was. Full recovery of native vegetation will take millennia, unless Nauruans decide to intervene.[29] This economically logical ecological barbarity is one of the indirect results of the livestock economy in Australia and New Zealand, and the dominance of the Pacific Rim over the Pacific islands (Hein 1990; MacDonald and Williams 1985: 61, 564–9; Mitchell 1989: 26–31).

REFLECTIONS ON THE ERA OF STEAMSHIPS AND PLANTATIONS

The driving forces behind the environmental changes in the Pacific after 1880 are the same as in the Age of Cook – with one alteration and one addition. The alteration is in the impact of population changes after 1880, as growth replaced secular decline. The addition derives from the geopolitical importance of Oceania to Rim powers.

Population, in the twentieth century as in the nineteenth, has crucially affected environmental change. However, the mechanism fundamentally altered: in the nineteenth century, population decline created environmental effects, whereas in the twentieth century it was population growth. In the nineteenth century depopulation created empty niches in the islands, which other species rushed to fill. In the twentieth century, population growth, from natural increase and immigration, filled most islands to historic maxima. By mid-century Oceania's populations were rising by 3 percent per annum; at the end of the century growth it is 2.5 percent in Melanesia, less in Micronesia and Polynesia. In most cases population growth has required an extension of cultivation, with unhappy consequences for native vegetation and soils. It has often led to intensified use of reefs and lagoons as well (Wiens 1962: 454–66).

In addition, temporary population surges – tourism or military presences – have affected environments in a few islands. Tahiti, Saipan, and Oahu have felt a good deal of both. Tourism has flourished since the 1970s, bringing millions, chiefly from Rim countries, to Pacific island shores (Daws 1977; Baines 1977; Peattie 1984: 210). By and large the Japanese predominate north of the equator and Australians south of it. Entrepreneurs and developers have radically redesigned coastal districts to accommodate the preferences of the tourists, leading to chain reactions of effects on coastal vegetation and soils, reefs and lagoons. Waste disposal on scales never before necessary now vex several islands. A minor current in the stream of tourists to the Pacific is drawn by the ecological distinctions of the islands, and consequently amounts to a force for nature conservation. The tourist boom is still very much in progress and its full effects remain to be seen.

Less seasonal and less predictable surges in temporary population have come with warfare. The Second World War brought sudden influxes that doubled or tripled island populations, straining local resources (among other things). Troops came and went swiftly, as whalers had done a century before. Sometimes they took local men with them, as the Japanese did in Micronesia when they recruited labor battalions for their Southeast Asian campaigns. The isolation of Japanese-held islands late in the war, when the Americans controlled air and sea, led to a situation of acute overpopulation and undersupply: all edibles were gathered or hunted by hungry locals and Japanese. At the war's end, islands of Japanese settlement, primarily in the Marianas, were suddenly deflated as their Japanese populations, as much as 90 percent of the total in some cases, departed for Japan. In the war years numerous islands, even remote ones that had felt little impact from trade or plantations, experienced the scouring ecological effects of population instability in a concentrated (if brief) form.[30]

More fundamentally, indigenous island populations fluctuated in the twentieth century in response to inducements and discouragements to migration. The most dramatic case is the Marianas, where Japanese settlement increased population tenfold between 1920 and 1935, and postwar repatriation almost emptied the islands. More recently, islanders everywhere have been migrating to the Pacific Rim and to cities. Samoans have moved in large numbers to New Zealand and the USA. Cook Islanders have left for New Zealand where they now outnumber those still at home by two to one. The decline of shipping and rise of long-haul trans-Pacific air traffic has economically isolated most of the islands, a bitter irony for those that had in the nineteenth century and the twentieth abandoned self-sufficiency for participation in the international economy. They can no longer export copra; they must export people (Ward 1989: 243–4; Peattie 1984: 210).

The impact of these population movements on islands' environments is twofold. It amounts to another widespread fallowing, a reduction of pressures on lands and lagoons, less sudden and as yet less profound than that of the Age of Cook. Once again, this has not necessarily translated into a resurgence of native vegetation and marine life, at least not in the short run, because exotic species are now present, entrenched, and in some cases nimble colonizers. On steep land, emigration has meant labor shortage, land abandonment, and accelerated erosion as terraces and irrigation channels suffer neglect. Migration to the cities has promoted a new kind of environment, with new problems, the most serious of which is waste disposal. The population mobility and instability of the twentieth century has produced its own environmental pressures, distinct from those of secular growth or decline.

The additional driving force in Pacific environmental change, conspicuous in the second Age of Cook and almost absent in the first, is the colonial and military presence. European colonialism after 1880 made simpler (if it did not make possible) the development of plantations, mines, and timber concessions. British power over Nauru allowed Australia and New Zealand their cheap phosphate. American dominion in Hawaii eased the way for sugar, pineapple, and cattle barons. Japanese control of the

Marianas permitted state-supported sugar plantations. But a great deal of the economic and environmental change that took place in the twentieth century did not require the colonialism of the great powers, only the linkage to the Rim's great economies.

The military impact of the great powers is another matter. Military occupations led to the forced depopulation of some islands (something the Spanish had done in the Marianas in the seventeenth century). Japanese occupation, although brief, brought some islands of Micronesia and Melanesia into more regular contact with the wider world. The Second World War helped materially in the dispersal of weeds, insects and pests throughout the Pacific (Dale and Maddison 1984: 253). Protracted combat, as on Guadalcanal or Okinawa, blistered some islands, with consequences still visible a half century later. Naval bombardment nearly obliterated vegetation on many atolls (Fosberg 1973: 213). The effects of combat, however intense, are often brief. On Saipan, the scene of bitter fighting in 1944, resurgent vegetation has erased almost all the scars of war (as well as the prewar canefields). Probably most consequential, and certainly most durable, is the environmental impact of the nuclear programs of the Americans, British, and French – all of which did require colonialism in one form or another.

Nuclear testing began in the Pacific in 1946 when the United States detonated a bomb at Bikini Atoll in the Marshall Islands. The first hydrogen bomb test, also American, came in 1952 on neighboring Eniwetok. It apparently eliminated the atoll's rat population (Jackson 1969). Britain's nuclear testing began in Australia in 1952, and British H-bomb testing took place in the Gilbert Islands, starting in 1957. The French moved their nuclear weapons testing to the Pacific in 1962 and took the precaution of incorporating their sites, the atolls of Moruroa and Fangataufa, into France in 1964. All in all, about 250 nuclear tests have taken place in the Pacific since 1945 (Firth 1987: 5–12, 24–7, 70–82, 94–108; Mitchell 1989: 212; Danielsson 1984; Danielsson and Danielsson 1986).

The full environmental effects of these tests are impossible to assess because the details are kept carefully secret. Atmospheric testing, abandoned last by France in 1974, dispersed fall-out throughout the global atmosphere and minimized the local effects. Undersea testing, abandoned in the 1960s, dispersed radiation with the ocean currents. Underground testing, practiced in the Pacific only by France, resumed in 1995 after the new Chirac government unilaterally withdrew from an international moratorium. The reefs of Muroroa are impregnated with highly lethal plutonium, some of which is slowly leaking into the sea. The consequences, great or small, will be durable: plutonium has a half-life of 24,000 years.

CONCLUSION

The environmental history of the Pacific exemplifies the costs of splendid isolation – or more accurately, of the end of isolation. Island ecosystems were highly labile, increasingly so west to east along the gradient of increasing isolation. This in effect equipped external agents of all biological ranks with extraordinary power. Similar patterns of isolation and its breakdown have produced cataclysmic change on many islands around the world, as in polar latitudes and in rainforest refugia. In every case, advances in transport, the process of economic integration, and to some extent the political links of colonial empires and war efforts, broke down the barriers of isolation, provoking sudden changes, most of them unfortunate for indigenous organisms – and societies. Ecosystems, individuals' immune systems, and sociopolitical systems all proved vulnerable to outside disturbance.

It could hardly have been otherwise. Once the oceanic islands' isolation was broken, biological invasion and economic extraction became irresistible. Islanders lacked the resources – and island rulers often did not wish – to forestall the economic changes that came first in Guam and then more widely. Equally, they could not prevent microbes, rats, and goats from prospering in the Pacific. Thus rapid and thorough ecological change swept through Oceania in recent centuries and continues to this day. Every year brings a few more biological invasions, and every year the islands lose more forests and soils so that the economic powers of the Rim can satisfy their need for timber and minerals.

NOTES

1 An environmental history of the Pacific Rim itself might be possible. The basic geology (mountains, vulcanism, earthquakes) and the climatic importance of ENSO events provide a certain unity to the Rim's environment. Numerous upwelling cold currents, full of nutrients and fish, combined with the downhill movements of water, nutrients, and soils from the coastal mountains have created an environmentally turbulent zone at the coasts, at sea and on land, where human beings over the centuries have found it attractive to make their livings. And in doing so, they have altered their environments, both locally and in recent centuries, more broadly.

2 The environmental impact of indigenous peoples in the Pacific is reviewed in McNeill (1994).

3 See Prieto (1975: 93–7), Spate (1979–88: I, 128–9, III, 56–8, 208 *passim*), and Merrill (1954: 239). Guam had perhaps 50,000 people before the Jesuit mission, about 4,000 in 1710. By 1786 only 1,318 Chamorros remained, but 2,626 were counted in 1810. After that, counts did not distinguish Chamorros from others in Guam (Spate 1979–88: II, 115–18).

4 Guzman-Rivas (1960: 92–133 and 195–208) discusses the biological exchange between the Americas and the Philippines.

5 Daniel Defoe's prototype for Robinson Crusoe, one Alexander Selkirk, was marooned in the Juan Fernández Islands early in the eighteenth century.

6 See Crosby (1986) for the concept of portmanteau biota, a complex of animal, plant, and microbial species that in effect work together as a team.

7 Rallu (1990) is the best guide.

8 This theme appears in Stannard (1989) and Crosby (1992).

9 See Shlomowitz (1989).

10 See also Cuddihy and Stone (1990: 40, 53–7) and Spriggs (1991). The impact of introduced grazing and browsing mammals on native plants is still strong. Wild horses are destroying vegetation in the Marquesas, especially Nuka Hiva; deer and possums are chewing away at New Zealand forests.

11 See Nagata (1985) and Cuddihy and Stone (1990: 73–91). Hawaii has a pan-tropical biota, with plants from India, China, Australia, the Americas, and not a few temperate invaders such as gorse and broom.

12 Here is Herman Melville on rats aboard whaling ships: "They stood in their holes peering at you like old grandfathers in a doorway. Often they darted in upon us at meal times and nibbled our food . . . every chink and cranny swarmed with them; they did not live among you, but you among them" (quoted in King 1984: 68). Two healthy rats in three good years can generate 20 million descendants; in ten years, if all went well – it never does – they could produce about 5×10^{17} (50 quadrillion) progeny (Druett 1983: 213).

13 Seabirds remained unaffected by the depredations of rats (and human beings).

14 This story (cane, rats, mongoose) was repeated in late nineteenth-century Jamaica as well.

15 Fosberg (1992) makes this clear for the Society Islands.

16 Ward (1972: 117–18) calculates that the Fijian trade required a million cubic feet of fuelwood, with "profound" implications for coastal vegetation.

17 See Shineberg (1967), Merlin and VanRavensway (1990), Kirch and Sahlins (1992: I, 57–97), Juvik and Juvik (1988: 381), and Cuddihy and Stone (1990: 39, 58). The trade was revived in 1988.

18 See Young (1967), Ward (1972), and Salvat (1981) on pearl.

19 See Klee (1980: 268–71) and Fosberg (1973). On tragedies of the commons, see Aristotle (*Politics* 2.3) and Hardin (1968).

20. An indication of the role of human transport in the dissemination of organisms is the speed at which influenza outbreaks travelled in the twentieth century. Early in the century until the late 1950s they spread at the rate of ship and rail traffic; after the 1960s the rate was determined by air transport (Goldsmid 1984: 196).

21 According to Alan Holt, Nature Conservancy, Honolulu (*Economist*, 10 April 1993).

22 *Economist*, 10 April 1993, reports 30,000 per square kilometer, or 300 per hectare.

23 See Rodda *et al.* (1992) and Savidge (1987). Several snakes have made it as far as the Honolulu airport, but none further, as far as is known (*Economist*, 10 April 1993, p. 92).

24 The saga of *Achatina fulica* is recounted in Dharmaraju (1984: 264–6) and Mitchell (1989: 204–6).

25 The sailing routes: France–Tahiti–New Caledonia; Australia–Solomons–Papua New Guinea; New Zealand–Tonga–Samoa–Fiji (Dale and Maddison 1984: 244–50). Some human pests spread too, such as the malaria-bearing *anopheles* mosquito, which since 1945 has colonized broad areas of the malaria-free Pacific from bases in Southeast Asia and Melanesia (Laird 1984: 303–9).

As yet, malaria plasmodium has yet to become established in Polynesia or Micronesia (Marshall 1993: 485).

26 See Purcell (1976: 202); Peattie (1984: 192–4). On the Society Islands' cotton, see Newbury (1972a).

27 The intense fire regime associated with plantation agriculture and ranching (or indeed any intense fire regime) has an effect upon ecosystems analogous to that of highly infectious disease. Upon its initial appearance it is highly destructive, but gradually, as it becomes endemic, it creates an ecosystem composed chiefly of species adapted to (or "immune" to) the effects of fire. Fiji, Hawaii, and much of the Pacific had to adjust to new disease regimes and new fire regimes between 1840 and 1950.

28 See Cuddihy and Stone (1990: 59–63). Sheep accounted for a small fraction of the conversion to pasture. Their numbers varied between 20,000 and 40,000 from 1870 to 1940.

29 See Manner *et al.* (1985). Abandoned mining zones do recover vegetation in Nauru. Initially 90 percent of the species are exotic weeds, but within decades some native species colonize where there is soil. Even in this extremely degraded environment, exotic species require the continued disturbance of human action; absent that, and native species can survive and flourish.

30 See Peattie (1984) for Japanese population and occupation in Micronesia.

BIBLIOGRAPHY

Baines, G.B.K. (1977) "The Environmental Demands of Tourism in Coastal Fiji," in John H. Winslow (ed.) *The Melanesian Environment*, Canberra: Australian National University Press.

Brodie, J.E. and R.J. Morrison (1984) "The Management and Disposal of Hazardous Wastes in the Pacific Islands," *Ambio* 13: 331–3.

Brookfield, Harold and John Overton (1988) "How Old is the Deforestation of Oceania?," in John Dargavel, Kay Dixon and Noel Semple (eds) *Changing Tropical Forests*, Canberra: Centre for Resource and Environmental Studies, Australian National University.

Campbell, I.C. (1989) *A History of the Pacific Islands*, Christchurch: University of Canterbury Press.

Crosby, A.W. (1972) *The Columbian Exchange: The Biological and Cultural Consequences of 1492*, Westport, Conn.: Greenwood.

—— (1986) *Ecological Imperialism: The Biological Expansion of Europe, 900–1900*, Cambridge: Cambridge University Press.

—— (1992) "Hawaiian Depopulation as a Model for the American Experience," in T. Ranger and P. Slack (eds) *Epidemics and Ideas*, Cambridge: Cambridge University Press.

Cuddihy, Linda and Charles Stone (1990) *Alteration of Native Hawaiian Vegetation: Effects of Humans, Their Activities and Introductions*, Honolulu: University of Hawaii Cooperative National Park Resources Study Unit.

Dale, P.S. and P.A. Maddison (1984) "Transport Services as an Aid to Insect Dispersal in the South Pacific," in M. Laird (ed.) *Commerce and the Spread of Pests and Disease Vectors*, New York: Praeger.

Danielsson, Bengt (1984) "Under a Cloud of Secrecy: The French Nuclear Tests in the Southeastern Pacific," *Ambio* 13: 336–41.

Danielsson, Bengt and Marie-Thérèse Danielsson (1986) *Poisoned Reign: French Nuclear Colonialism in the Pacific*, Harmondsworth: Penguin.

Daws, Gaven (1977) "Tourism in Hawaii: Benefits and Costs," in John H. Winslow (ed.) *The Melanesian Environment*, Canberra: Australian National University Press.

Dharmaraju, E. (1984) "Transport and the Spread of Crop Pests in Tropical Polynesia," in M. Laird (ed.) *Commerce and the Spread of Pests and Disease Vectors*, New York: Praeger.

Dodge, Ernest S. (1965) *New England and the South Pacific*, Cambridge, Mass.: Harvard University Press.

Druett, Joan (1983) *Exotic Intruders: The Introduction of Plants and Animals into New Zealand*, Auckland: Heinemann.

Firth, Stewart (1987) *Nuclear Playground*, Sydney: Allen & Unwin.

Flynn, Dennis and Arturo Giraldez (1995) "Born with a 'Silver Spoon': The Origins of World Trade in 1571," *Journal of World History* 6: 201–22.

Fosberg, F.R. (1973) "Past, Present, and Future Conservation Problems of Oceanic Islands," in A.B. Costin and R.H. Groves (eds) *Nature Conservation in the Pacific*, Canberra: Australian National University Press.

—— (1988) "Vegetation of Bikini Atoll," *Atoll Research Bulletin* 315: 1–28.

—— (1992) "Vegetation of the Society Islands," *Pacific Science* 46: 232–50.

Gilles, P.J. (1977) "Environmental Planning at Bougaineville Copper," in John H. Winslow (ed.) *The Melanesian Environment*, Canberra: Australian National University Press.

Goldsmid, J.M. (1984) "The Introduction of Vectors and Disease into Australia: An Historical Perspective and Present-day Threat," in M. Laird (ed.) *Commerce and the Spread of Pests and Disease Vectors*, New York: Praeger.

Guzman-Rivas, Pabio (1960) "Reciprocal Geographic Influences of the Trans-Pacific Galleon Trade," Ph.D. dissertation, University of Texas.

Hardin, Garrett (1968) "The Tragedy of the Commons,"*Science* 162: 1243–8.

Hein, Philippe L. (1990) "Between Aldabra and Nauru,"in W. Beller, P. d'Alaya and P. Hein (eds) *Sustainable Development and Environmental Management of Small Islands*, Paris: UNESCO and Parthenon Publishing (Man and the Biosphere Project, Vol. 5).

Hindwood, K.A. (1940) "The Birds of Lord Howe Island," *Emu* 40: 1–86.

Howe, K.R. (1984) *Where the Waves Fall: A New South Sea Islands History from the First Settlement to Colonial Rule*, Sydney: Allen & Unwin.

Jackson, W.B. (1969) "Survival of Rats at Eniwetok Atoll," *Pacific Science* 23: 265–75.

Juvik, Sonia P. and James O. Juvik (1988) "Images and Valuations of Hawaiian Rainforests: An Historical Perspective," in John Dargavel, Kay Dixon and Noel Semple (eds) *Changing Tropical Forests*, Canberra: Centre for Resource and Environmental Studies, Australian National University.

King, Carolyn (1984) *Immigrant Killers: Introduced Predators and the Conservation of Birds in New Zealand*, Auckland: Oxford University Press.

Kirch, P.V. and Marshall Sahlins (1992) *Anahulu: The Anthropology of History in the Kingdom of Hawaii*, Chicago: University of Chicago Press, 2 vols.

Klee, Gary (1980) "Oceania," in Gary Klee (ed.) *World Systems of Traditional Resource Management*, London: Edward Arnold.

Laird, M. (1984) "Overview and Perspectives," in Marshall Laird, (ed.) *Commerce and the Spread of Pests and Disease Vectors*, New York: Praeger.

McCall, Grant (1976) "European Impact on Easter Island: Response, Recruitment and the Polynesian Experience in Peru," *Journal of Pacific History* 11: 90–105.

MacDonald, Barrie and Maslyn Williams (1985) *The Phosphateers*, Melbourne: Melbourne University Press.

McNeill, J.R. (1994) "Of Rats and Men: A Synoptic Environmental History of the Island Pacific," *Journal of World History* 5: 299–349.

Manner, H.I., R.R. Thaman and D.C. Hassall (1985) "Plant Succession after Phosphate Mining on Nauru," *Australian Geographer* 16: 185–95.

Marshall, Leslie B. (1993) "Disease Ecologies of Australia and Oceania," in Kenneth F. Kiple (ed.) *The Cambridge World History of Human Disease*, New York: Cambridge University Press.

Merlin, Mark and Dan VanRavensway (1990) "The History of Human Impact on the Genus *Santalum* in Hawai'i," in *Proceedings of the Symposium on Sandalwood in the Pacific*, Berkeley: United States Forest Service Pacific Southwest Research Station.

Merrill, Elmer Drew (1954) "The Botany of Cook's Voyages, and its Unexpected Significance in Relation to Anthropology, Biogeography, and History," *Chronica Botanica* 14, 5–6: 161–384.

Mitchell, Andrew (1989) *A Fragile Paradise: Nature and Man in the Pacific*, London: Collins.

Nagata, K.M. (1985) "Early Plant Introductions in Hawai'i," *Hawaiian Journal of History* 19: 35–61.

Newbury, Colin (1972a) "Trade and Plantation in Eastern Polynesia," in R.G. Ward (ed.) *Man in the Pacific: Essays on Geographical Change in the Pacific Islands*, Oxford: Clarendon Press.

—— (1972b) "The Makatea Phosphate Concession," in R.G. Ward (ed.) *Man in the Pacific: Essays on Geographical Change in the Pacific Islands*, Oxford: Clarendon Press.

Northup, David (1995) *Indentured Labor in the Age of Imperialism, 1834–1922*, New York: Cambridge University Press.

Nunn, Patrick D. (1990) "Recent Environmental Changes on Pacific Islands," *Geographical Journal* 156: 125–40.

Peattie, Mark R. (1984) "The Nan'yo: Japan in the South Pacific, 1885–1945," in Ramon H. Myers and Mark Peattie (eds) *The Japanese Colonial Empire, 1895–1945*, Princeton: Princeton University Press.

Prieto, Carlos (1975) *El Océano Pacífico: Navegantes españoles del siglo XVI*, Barcelona: Alianza.

Purcell, David (1976) "The economics of Exploitation: The Japanese in the Mariana, Marshall and Caroline Islands," *Journal of Pacific History* ll: 189–211.

Rallu, J.L. (1990) *Les populations océaniennes aux XIXe et XXe siècles*, Paris: INED.

Rodda, G.H., T.H. Fritts and P.J. Conry (1992) "Origin and Population Growth of the Brown Tree Snake, *Boiga irregularis*, on Guam," *Pacific Science* 46: 46–57.

Routley, R. and V. Routley (1977) "Destructive Forestry in Australia and Melanesia," in John H. Winslow (ed.) *The Melanesian Environment*, Canberra: Australian National University Press.

Salvat, B. (1981) "The Living Marine Resources of the South Pacific – Past, Present, and Future," in N.A. Shilo and A.V. Lozhkin, *Ecology and Environmental Protection in the Pacific Region*, Moscow: Nauk.

Savidge, Julie A. (1987) "Extinction of an Island Forest Avifauna by an Introduced Snake," *Ecology* 68: 660–8.

Shineberg, Dorothy (1967) *They Came for Sandalwood: A Study of the Sandalwood Trade of the South-West Pacific, 1830–1865*, Melbourne: University of Melbourne Press.

Shlomowitz, Ralph (1989) "Epidemiology and the Pacific Labor Trade," *Journal of Interdisciplinary History* 19: 585–610.

Spate, O.H.K. (1979–88) *The Pacific Since Magellan*, Minneapolis: University of Minnesota Press, 3 vols.

Spriggs, Matthew (1991) "Preceded by Forest: Changing Interpretations of Landscape Change on Koho'olawi," *Asian Perspectives* 30, 1: 71–116.

Stannard, David E. (1989) *Before the Horror: The Population of Hawai'i on the Eve of Western Contact*, Honolulu: University of Hawaii Social Science Research Institute.

Thaman, R.R. (1992) "Vegetation of Nauru and the Gilbert Islands: Case Studies of Poverty, Degradation, Disturbance and Displacement," *Pacific Science* 46: 128–58.

Ward, R.G. (1972) "The Pacific Bêche-de-mer Trade with Special Reference to Fiji," in R.G. Ward (ed.) *Man in the Pacific: Essays on Geographical Change in the Pacific Islands*, Oxford: Clarendon Press.

—— (1989) "Earth's Empty Quarter? The Pacific Islands in a Pacific Century," *Geographical Journal* 155: 235–246.

Wester, Lyndon (1991) "Invasions and Extinctions on Másatierra (Juan Fernández Islands): A Review of Early Historical Evidence," *Journal of Historical Geography* 17: 18–34.

Wiens, H.J. (1962) *Atoll Environment and Ecology*, New Haven: Yale University Press.

Wilkes, Charles ([1845] 1970) *Narrative of the United States Exploring Expedition During the Years 1838, 1839, 1840, 1841, 1842*, Upper Saddle River, N.J.: Gregg Press, 5 vols.

Young, John M.R. (ed.) (1967) *Australia's Pacific Frontier: Economic and Cultural Expansion into the Pacific, 1795–1885*, Melbourne: University of Melbourne Press.

6

THE AMERICAN PACIFIC

Where the West was also won

Arthur P. Dudden

Perhaps the most unsatisfactory element of American history as we customarily find it structured and presented is the treatment historians accord the nation's Western history. Both the Continental West of the forty-eight contiguous states and the Pacific Oceanic West of Alaska, Hawaii, and beyond are conspicuously shortshrifted or, at times, overlooked altogether. This holds true especially for histories of the twentieth century, even more particularly for the half century since Japan's capitulation ending the Second World War.

The sagas of nineteenth-century westward movements are fully incorporated. Stereotyped into popular folklore, the hazardous wilderness adventures undergone generations ago blend with modern travails to provide the stuff of the earlier Hollywood's endless cycle of westerns. Pathfinders, prospectors, trappers, ranchers, cowboys, crooks, vagrants, Indians, soldiers, gamblers, prostitutes, and schoolteachers crisscross innumerable frontiers to compete against each other. In books, schoolrooms, and movies, this folklore dwells on the well-nigh universal epic – How the West Was Won – and it continues, in large part, to define the American West in popular imagination.

Much less familiar is the historic West encompassed by the Pacific Ocean Basin. Yet the histories of Alaska's Inuits, Aleuts, and Indians, Hawaii's and Samoa's Polynesians, the Filipinos and other colonial islanders, in addition to the Chinese, Japanese, and Koreans encountered by merchants, missionaries, soldiers, and sailors in their homelands recount the fullest dimensions of America's westward adventuring. Alaska and Hawaii, as the forty-ninth and fiftieth states respectively, have been integrated into the Union, even though, by great distances, they lie farther to the West than all the better-known western states and regions. Manifest Destiny never halted at the Pacific shores of California, Oregon, and Washington. Neither has the history of the United States.

The call of Cathay's riches hearkened back, siren-like, at least to Marco Polo's time. Shortly before 1700, the East India Company had introduced its American colonists to Great Britain's soaring addiction for Chinese teas.

Thereafter, in addition, luxury goods flowed increasingly from Canton into the homes of prospering British Americans. Finely carved lacquerwares, ivories, and jades, lustrous silks, cottons, and tapestries, scrolls, screens, and intricately woven carpets were unloaded at Boston, New York, Philadelphia, and Charleston, together with porcelain tablewares, vases, and ornamental bowls. But the American Revolutionary War, from 1775 until 1783, interrupted that traffic. When its own China trade commenced, the newly independent United States of America effectively embraced scarcely more than a strip of seaports, farms, plantations, and inland market towns from New Hampshire to Georgia. Yet from the republic's inception, a seagoing American empire began to take shape, half a century before Texas, California, or Oregon entered the Union.

The first ship to fly the Stars and Stripes in East Asia, the *Empress of China*, was underwritten by the enterprising Robert Morris of Philadelphia. Outbound from New York, on February 22, 1784, laden with her cargo of ginseng root (the wild-growing North American variety) prized by China's apothecaries, the *Empress* reached Macao, the Portugese trading factory on the estuary of the Pearl River, on August 23. Four months later, the vessel set sail from Whampoa, the anchorage for Canton (now Guangzhou), and arrived home on May 11, 1785. A regular commerce ensued in her wake. Merchantmen from Philadelphia, New York, and Boston coursed southeastward down the Atlantic Ocean around Africa's Cape of Good Hope into the Indian Ocean, then through Sunda Strait between Java and Sumatra into the western Pacific, and, finally, to Canton, where, somehow for Americans, the Far East turned magically into the farthest West.

By 1800, American ships were also rounding Cape Horn, South America's dangerous tip, to navigate northwestward from there directly across the Pacific Ocean. Yankee seal hunters and whalers at the same time began to seek their prey along the "onshore" fishery of South America's western coastline and off the rocky islands bordering Antarctica. During the War of 1812, Captain David Porter, USN, without authorization, brazenly took his frigate into Pacific waters, to destroy more than a dozen British ships and even to lay an abortive claim to the island of Nuka Hiva in the Marquesas archipelago. Merchants and sailors from the earliest trans-Pacific China trading vessels were soon putting ashore in Honolulu, and crewmen from whalers followed their example. By 1820, Americans were flocking into the Hawaiian Islands to compete with their British and French counterparts for the trade and allegiance of the Kanakas, as Polynesians were generally known throughout the Pacific. After lengthy voyages, ship captains headed their vessels to the sheltering waters of Honolulu on Oahu and Lahaina on Maui, where their crews could recuperate ashore after long months at sea.

Other restless wanderers drove themselves farther and farther across the vast reaches of the Pacific Ocean toward the exotic enticements of fragrant woods and spices and dusky-skinned islanders. Evangelical urges welled up among them to rescue those termed 'pagans' for Christian salvation. Indefatigably, for Americans of the nineteenth century, this spiritual mission combined itself with Manifest Destiny's westward thrusts to forge their imperialist impulses.

In 1854, Commodore Matthew Calbraith Perry, USN, employed gunboat diplomacy to wrest the earliest modern treaties of commerce from the longtime isolationist Tokugawa Shogunate of Japan. Thirteen years later, in 1867, Secretary of State William Henry Seward contrived to purchase Alaska from Russia, the great land bridge between the hemispheres that stretches westward from North America to within three miles of Siberian Asia – the very land bridge that diverted the ancient descent of the Korean peoples and the Native Americans from a common ancestry.

With its extensive new western territories, the Federal Republic at last spanned the North American continent. California entered the Union in 1850 as the thirty-first state. Oregon, the thirty-third, joined in 1859 on the eve of Lincoln's election and the triumph of the secession movement. Inside of two decades, arguably as significant for the future as the impending breakup of the Union, the admissions of California and Oregon, together with the acquisition of Alaska, made the United States into a North Pacific Rim country. Yet the place of the United States in the Pacific Basin, its far western history in fact, is by most Americans neither well enough known nor well enough understood.

In particular, three imperial imperatives, often overlapping, drove American ventures into Pacific Oceania, and inspired official policies toward East Asia until Japan's attack against Pearl Harbor in 1941. These were: (1) an uneven mixture of commercial and evangelical zeal, (2) naval and military strategy, and (3) the prescription for China of the Open Door Policy. When read in the light of American spiritual and secular proselytizing, which peaked in China during the 1930s, and the anti-oriental, racist animosities embodied in legislation such as the Immigration Act of 1924, the unstated principle underlying Washington's policies for the nation's westernmost concerns was competition not cooperation. And competition, by 1919 after the First World War and the Russian Revolution, came to mean competition almost exclusively against Japan over China.

Earlier in US history, shortly after 1820, Senator Thomas Hart Benton of Missouri had grandly announced the primary American motivation in the Pacific: "Upon the people of Eastern Asia the establishment of a civilized power on the opposite coast of America could not fail to produce great and wonderful benefits. Science, liberal principles in government, and the true religion might cast their lights across the intervening sea. The valley of the Columbia might become the granary of China and Japan, and an outlet to their imprisoned and exuberant population." Soon leaders of both political parties were hoping publicly that the North Pacific Ocean might become, in

William H. Goetzmann's term, "a vast American lake," a watery bridge extending westward maintained by the profits of whaling and trading, to tap Asia's treasures while converting Asia's peoples to republicanism and Christianity.

Thereafter, for a century and more, the vision of a western commercial empire laid down by William Henry Seward, first as United States senator from New York and next as secretary of state under Abraham Lincoln and Andrew Johnson, would conspicuously define American policy toward Asia. The contest for world power, Seward had convinced himself, would one day be won or lost in Asia after commerce between them united the hemispheres. Seward's goal was to prepare his country for its imperial destiny by moving America stage by stage from its internal bastions of economic might across the stepping stones of the Pacific toward an ultimate triumph in Asia.

The role for Alaska would be to guard the northern flank along the seaward approaches to Japan and China, while before long an isthmian canal across Central America would need to be opened for defending the southern corridor. Seward's proposed avenue for trade with East Asia depended also on completing the transcontinental railroad from New York to San Francisco to link the flow of goods with the oceanic highway from the Golden Gate to Honolulu and beyond. (Ironically, thousands of Chinese immigrants eventually labored to lay western stretches of railroad track.) In 1867, Seward directed the takeover of Midway Island for a mid-Pacific naval bastion, but the atoll's coral-floored lagoons proved undredgeable. His final step called for acquiring the Hawaiian Islands for a way station and naval base. Yet this feat, because of the kingdom's cherished independence, could not be accomplished quickly.

Nevertheless, the United States government in 1887, by tightening the bonds of trade reciprocity against Hawaii's sugar exporters, won that monarchy's concession to shelter American warships inside Pearl Harbor, thereby pushing the nation's strategic frontier substantially westward toward Japan and China, whose harbors by treaty rights already sheltered foreign commercial vessels. Secretary of State Thomas F. Bayard realized that to annex Hawaii itself he had but to wait patiently, quietly letting the islands fill up with American planters and industries, until they should be wholly identified with the United States. It was, he gloated, "simply a matter of waiting until the apple should fall."

In 1898, as unintended fruits of the Spanish–American–Filipino War, the Hawaiian Islands virtually fell into American hands precipitated by Commodore George Dewey's destruction of Spain's fleet at Manila Bay. Strategists for several years had identified Hawaii with the nation's security, and central also to the defense of the as yet unbuilt isthmian canal which, as Captain Alfred Thayer Mahan, USN, and others argued, was essential for safeguarding the republic. Following Spain's surrender, Congress simply annexed the Hawaiian Islands outright, on July 6, 1898, to gain Pearl Harbor for a vital naval base and coaling station astride the seaway to the Philippines.

In the following weeks and months, President William McKinley pressed the hapless Spanish government to grant the Philippine Islands (for $20 million), Puerto Rico, Guam, and Wake islands to the United States, in addition to its concession of the original American war aim – the independence of Cuba. The brutal crushing of the ensuing Filipino independence movement was euphemistically dismissed as the legitimate suppression of an unlawful insurrection on the natives' part. What was important for undertaking such a giant step 7,000 miles southwestward from San Francisco was the closeness of the Philippines to China and Japan, together with a newly discovered destiny to take up the white man's burden.

On February 6, 1899, the Senate ratified the treaty with Spain ceding the Philippine Islands to the United States. Later in the same year, the United States negotiated a treaty with Germany and Great Britain to obtain sovereignty over the six eastern Samoan Islands, where, midway in the South Central Pacific Ocean, the United States Navy had been operating its base at Pago Pago on the island of Tutuila since 1878. The westward expansionist movement now subsided in order to digest and exploit the nation's enormous territorial gains. But the tasks of subjugating and governing the islands constituted only part of the picture. Seward's half-century old dream of erecting a trading empire with China galvanized his countrymen's opinion. For interested Americans, China's proximity to Manila was the primary attraction the Philippine Islands had to offer.

At the same time, officials in Washington worriedly watched the European powers and Japan prepare to partition China among themselves into spheres of influence, undoubtedly with exclusive privileges for their own nationals. The 2,100-year-old Empire of China was threatening to disintegrate, already debilitated by its lengthy decline and recently rendered almost helpless by the devastating defeat suffered in the Sino-Japanese War of 1894–5.

Secretary of State John Hay thereupon circulated his soon-to-be celebrated "Open Door" notes. Hay's first note, dated September 6, 1899, requested Japan, Russia, Germany, Great Britain, France, and Italy each to sustain the policy of equal trading opportunity for all nations within their own spheres. Brashly overriding the noncommittal, evasive replies he received, Hay proclaimed the international adoption of his Open Door Policy for China. Hay's second Open Door note was issued, July 3, 1890, during the Boxer uprising, when American naval and military forces joined the international expedition formed to rescue diplomats and their families trapped by rebels inside the legations at Peking (Beijing). This time Hay appealed for China's independence, in sum to maintain China territorially and administratively intact, in order to keep open the trading door.

Although outwardly triumphant, Hay's policy of the Open Door for China could not then shape international politics but, like the Monroe Doctrine, it would grow to become increasingly popular at home, a morally patriotic principle for America's leaders and diplomats to uphold. John Hay's Open Door Policy over the next four decades would harden into a sloganized shibboleth that other great powers would learn to take seriously. The imperatives driving American ventures across the Pacific Ocean and into East Asia were now fully operational.

Asian developments, however, not the Open Door Policy, determined the fate of China. Commencing with China's revolution of 1911 and closing with Japan's thwarted attempts from 1931 to 1945 to colonize the onetime Celestial Empire, America's hopes and expectations had, in truth, little prospect of fulfillment. Ironically, the Nine-Power Treaty signed at Washington, in 1922, ostensibly internationalized the Open Door Policy by pledging its signatories (Britain, the United States, Japan, France, and Italy, Belgium, the Netherlands, Portugal, and China) to guarantee China's sovereignty, independence, and territorial integrity. Only the neighboring Soviet Union, the globe's pariah, was excluded from participation. Its omission would prove to be crucial.

The fundamental futility of the Open Door Policy was evident in the decisions made to annex and fortify the Philippine Islands, but most leaders never grasped this fact. Theodore Roosevelt had perhaps done more than anyone else to acquire the Philippines, but he changed his mind quickly when, in 1905, Japan defeated Russia and proceeded to swallow up Korea. He recognized the virtual impossibility in such a predatory world of upholding a distant empire by means of wishfully pious policies backed up by only a third-rate navy and a sixth-rate army. In the absence of public support for a grand imperial design with the force to sustain it, Roosevelt recognized that the Philippine Islands were, in truth, "our heel of Achilles," making any confrontation with Japan inflammably dangerous.

Moreover, following the First World War, the United States subscribed to warship tonnage limitations that left Japan's navy paramount in the western Pacific Ocean, while installing humiliating barriers at home both against Japanese immigration and Japanese trade. Possibly a farsighted program of economic development joined to a fundamental Filipinizing of the colonial regime might have centered East Asia's co-prosperity sphere in Manila before Tokyo cornered the concept. Instead the government in Washington wavered between its unreadiness to emancipate the Filipino colonials yet blindly unprepared to defend them or even itself against an aroused Japan.

To maintain China intact as a sovereign state, though freely open to foreign penetration, as John Hay's precepts demanded, all of the great powers involved in China would have to respect the Open Door Policy, or otherwise it would cease to exert any influence. Between 1905 and 1940, however, wars and revolutions sidelined Russia, Germany, France, and

Great Britain in turn, to leave only Japan and the United States capable of executing any significant policy whatever over China. Internally chaotic and torn with fighting among nationalists, warlords, and communists, China meanwhile was growing too xenophobic and nationalistic to tolerate the foreign influences that since 1842 under the unequal treaty system had exploited her people. Nevertheless, unless the Chinese could somehow pull themselves together against the foreign powers overrunning them, outside intruders would continue to determine China's destiny. After the outbreak of the Second World War, the United States and Japan competed directly for China against each other. By that time, Japan was allied through the Axis Pact to Germany and Italy, and insisting on the right to obtain essential supplies of oil, rubber, tin, and rice from the embattled French, Dutch, and British colonies in Southeast Asia.

Throughout the prolonged negotiations of 1941 between the United States and Japan, Secretary of State Cordell Hull doggedly reiterated the substance of the Open Door Policy, to which the Japanese policy planners could never accede without relinquishing altogether their military government's pan-Asianist designs. Japan's Ambassador Kichisaburo Nomura failed to impress his superiors with the commitment of the United States to its traditional stand, while Hull ignorantly believed that his posture of firmness based on moral rectitude would deter the Japanese. In truth, President Franklin D. Roosevelt's embargo on petroleum exports and his order freezing Japan's assets in the United States had virtually killed any prospects for diplomacy. What is astonishing is that no genuine peacemaking efforts were put forward by either the Japanese or the Americans before Japan had to face the prospect of running out of oil for fuel. Japan's attack on Pearl Harbor proved to be the tragic result.

From December 1941 to September 1945, United States and British Empire forces struggled successfully to thwart Imperial Japan's colossal efforts to conquer China and expel the western nations from their Pacific and Asian colonies. In the end, in a cataclysmic catastrophe, Japan lost both its Fifteen Year War to subjugate China and also the Great Pacific War against the United States and its allies, and suffered the humiliation of an American occupation of its homeland.

Imperial supremacy in the western Pacific region now passed for a time to the United States. The war had not only occasioned the fall of Japan's empire, but also the destruction of the British, French, and Dutch empires in the Far East. The dual threat of Soviet and Chinese communism led the United States next, in its militant anti-communist containment policy of the Cold War era, into the inconclusive Korean War, a so-called "police action," and into the morasses of Indo-China. The Vietnam War, it is now clear, assumes more than a singular significance. For twenty-five years after 1950, the struggle for Indo-China measured the limits of containment against communism. Saigon's fall to the Viet Minh, in 1975, marked the tidal retreat of the American imperial frontier from East Asia and the western Pacific, the end of the epoch of westward destiny.

Commercial and religious opportunities were hereafter no longer apparent, as for Benton, Seward, and Hay they had been. Military and naval forces have straggled home from the imperial world that George Dewey, Arthur and Douglas MacArthur, William Howard Taft, Chester Nimitz, Dean Acheson, John Foster Dulles, John F. Kennedy, and Lyndon Baines Johnson had made. The stirring appeals of duty, the Open Door Policy, and containment sounded quaint. Pacific Basin civilizations seemed almost wholly transformed from the exotic worlds encountered by the American republic's earliest westward-heading adventurers.

Folk loyalties and nationalisms have persistently proved themselves durable even against the onslaughts of capitalism and communism, while indigenous religions still fortify ancient traditions. From the United States and Western Europe, the peoples of East Asia and the Pacific islands have borrowed technology, education, and popular culture, yet frequently deprecate their accompanying value systems. With jet airplanes and satellite communications networks spinning new linkages between them and their former overlords, Asians and Pacific islanders alike were endeavoring to reconcile their novel circumstances with older ways, as were Americans.

In the future, the West of the Pacific Basin will undoubtedly continue to be as important for the United States as it has been for previous generations. Immigration from Asia, in addition, has become almost as important as European immigration was for earlier periods of history. The breakup of the Soviet Union has thawed the "ice curtain" dividing the hemispheres, to permit Siberians and Alaskans freely once more to cross the Bering Straits to reclaim long-separated relatives and friends, while North American sportsminded individuals are being lured to fish and hunt in Siberia's wilderness. But what does the future hold for Pacific Siberia itself? Will Asians and Americans link themselves together again along Alaska's Aleutian Islands causeway? Merely to raise such a once far-fetched thought serves to estimate the magnitude of the changes currently underway.

Even if capitalism defines East Asia's future, it seems probable for the nations involved that relations with the United States will continue to be troublesome. Japan's triumph may well be at hand, yet Japanese producers still lack the natural resources sufficient to ensure national supremacy. And two acutely sensitive points plague Nipponese relations with the United States: the colossal trade imbalance between them and the American, treaty-bound, responsibility for Japan's defense. China's path is even less discernible. Ill feelings persist over Taiwan, the "lost province," while the frequent censures delivered against Beijing's trading and human rights practices agitate Sino-American relations. Nonetheless, at long last, China's door to the world outside is free from foreign intrusion, China's alone to open or close. Nearby, the harsh division of Korea between North and

South has withstood pressures of all kinds for nearly five decades. But more than thirty thousand uniformed American military personnel are still stationed there prepared to help defend South Korea against nuclear threats from North Korea, in upholding the bitter armistice between the rival Pyongyang and Seoul governments.

Nowadays, America's far western initiatives are expressed in less proprietary or acquisitive terms. The conservative change is evident from the independence granted, in 1946, to the Philippines followed decades later, with volcanic urgings from Mount Pinatubo, by the closing throughout the former American colony of American military installations, while statehood for Alaska and Hawaii translates into a similar signal. In South-East Asia, Vietnam, Laos, and Cambodia, after decades of horrifying bloodletting, are struggling to be reborn as viable societies, while Uncle Sam, inwardly tortured by guilt over the largely repudiated Indo-China War, fumbles to foster a realistic postwar policy toward them. Even Thailand, a major, if clandestine, ally of the United States, has adjusted to the wholesale withdrawals of American aerial combat squadrons and undercover operations.

Two hundred years ago, on September 17, 1787, while the last members of the Convention in Philadelphia were signing the Constitution of the United States of America and the China trade was scarcely begun, the venerable Benjamin Franklin, according to Madison's notes, gazed at the presiding officer's chair, whereon a decorative sun was painted. He observed, "I have often and often, in the course of the session, and the vicissitudes of my hopes and fears as to its issue, looked at that behind the President without being able to tell whether it was rising or setting, but now at length I have the happiness to know that it is a rising and not a setting sun." Today's Americans might well wonder, as Dr Franklin did, if their prospects are still rising to the West, like generations before them, somewhere toward Asia, far across their ocean of destiny – across the American Pacific, where their West was also won.

BIBLIOGRAPHY

Beasley, W.G. (1995) *The Rise of Modern Japan*, 2d edn, New York: St Martin's Press.

Borthwick, M. *et al.* (1992) *Pacific Century*, Boulder, Colo.: Westview Press.

Caruthers, J.W. (1973) *American Pacific Ocean Trade*, New York: Exposition Press.

Cohen, W.I. (1990) *America's Response to China*, 3d edn, New York: Columbia University Press.

Cumings, B. (1981, 1990) *The Origins of the Korean War*, 2 vols, Princeton, N.J.: Princeton University Press.

Daws, G. (1974) *Shoal of Time*, Honolulu: University of Hawaii Press.

Dennett, T. (1922) *Americans in Eastern Asia*, New York: Macmillan.

Dudden, A.P. (1992) *The American Pacific*, New York and Oxford: Oxford University Press.

Fairbank, J.K. (1983) *The United States and China*, 4th edn, Cambridge, Mass.: Harvard University Press.

Field, N. (1993) *In the Realm of a Dying Emperor*, New York: Vintage Books.
Fuchs, L.H. (1961) *Hawaii Pono*, New York: Harvest/Harcourt, Brace, Jovanovich.
Gardner, L.C. (1995) *Pay Any Price: Lyndon Johnson and the Wars for Vietnam*, Chicago: Ivan R. Dee.
Gibney, F. (1992) *The Pacific Century*, New York: Charles Scribner's Sons.
Goetzmann, W.H. (1986) *New Lands, New Men*, New York: Viking Penguin.
Hogan, M.J. (ed.) (1995) *Hiroshima in History and Memory*, New York and Cambridge: Cambridge University Press.
Hsü, I.C.Y. (1995) *The Rise of Modern China*, 5th edn, New York and Oxford: Oxford University Press.
Johnson, D.D. (1995) *The United States in the Pacific*, Westport, Conn.: Praeger Publishers.
Karnow, S. (1989) *In Our Image, America's Empire in the Philippines*, New York: Random House.
—— (1991) *Vietnam*, rev. edn, New York: Viking.
LaFeber, W. (1989) *The American Age*, New York: W.W. Norton.
Lower, J.A. (1978) *Ocean of Destiny*, Vancouver: University of British Columbia Press.
McDougall, W.A. (1993) *Let the Sea Make a Noise*, New York: Avon Books.
Miyoshi, M. and Harootunian, H.D. (eds) (1993) *Japan in the World*, Durham, N.C.: Duke University Press.
Naske, C.M. and Slotnick, H.E. (1987) *Alaska*, 2d edn, Norman: University of Oklahoma Press.
Neu, C.E. (1975) *The Troubled Encounter: the United States and Japan*, New York: John Wiley & Sons.
Patterson, T.G. *et al.* (1995) *American Foreign Policy*, 2 vols, 4th edn: Lexington, Mass.: D.C. Heath.
Prange, G.W. *et al.* (1981) *At Dawn We Slept: the Untold Story of Pearl Harbor*, New York: McGraw-Hill.
Reischauer, E.O. and Jensen, M.B. (1995) *The Japanese Today*, enl. edn, Cambridge, Mass.: Belknap/Harvard University Press.
Schaller, M. (1985) *The American Occupation of Japan*, New York and Oxford: Oxford University Press.
Spence, J.D. (1990) *The Search for Modern China*, New York: W.W. Norton.
Toland, J. (1991) *In Mortal Combat: Korea*, New York: Quill/William Morrow.

Part II

SELECTED ECONOMIC ISSUES IN PACIFIC RIM HISTORY

7

THE FRENCH PRESENCE IN THE PACIFIC OCEAN AND CALIFORNIA, 1700–1850

Annick Foucrier

The current presence of France in the Pacific Ocean is well acknowledged, but its beginnings are often ignored. The subject of this chapter is not limited to the French territories in the Pacific Ocean, nor to the presence of French residents in California. It must be understood as a study of the relationship between the French presence in the Pacific Ocean and the French presence in California. The French were in California because they were in the Pacific Ocean, obviously, but inversely their presence in California helps us understand why they were in the Pacific Ocean (Foucrier 1991).

French ships started to sail the waters of the Pacific Ocean at the end of the sixteenth century. The mariners of St Malo took special advantage of the good relations then existing between France and Spain to trade in the South American ports. Eventually their success was such that their competitors repeatedly asked the French government to keep them away. Meanwhile, however, one of them, Nicolas Frondat, who was captain of the *Saint Antoine*, had gone as far as China and Japan to trade (1707–1711) (Dahlgren 1909). On his way back, following a northern route, even more northern than the route taken by the Manila Galleon, he was able to observe the islands off California (San Clemente Island), as stated in his logbook. He was the first Frenchman to do so. The map shown in Figure 7.1 was drawn from that data and it added to the knowledge of, and to the interest in, these far away lands.

The eagerness of the Spanish crown for secrecy had maintained a veil of obscurity over these regions. Yet the eighteenth century was a time of discoveries for Western European maritime nations (Friis 1967; Spate 1988). The third exploratory trip of James Cook, the English captain, is especially notable. Apart from the fateful death of the famous navigator, it led to the discovery by Western Europeans of the great value of sea otter furs on the Chinese market. (The Russians already knew about it, after an exploratory journey that led to the death in 1741 of another important

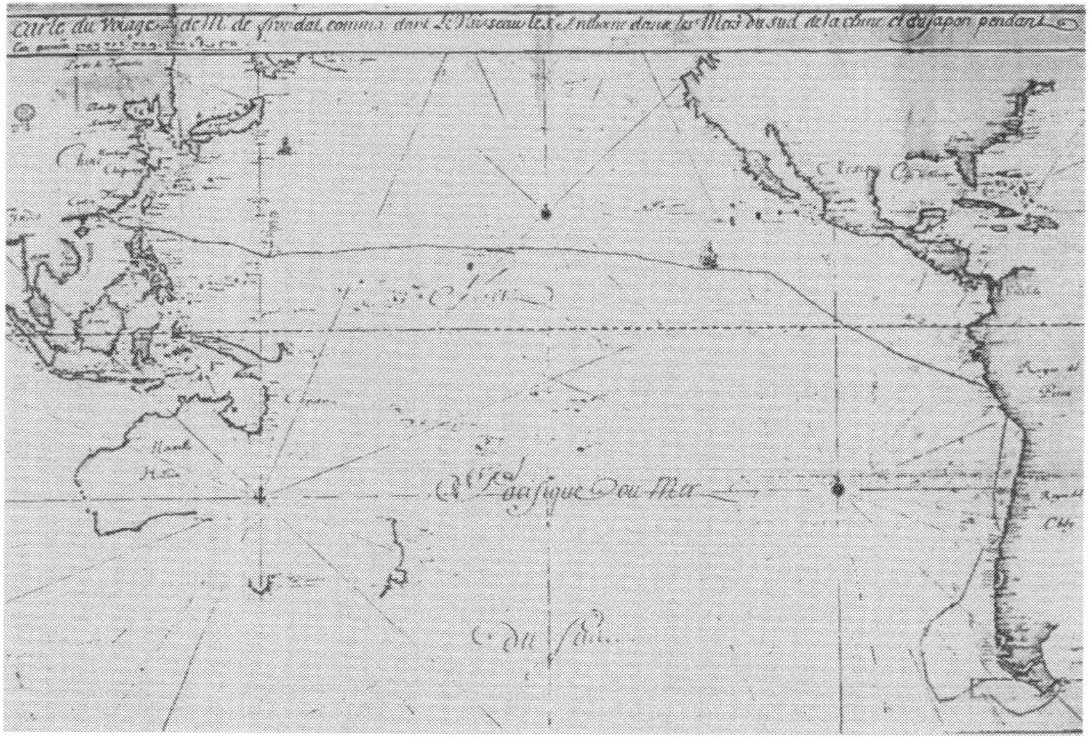

Figure 7.1 The voyage of the *Saint Antoine*, 1713, captained by Nicolas Frondat

discoverer, Vitus Bering.) Cook had stopped at Nootka Sound, avoiding California which was then in the process of being colonized by the Spaniards.

The King of France, Louis XVI, a distinguished amateur geographer, then took the opportunity to challenge the prestige the English crown had garnered from Cook's voyages (Garry 1967; Gaziello 1984; Dunmore 1985). The well-known navigator Jean François de Lapérouse was assigned an ambitious project of gathering data on lands then unknown, or scarcely known, and on sea otters. Since the Family Compact of 1661 had established good relations between France and Spain, California was chosen for scrutiny. Although he eventually died in a shipwreck off the island of Vanikoro, Lapérouse followed his instructions, and his stay in Monterey (September 15–24, 1786) was a welcome opportunity for gathering much information (Figure 7.2). But while it certainly was a step forward, much more remained to be uncovered.

It was 1837 before another French round-the-world expedition took the opportunity to visit California in order to draw more maps, like the one of Monterey Bay (see Figure 7.3) that we can compare with those of Lapérouse, and also of San Francisco Bay, the entrance to which Lapérouse missed. This expedition, headed by Captain Dupetit-Thouars, was the first official French one to call at California ports since Lapérouse (Dupetit-Thouars 1840–1864. Some excerpts concerning the sojourn of the *Venus* in California have been translated by Rudkin 1956). However, these ports had been already visited by a number of other French ships. The first to appear after the Great Revolution and the Napoleonic wars was the *Bordelais* (1816–1819), whose captain was Camille de Roquefeuil (Roquefeuil 1823. The chapters relating to California have been translated and edited by Rudkin 1954). Roquefeuil's purpose was to gather sea otter pelts as items of trade in China, and although he was not very successful in this endeavor (the sea otters had already been largely depleted), he led a voyage round the world that provided invaluable information for the French navy for years to come. Other merchant ships headed to California to exchange French goods for sea otter pelts, and later they engaged in the hide and tallow trade, as did the *Héros* (1826–1829) (Duhaut-Cilly 1834–1835).

Actually, the predominant activity that attracted French ships to California in the 1830s and 1840s was whaling. Eighteen whalers called at Californian ports between 1825 and 1846 (Foucrier 1990a, 1990b). The *Triton* was the first of these French whaling ships to reach the northern Pacific Ocean waters and San Francisco Bay in 1825, although the crew had been quite reluctant to undertake such a long trip. They found that whales were too fierce and too strong for their equipment, and they resorted to hunting sea elephants on the shores of Baja California. Many more whalers were drawn to the northern Pacific, and one of them, the *Gange*, is credited with having opened the whaling fields of the Gulf of Alaska (Webb 1988). That

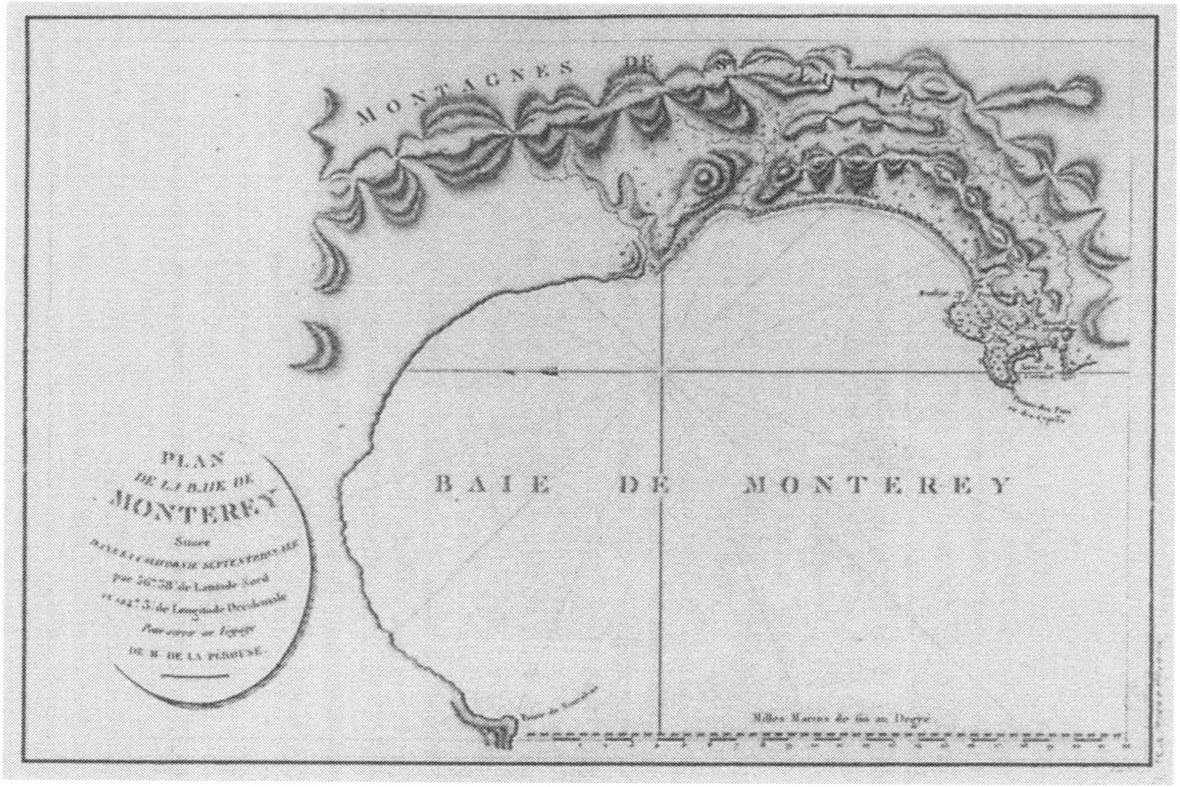

Figure 7.2 Map of Monterey Bay, California, as drawn by Jean François de Lapérouse

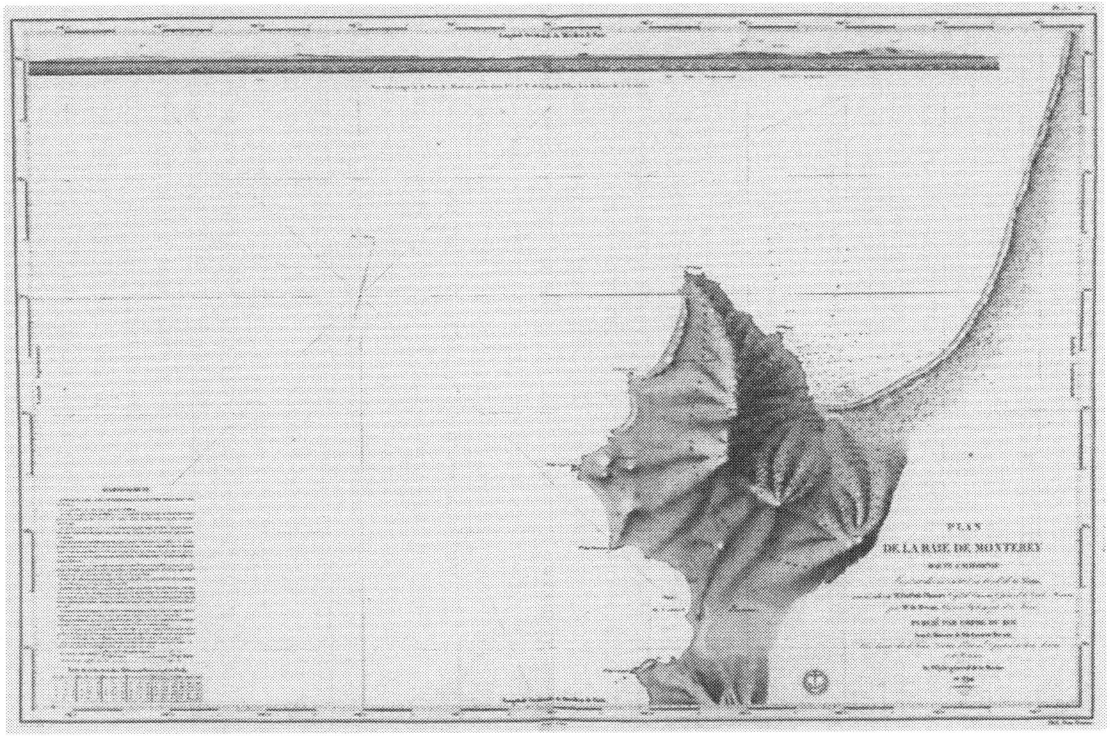

Figure 7.3 Map of Monterey, California, drawn as a result of the Dupetit-Thouars expedition

campaign was typical of the late 1830s. California would provide fresh food and a resting place for the crews and an opportunity to repair the ships at the end of the hunting season.

The French government took much interest in protecting French whaling. Navy ships were sent to the Pacific Ocean, and in 1839 the Ministry of Foreign Affairs appointed an attaché to go to California and Oregon to ascertain the political and economic climate (Foucrier 1992b). Thus Eugène Duflot de Mofras visited the west coast from San Blas to the mouth of the Columbia River. Eventually he published two volumes illustrated with drawings and maps (Duflot de Mofras 1844), such as Figure 7.4, on which two major features should be noted: the emphasis on whaling, by the location of the new hunting fields, and the highlighting of the islands as strategic stopping places for voyages between the Philippines, the Isthmus of Panama, Mazatlán and San Francisco. He does not neglect the advance of the Russians.

Indeed, the islands were to become the focus of French diplomacy in the Pacific Ocean. The French Navy needed a safe place to stop and repair ships, and in 1840 an attempt to gain a foothold in New Zealand had been prevented by the British (Dunmore 1990). On May 1, 1842, Vice-Admiral Dupetit-Thouars, chosen because of his previous knowledge of the region, took formal possession in the name of France of the islands of the Marquesas. And on September 9 of the same year, he made the decision on his own to establish a protectorate over Tahiti as asked by the local chiefs. The French authorities were too far away to be consulted in a timely manner. Dupetit-Thouars feared that the security of the Marquesas might be threatened by the presence of foes in near-by islands.

The French possession was confirmed by sending armed forces to the islands, but they required food and shelter. Most of the supplies came from Chile, but the governor dispatched two merchant ships to California to buy cattle and wood. The *Médicis* (1844–1846) made one round trip (see Figure 7.5) and brought back cows and timber. The other one, the *Lion*, made six round trips (two each year) in three years, each time bringing back more cattle and wood. On the way to California, the ship would stop at Honolulu in order to buy hay for the animals. Such a ship, loaded with highly combustible hay and as many as 300 animals, was a tinderbox waiting to burn, indeed a very dangerous situation. Once, a storm was encountered, and the ship had great difficulty in reaching the islands. It finally did so in very bad condition, with the main mast broken, but having lost only twenty animals out of 300. No wonder the sailors tried to desert.

Economic and diplomatic interests led to the creation by the French government of several consulates in the Pacific arena, one of them in Monterey, then the capital of California, on September 21, 1842. However, the early nominees refused to travel such a long distance. The first to occupy the position was acting consul Louis Gasquet, and it took him

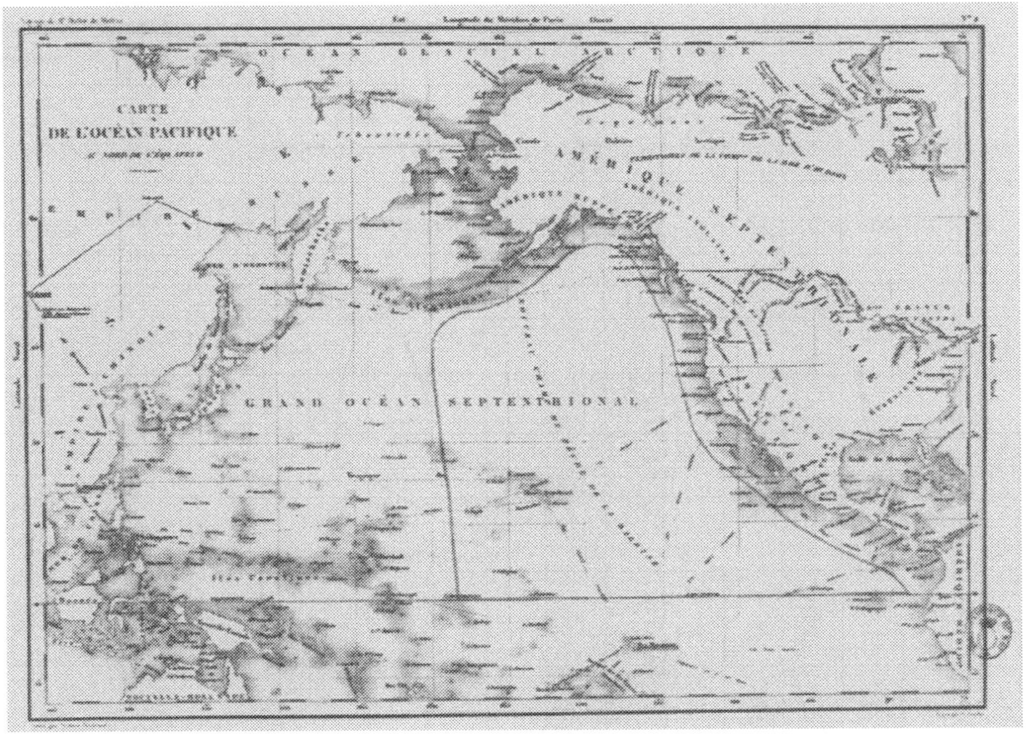

Figure 7.4 Map of the Pacific Ocean north of the equator, published in 1844 by Eugene Duflot de Mofras

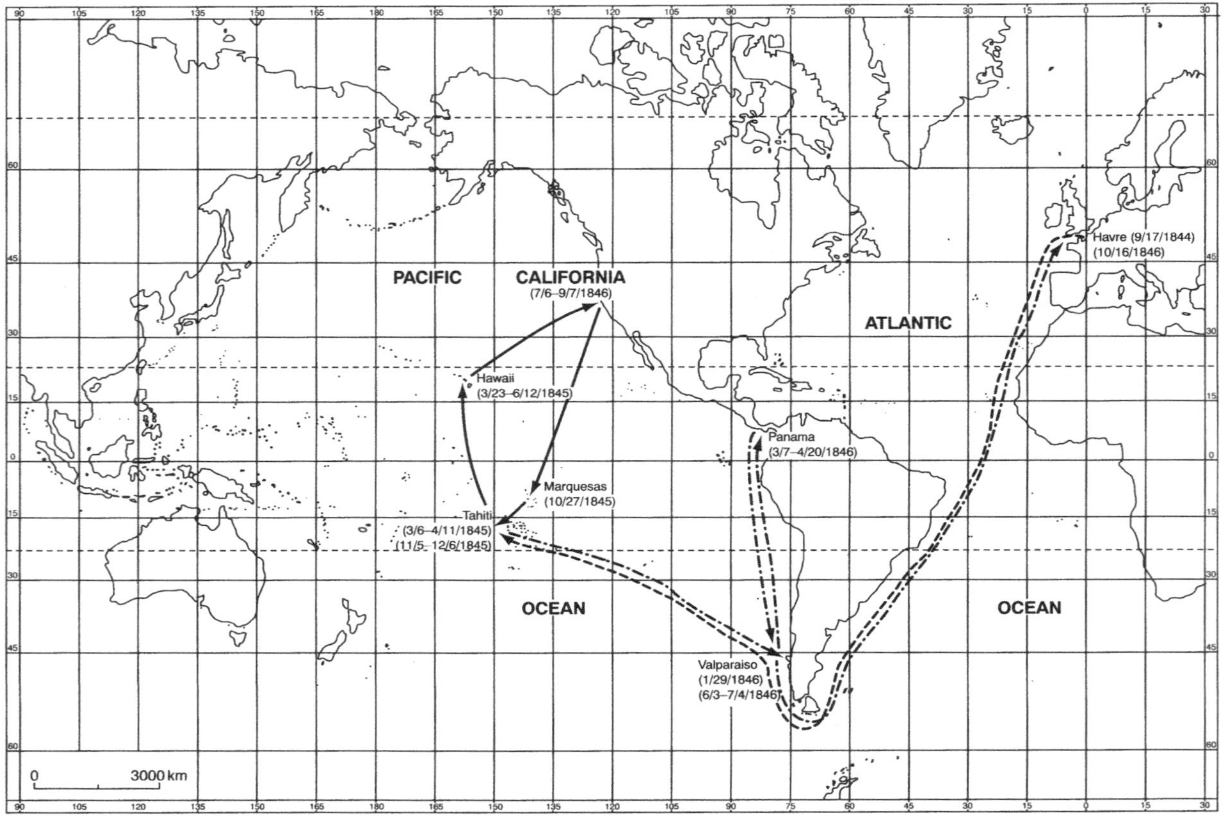

Figure 7.5 The voyage of the *Médicis*, 1844–46

almost two years, following his departure from Le Havre on August 9, 1843, until his arrival at Monterey on May 5, 1845. Meanwhile, he had to stay in Mexico City longer than expected because of the lack of funds to pursue his trip. In California he would witness the major changes that affected the country in 1846.

The two maps of California are syntheses of major events that occurred in the region around 1790 and in 1846 (see Figure 7.6). At the end of the eighteenth century, a few years after Lapérouse's sojourn, a clear convergence of Russian, British and Spanish activities can be seen. In 1846, the major rivals were Great Britain, Mexico and the United States, although this does not mean that France was totally absent, as the presence of an acting consul and of French residents testifies.

To understand fully what was happening in the northern Pacific, it is necessary to consider the events taking place on a world-wide scale and to view them in a manner which encompasses the metropolises as well (Foucrier 1992a). Figure 7.7 shows the progression and retreat in the Pacific arena of the major powers from the sixteenth century to the mid-nineteenth century.

The Russians progressed eastward across Siberia and reached Alaska in the eighteenth century, and although in the beginning of the nineteenth they were able to build Fort Ross north of San Francisco, their ability to protect this new territory was diminishing (Chevigny 1965; Tikhmenev 1978).

In response, the Spaniards moved north from New Spain to establish missions in Alta California, principally to thwart any settlement there by rivals. That, too, was a move which stretched their resources beyond their means (Cook 1973). Following the wars of independence, when Spanish authority was defeated, new nations emerged in the Americas, with California becoming a Mexican province in 1821.

Meanwhile, the British had moved across Canada from the east. In 1793 Alexander Mackenzie, while exploring, opened the way to the west coast where the English government had already challenged the Spanish domination at the time of the Nootka Sound conflict in 1789 (Manning 1905; Sheppe 1962; Pethick 1980). From 1821, the Hudson Bay Company was dominant in Oregon, and the trappers while trading with Indian tribes went south as far as California. A large number were French Canadian, and French Camp, just a few miles south of Stockton, owes its name to the fact that it was used as a rendezvous for a party led by Michel Laframboise between 1828 and 1843 (Chaput 1985). At the beginning of the nineteenth century, the British also used India as a base in their advance southward to Australia and New Zealand. In the 1840s they were still moving forward and had already established outposts on the Pacific Rim, giving themselves a foothold in places as significant as China (1842) and Chile (Brookes 1941; Steven 1983).

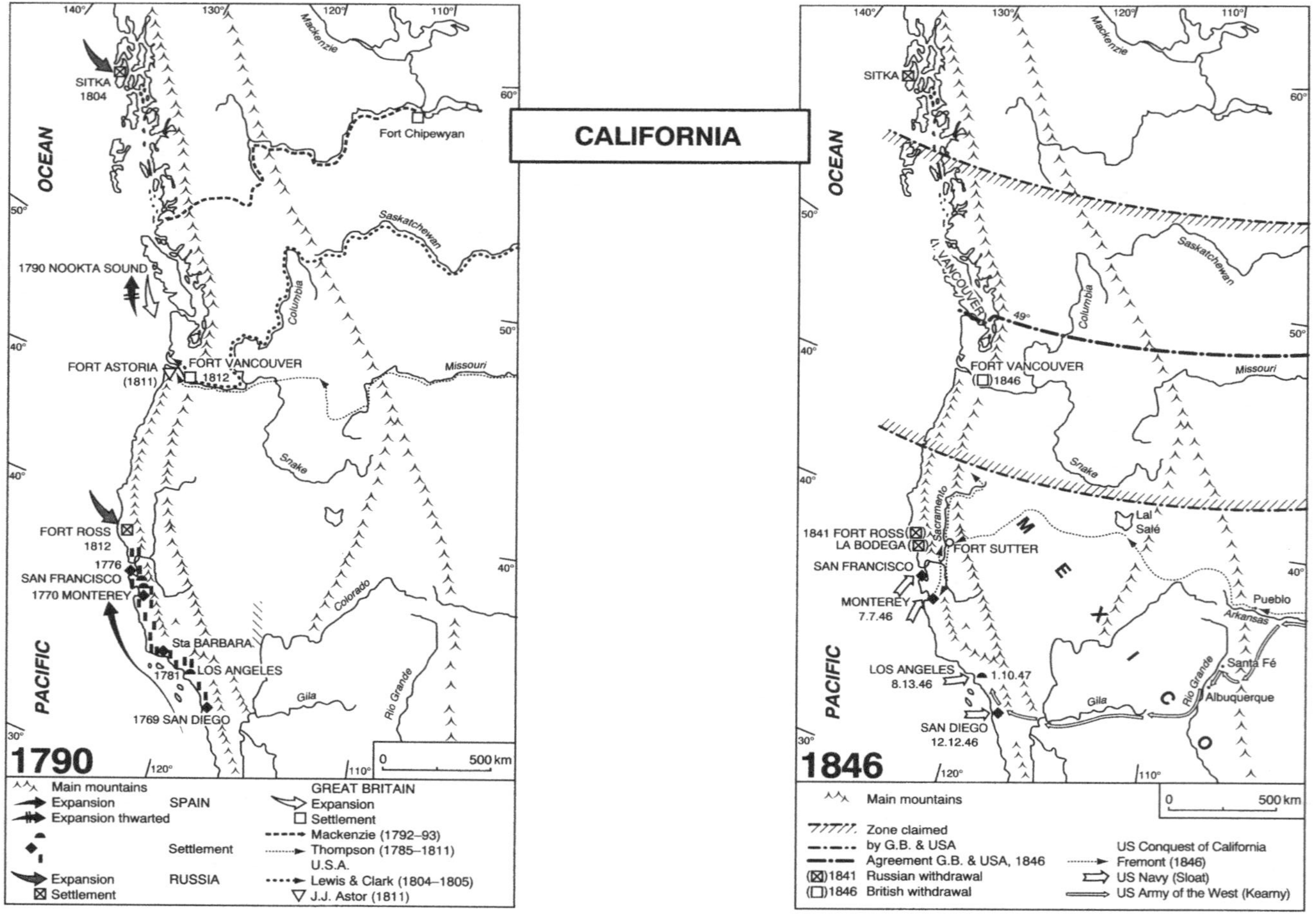

Figure 7.6 Maps of California, depicting 1790 and 1846 circumstances

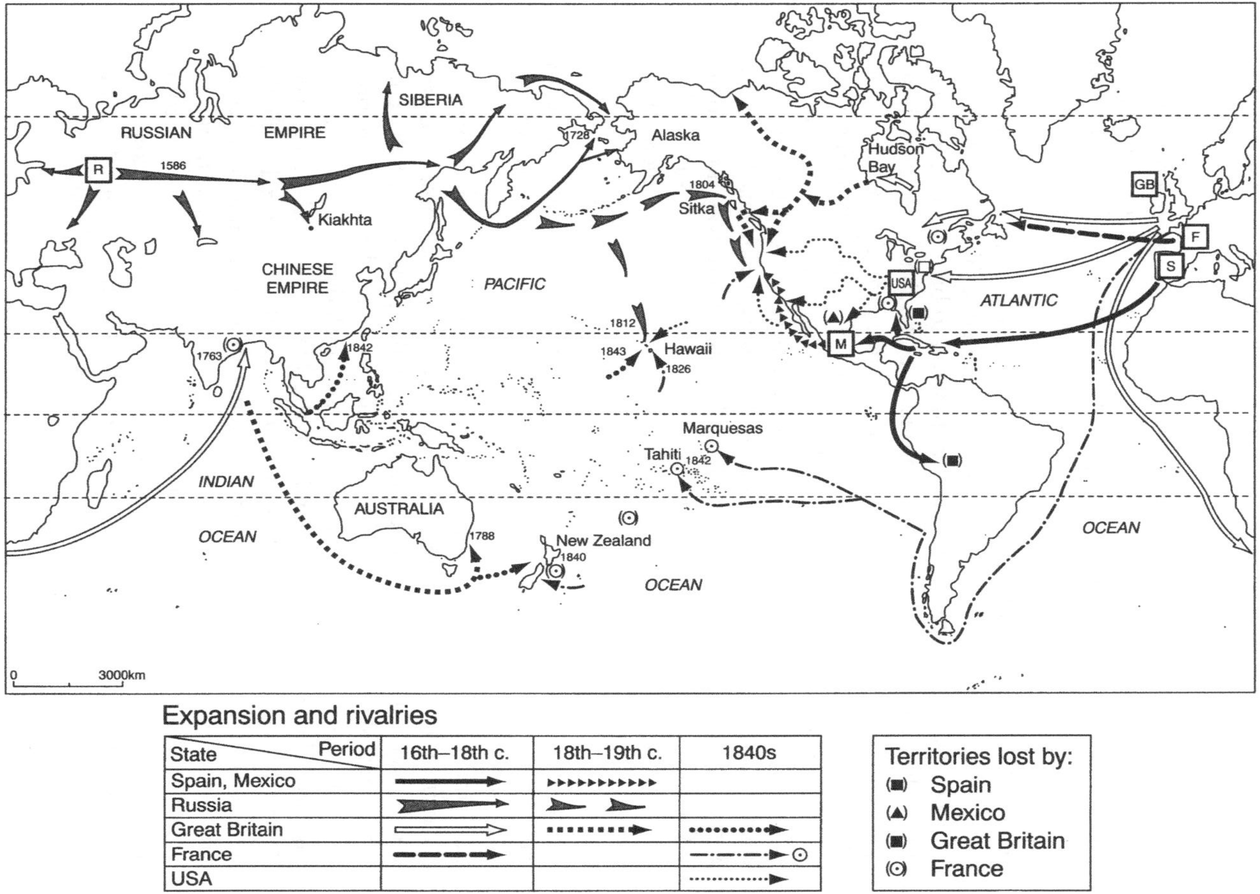

Figure 7.7 Ebb and flow of empires from the sixteenth century to the nineteenth

From another direction, the United States, following the principle of Manifest Destiny, advanced westward to the Pacific Ocean (Heffer 1995; Dudden 1992). Although crossing the Rocky Mountains proved no small task, explorers led the way for the settlers of this new, challenging power, the goal of which was eventually to occupy the territories Mexico had inherited from Spain. This young nation, torn apart by internal strife, seemed easy prey to its northern neighbor. The treaty of Guadalupe Hidalgo, February 2, 1848, which ended the war between the United States and Mexico, allowed the former to annex half of the Mexican territory, including California (Graebner 1955).

As for France, until the end of the eighteenth century this powerful country held significant territories in North America. Then, in 1803, the sale of Louisiana brought to an end any ambition to build an empire there. In the 1840s, the acquisition of the Marquesas and Tahiti reflected a desire to play a role in the Pacific Ocean arena (Faivre 1953). As for California, some historians have interpreted the agitation by French residents for a French protectorate as proof of French designs on that territory (Nasatir 1945). However, documents show that there was no official backing. The French government had no intention of colonizing California because it was too far from the capital to be defended, and there was not enough population to send there. Nevertheless, the ministries of the Navy and of Foreign Affairs would have considered favorably the acquisition of La Bodega Bay, sold by the Russians to Sutter in 1841, as an access to a source of wood and cattle (Foucrier 1992b). In any event, French Navy captains stationed in the Pacific ignored orders to investigate the feasibility of such an acquisition because they were more involved with events in the South Pacific.

California played an important role in the competition for the control of the Pacific Ocean. France showed some interest in California, but the French government did not seriously consider the possibility of the conquest of this Mexican province. The main focus of the French authorities was the protection of French whaling and trade, including French traders in California. The South Pacific islands of the Marquesas and Tahiti were sufficient as safe places for ships, and the war that occurred with the natives at Tahiti demonstrated the difficulties of maintaining colonies so remote from the metropolis. Nevertheless, the suspicious activities of French and British residents in California and Mexico were a welcome argument for those in the United States who planned to extend the boundaries of the Union to the shores of the Pacific Ocean. This was eventually accomplished through the conquest of the nothern regions of Mexico, from Texas to California.

BIBLIOGRAPHY

Brookes, Jean Ingram (1941) *International Rivalry in the Pacific Islands, 1800–1875*, Berkeley: University of California Press.

Carter, Charles Franklin (1929) "Duhaut-Cilly's Account of California in the Years 1827–1828," in *California Historical Society Quarterly*: 130–166, 214–250, 306–338.

Chaput, Donald (1985) *French Canadian Contribution to Winning the American West, Biographical Notes*, Québec: Bibliothèque nationale.

Chevigny, Hector (1965) *Russian America. The Great Alaskan Venture, 1741–1867*, New York: The Viking Press.

Cook, Warren (1973) *Flood Tide of Empire: Spain and the Pacific Northwest, 1543–1819*, New Haven: Yale University Press.

Dahlgren, Erik W. (1909) *Les relations commerciales et maritimes entre la France et les côtes de l'océan Pacifique. T.I. Le commerce de la mer du Sud jusqu'à la paix d'Utrecht*, Paris: E. Champion.

Dudden, Arthur (1992) *The American Pacific: From the Early China Trade to the Present*, New York: Oxford University Press.

Duflot de Mofras, Eugène (1844) *Exploration du territoire de l'Orégon, des Californies et de la mer Vermeille, exécutée pendant les années 1840, 1841 et 1842*, 2 vols, Paris: Arthus Bertrand. Translated with an introduction by M.E. Wilbur 1937.

Duhaut-Cilly, Auguste Bernard (1834–1835) *Voyage autour du monde principalement à la Californie et aux îles Sandwich pendant les années 1826, 1827, 1828 et 1829*, 2 vols, Paris: Arthus Bertrand. The chapters relating to California have been translated with an introduction by Charles Franklin Carter (1929).

Dunmore, John (1985) *Pacific Explorer: The Life of Jean-François de La Perouse, 1741–1788*, Dunmore Press.

—— (ed.) (1990) *New Zealand and the French: Two Centuries of Contact*, Waikanae, NZ: Heritage Press.

Dupetit-Thouars, Abel Aubert (1840–1864) *Voyage autour du monde sur la frégate la Vénus pendant les années 1836–1839*, Paris: Gide. Some excerpts concerning the sojourn of the Venus in California have been translated by Rudkin (1956).

Faivre, Jean-Paul (1953) *L'expansion française dans le Pacifique, 1800–1842*, Paris: Nouvelles éditions latines.

Foucrier, Annick (1990a) "Baleiniers français en Californie (1825–1848)," in *Revue d'histoire moderne et contemporaine* 37: 239–252.

—— (1990b) "Adventures on the California Coast: French Whalers from 1825 to 1848," in *The Californians* 8, 3: 30–36.

—— (1991) "La France, les Français et la Californie avant la ruée vers l'or (1786–1848)", Unpublished Ph.D., EHESS, Paris.

—— (1992a) "La Californie, noeud gordien du Pacifique Nord (1769–1848)," in *Marins et Océans* (CFHM), t.III, Paris: Economica: 123–149.

—— (1992b) "Spy or Explorer? The True Mission of Eugene Duflot de Mofras," in *The Californians* 9, 4: 17–26.

Friis, Herman Ralph (ed.) (1967) *The Pacific Basin: A History of its Geographic Exploration*, New York: American Geographical Society.

Garry, Robert J. (1967) "Geographical Exploration by the French," in H.R. Friis (ed.), *The Pacific Basin. A History of its Geographic Exploration*, New York: American Geographical Society.

Gaziello, Catherine (1984) *L'expédition de Lapérouse, 1785–1788, réplique française aux voyages de Cook*, Paris: Comité des Travaux Historiques et Scientifiques.

Graebner, Norman (1955) *Empire on the Pacific: A Study in American Continental Expansion*, New York: Ronald Press.

Heffer, Jean (1995) *Les Etats-Unis et le Pacifique. Histoire d'une frontière*, Paris: Albin Michel.
Manning, William R. (1905) "The Nootka Sound Controversy," in *Annual Report of the American Historical Association for the Year 1904*, Washington.
Nasatir, Abraham P. (1945) *French Activities in California: An Archival Calendar-Guide*, Stanford: Stanford University Press.
Pethick, Derek (1980) *The Nootka Connection: Europe and the Northwest Coast, 1790–1795*, Vancouver: Douglas & McIntyre.
Roquefeuil, Camille de (1823) *Journal d'un voyage autour du monde pendant les années 1816, 1817, 1818, et 1819*, 2 vols, Paris: Ponthieu. The chapters relating to California have been translated and edited by Rudkin (1954).
Rudkin, Charles N. (1954) *Camille de Roquefeuil in San Francisco, 1817–1818*, Los Angeles: Glen Dawson.
—— (1956) *Voyage of the Venus, Sojourn in California*, Los Angeles: Glen Dawson.
Sheppe, Walter (1962) *First Man West: Alexander Mackenzie's Journal of His Voyage to the Pacific Coast of Canada in 1793*, Berkeley: University of California Press.
Spate, O.H.K. (1988) *The Pacific since Magellan*, Vol. III, Minneapolis, University of Minnesota Press.
Steven, Margaret (1983) *Trade, Tactics and Territory: Britain in the Pacific, 1783–1823*, Melbourne: Melbourne University Press.
Tikhmenev, P.A. (1978) *A History of the Russian-American Company*, Seattle and London: University of Washington Press.
Webb, Robert L. (1988) *On the Northwest: Commercial Whaling in the Pacific Northwest, 1790–1967*, Vancouver: University of British Columbia Press.
Wilbur, M.E. (1937) *Duflot de Mofras' Travels on the Pacific Coast*, 2 vols, Santa Anna, Calif.: Fine Arts Press.

8

'EASTWARDS OF THE CAPE OF GOOD HOPE'[1]

British overseas banking on the Pacific Rim, 1830–70

Frank H.H. King

Such disparate territories as Australia, China, British Columbia, Chile, California, the Dutch East Indies, Japan, the Philippines, and the Straits Settlements – virtually covering the Pacific Rim – were served by British overseas banks characterized by common regulatory origins. As the years passed, this virtual 'system' of banks expanded and developed but always in the particular context dictated by the legislation, which, however diverse, attempted to ensure sound banking practices throughout the British Empire, in territories where Britain had extraterritorial privileges, and, through agencies, even in foreign countries. Although British overseas banks on occasion failed or required reorganization, their contribution to intra-regional trade, including trans-Pacific exchange operations, was significant. The study of their origins and regulatory evolution is therefore of importance in any understanding of the developing economy of the Pacific Rim.

The early history of the system in the Pacific Rim can be studied by focusing on the Eastern exchange banks and on the colonial banks of Australasia, but in the process reference must be made to developments both in London and in other parts of the Empire, formal and informal. British banks in, say, Hong Kong were directly influenced by regulations promulgated to meet problems experienced in, say, the West Indies. This study may of necessity move far from the Pacific Rim, but it returns, enriched, to explain banking developments in our area of prime concern.

The years selected cover a period of evolution, but they also mark a stage in the history of banking on the Pacific Rim. These are the years in which, almost without exception, international banking was firmly in the hands of British or British imperial institutions. The French had their Comptoir d'Escompte with offices in Mauritius and the Far East – on occasion staffed by Germans, but so great was the advantage of the British network and its London facilities that banking had not become a field of effective international rivalry; non-British merchants and others patronized and, on occasion, were directors of British overseas banks, especially in the case of the Hongkong and Shanghai Bank, founded in 1864. United States banks remained state-based, the National Banking Act prohibiting overseas branches; Germany and Italy, both in the process of political unification, lacked the overseas interests; Spain and Portugal restricted their operations and lacked a Pacific Rim network; Japan had yet to experience the necessary modernization. Local or 'native' banks flourished in China and elsewhere, but they were conceptually and organizationally unsuited for redefinition, much less for expansion.

The years to 1870 established the overwhelming British banking presence. The events of this period explain in part the reasons behind continued British banking dominance on the Pacific Rim in later periods when European and, eventually, American competition was significant.

And yet despite the importance of British banking in the development of these territories East of Suez – or, as the royal charters would have it, 'Eastwards of the Cape of Good Hope', the subject has not been one of continuous academic focus. The pioneering work of Baster in the early 1930s was allowed to stand for many years and has only recently been reconsidered in a work on British multinational banking by Geoffrey Jones of Reading University, a work which makes considerable use of case studies, individual bank histories, by Jones himself and by others.[2] Nevertheless, the consideration of banking before 1870 has not as yet been put into full context, and in this chapter I shall mention several of the outstanding problems, depending on my own studies primarily of the files of the Board of Trade, the Treasury, the India Office, as well as of the Chancery Rolls themselves.[3]

The period chosen, 1830–70, covers the developments from the earliest British overseas banks subject to the Colonial Banking Regulations (CBR) to the passage of the general banking Act of 1862 and the immediate consequences thereof.[4] In this period the legal context in which the banks operated and the colonial (or other host) political systems changed to such an extent that imperial banking policy itself changed, either because the earlier policies had become irrelevant or because they were no longer enforceable *vis-à-vis* the foundation of new banks. In considering this evolution the historian should remember that application of the CBR was not wholly consistent, in part because of the recognition of special factors and in part because those determining policy had not fully understood the situation, had failed to coordinate, or had not read the files.[5] The case of the Agra and United Service Bank, Ltd is a perfect example of potential confusion realized, and the case is stated briefly in the context of other Agra problems later in this chapter.

The historian should also remember that the British government's apparently erratic course was in part a reflection of the Treasury's preoccupation of the moment. For example, when a bank was apparently refused a charter for one reason, an examination of the files may indicate that there were, in fact, several other reasons, each sufficient for the refusal but which the Treasury had not thought necessary to incorporate in the final correspondence.

These eccentricities resulted, at least in part, from the increasingly time-consuming consultation required. The Committee of the Privy Council for Trade had the prime responsibility for vetting joint-stock banking applications in England, but, following the Prime Minister's minute of April 9, 1833, charters for colonial banks required the Board to consult the Treasury; the latter, indeed, became responsible for preparing the warrant for the royal signature and the warrant was issued under authority of the Treasury Board.[6] The Treasury, in turn, would consult with the colonial and/or Indian governments. The consequent deviations from the standard model envisaged in the basic statutes and regulations illustrate the complexity of administering an imperial banking system.

The Treasury, for example, tended to be favourably inclined to banks already in successful operation, permitting them to include certain of their peculiarities in the royal charter – as for example the location of branches.[7] One key provision of the CBR set a time limit for the paying up of subscribed capital; additional time would be permitted if the bank could show that a trade downturn had made the full amount in excess of immediate needs, the Treasury recognizing that superfluous capital was expensive and could tempt the bank into speculative activities.[8] The limited liability granted shareholders by the charters was almost without exception a double liability; the Colonial Bank's shareholders were, however, granted single liability on the interesting grounds that the bank had an exceptionally large subscribed capital.[9] Exceptions were noted as such and not permitted as precedents.

As for provisions relative to the note issue, that is a subject in itself; here there were few exceptions but, surprisingly, in the case of the Oriental Bank, the Treasury permitted it, in Ceylon, to issue ten-shilling notes, a smaller denomination than usual, on the grounds it was already doing so – and there were other exceptions permitted.[10] Furthermore, not only were charter provisions not uniform as between the different banks, but they evolved and were particularly sensitive to the controversy as to whether notes should be issued by private banks or by the government – and, if the former, what constituted an acceptable bank for the purpose of note issue.[11]

Terminology By 'British overseas bank' we intend a general, non-legal term, to describe a bank which operated wholly or partly outside of the United Kingdom and was either owned by a majority of British shareholders or was accepted as 'British' by the authorities. From this general definition we shall exclude, in this chapter, consideration of the local Indian banks and the Presidency banks; we shall confine consideration to joint-stock operations. The term 'exchange bank' is used with particular reference to 'London and "X" banks': that is, banks which financed trade involving an exchange risk due to different or varying currency standards as between London and the overseas point(s) of operation.[12] Other types of British overseas banks would include local colonial joint-stock banks which remained subject to some form of direct or indirect Treasury interest.

Is the term 'multinational' appropriate for British overseas banks? Probably not in the early years. Colonial joint-stock banks were so tied into the imperial system that their control was parallel to federal government control in a federal state. This would remain true so long as (a) banking remained a 'reserved subject' *and* (b) the Treasury remained willing to advise disallowance as opposed to merely offering comments. As for the banks designed to finance trade between the colonies and the United Kingdom, they too had the characteristics of a single-jurisdiction bank except where the problem of exchange became a real factor affecting policy and profitability. Thus banks operating between England and India would be, from the first, multinational, since the Indian government, under the provisions of 3&4 William IV, *c.* 85, acted in trust for the Crown and was recognized as an independent authority *de facto*, a judgement valid despite the fact that Parliament reserved its rights and a Crown charter issued under the authority of a Parliamentary act could be made to apply in India.[13]

English v. imperial banking The question arises, therefore, as to why a separate category is necessary or, indeed, why a separate study of organizational development is necessary in consideration of British overseas banks. Basically, British overseas banking policy was controlled by the Treasury as influenced by the Colonial Office, the governments of the various territories and, to a limited extent, the Foreign Office. Consequently, the English and imperial banking had different histories. There was also interaction; by the end of our period, British overseas banks had either settled themselves as domestic banks in a foreign, that is, colonial self-governing situation or had become multinationals. This reflects the fact that although policy towards bank incorporation and regulation differed as between English, Scottish, Indian, and other overseas banks, it moved, at an uneven pace, in the same direction. Thus from the early 1830s there was recognized joint-stock banking in England; in 1844 and again in 1857, 1858 and 1862 there were significant changes including the granting of limited liability. Colonial requirements as embodied in charters were from the earliest years more specific, and also from the first overseas banks enjoyed limited liability.

This play between domestic English and Treasury overseas policy and the state of English banking and the requirements of the overseas banks dictated the form which the overseas banks took and the role they played in English domestic banking. The free-standing multinational form is one way of describing the fact that at least until the 1862 general banking Act royally chartered and overseas chartered banks could not, on the basis of those charters, themselves undertake banking in England – although they could, as customers, have banking undertaken for them by a domestic bank. That the Agra and United Service Bank attempted to resolve this problem by incorporating in England under English legislation is an indication of the eventual legal solution, although permission did not usually lead to implementation (see below).

British overseas banks did not, with the short-lived exception of the Agra and United Service Bank, develop a British domestic banking presence; domestic banks did not establish overseas branches. In the case of the former, a bank with limited liability would have been operating in the United Kingdom; in the case of the latter, it would be operating with unlimited liability in an area where shareholders expected protection. Royally chartered banks were permitted to issue banknotes despite having a London office; that is, despite the provisions of 7 George IV, *c.* 46, subject to increasingly stringent conditions and limits. This was not merely a concession to private enterprise; the Treasury considered, at least until failure of the Oriental Bank in 1884, that such note issues were beneficial. At the same time in England the note issue was differently conceived and differently controlled in the relevant legislation. As an Indian-based bank, the Agra was threatened with an injunction were it to continue London operations without an English domestic charter; on the other hand banks incorporated under 1862 legislation might issue notes overseas but these were not permitted acceptance by the colonial treasuries. The legislative and regulatory mix made it impractical for any bank to operate both in England and overseas until 1862, by which time the pattern had been set and the example of differentiation as practised in the City prevailed.

Incorporation, the alternatives Another approach to the study of British overseas banking is through examination of the alternatives facing bank promoters interested in establishing a bank which would operate overseas; that is, beyond England (and the British Isles).

The imperial regulatory authorities, the Board of Trade and the Treasury, observed that those promoting joint-stock banks wanted one or more of the following privileges, (a) limited liability, (b) the right of note issue, and (c) the acceptance of those notes by the relevant colonial treasuries. Since these privileges involved the monetary system and the public sector, the regulators established a set of rules, the CBR, which (a) gave, if the promoters requested them, the privileges listed above, but (b) required the charter of incorporation to include terms which the regulators considered made the banks sounder institutions. So long as these provisions (or allowed variations) of the CBR were incorporated in the terms of the new bank's charter, the regulators were not concerned as to who issued the charter.

1 If the projected bank's head office were to be in London, the imperial authorities incorporated the bank through a royal charter, which forbade banking in England on the basis of the charter. The 1844 joint-stock bank Act effectively left this prohibition unchanged.

After the 1862 bank Act, if promoters wanted a London head office *and* the privileges listed, they had still to seek a royal charter, the privileges of which would be first agreed with the host territorial governments. If they were willing to operate overseas without privileges (b) and (c), they could seek incorporation under the general Act, but this would not 'protect' them overseas: there such a bank would be a foreign corporation subject to whatever prohibition or restriction, etc., the host government imposed.

2 If the projected bank's head office were to be in an overseas territory, the promoters would approach the relevant local colonial authorities, who would either incorporate the bank through a special Act or pass a general banking Act under which the specific promotion would then be incorporated. However, the Colonial Office would pass such Acts to the Treasury for approval; the Treasury would advise disallowance unless the provisions of the CBR had been included. In anticipation, the Treasury would have copies of approved charters and/or the regulations themselves forwarded to the colony. In consequence the new bank would have exactly those provisions, with their restrictions and privileges, as the model royally chartered bank. By decision of its government, this alternative was not available in India.

3 If the projected bank's head office were to be in an overseas territory in which the governor were responsible to the legislature, the promoters would have to determine whether they wished to operate outside the territory. Only in such circumstances would the promoters need to consider the imperial banking regulations. The Treasury wished to impose the CBR terms on all banks, but usually restrained itself if the colony's legislature insisted on its own terms for a local bank operating in that colony only.

4 After passage of the 1862 general companies legislation in England, colonies might individually introduce similar legislation. The Treasury, however, would recommend disallowance if banking companies were included.[14] Thus a difference developed as between banks with a head office in England under the 1862 Act and those with a head office in a colony where the CBR terms were still insisted on. However, this

difference lasted but a few years, say to 1866. With the passage of the appropriate legislation, a territory could prevent the operation of any 'foreign' bank to which it objected, and this route to regulation appeared more satisfactory to the Treasury than forbidding the original incorporation. Such certainly was the case in territories with responsible governments.

So much may be said without consideration of management problems and management and shareholder interests and expectations.

Banking regulations differed as between England and other European countries. Therefore in support of the proposition that the separation between domestic and multinational banking transcended legislative prohibitions, note that the attempts of the German Deutsche Bank and the French Crédit Lyonnais to found branches in the East proved unprofitable; the banks of both nations resorted to broadly based national consortium banks – the Deutsch-Asiatische Bank and the Banque de l'Indo-Chine respectively.

The CBR were not designed for British banks only. The Bank of Rotterdam, which was Dutch, was informed they would be permitted to establish a branch in Singapore if the conditions of the CBR were incorporated in their charter![15] The basis of the policy insisting on the CBR terms was the Treasury's judgement of their soundness. Economic historians have argued that the British government, frustrated in its hopes of implementing sound economic policy in England where interests and precedents proved implacable, attempted to put the latest theories into practice overseas.[16] The Colonial Banking Regulations and their implementation support this thesis.

Before considering specific issues and to recapture the enthusiasm of the time, the following typical quotation comes from the writing of Robert Montgomery Martin:

> By means of these Colonial Banks I wished to strengthen the connection between the Colonies and the Parent State, – to create a moneyed influence in England, interested in and identified with, the progress and prosperity of the Colonies, – to direct unemployed wealth to the vast and rich fields of the British possessions, rather than it should be sunk and utterly lost in foreign loans and South American mining speculations; – I wished to see the exchange steadied and equalized as much as possible between the different parts of the British Empire, – to prevent the necessity for exporting specie to or from the Colonies, – and by separating the functions of banker and merchant, to induce the latter to direct and employ all his means, skill and energies, to the advancement of the commerce between the mother country and the distant dependence, thus strengthening their mutual relations and binding them closely together by the strong feelings of reciprocal friendly interests.[17]

IMPERIAL UNIFORMITY

In the previous section we considered the question of the uniformity of the CBR and concluded that (a) there was evolution and (b) at any one time there were variations. Policy, however, intended uniformity. Certainly policy was considered in imperial or Empire-wide terms – always with the exception of India. For example: (a) at least until the late 1840s there existed a presumption of currency uniformity as reflected in the similarity of units of account, and, therefore, a minimum of exchange risk in the transfer of funds between London and a particular colony – even silver-based Hong Kong government accounts had to be kept in pound/shilling/pence units of account; (b) banking – there were basic principles of banking which could be enshrined in a single document – namely, the Colonial Banking Regulations, which, since money and banking legislation was a reserved subject and no general companies Acts existed, could be enforced by the Imperial government.

All this changed as territories evolved responsible legislatures, as limited liability became general, and as British banking contacts developed in cities dealing in a currency area which was beyond Imperial control, e.g. Hong Kong for China, Singapore for the East Indies and the Malay States. Exchange operations were to become important, potentially speculative, and hence questionable as a banking activity. This will be considered further.

The Colonial Banking Regulations had, however, a longer life and were in themselves, whether enforceable or not, an acceptable exposition of reasonable criteria for a sound banking company. But their enforcement – that is, their required inclusion in the charters or articles of association of new banking companies – rested on two assumptions: (a) that bank organizers required limited liability, for which privilege they were willing to subject themselves to restrictions which, while authorities considered them sound, promoters might consider unnecessary, (b) the political entities in which they operated would cooperate either because they were subject to the Imperial government in London (or were, in fact, London itself), or because they accepted the validity of the provisions contained in the regulations. Regulatory control was exercised from London either by the need for the banking company to obtain a charter of incorporation in London itself or, if it were a local colonial bank, the need to obtain the sanction of that colony's government – as such matters were 'reserved' (that is, had to be referred to London) the Treasury and the Colonial Office could in the early years be responsible for a final decision. As for London, the coming of general limited liability for banking companies in the 1858 and 1862 banking legislation seemed to eliminate the one effective factor ensuring imperial control.[18] As for the colonies, as their executives became responsible to the local legislature, especially after 1849, in cases where the legislature did not accept the restrictions of the banking regulations, the British Treasury was limited to remonstrating or warning of the consequences (a) to the shareholders about to embark on an unsound banking project and (b) to the colony's economy itself.[19]

A member of Parliament expressed the view that Treasury interference was 'ridiculous' were it not serious, a view with which James Stephen, the redoubtable permanent under-secretary and legal adviser of the Colonial Office, agreed.[20] However, in cases where the bank was intended to operate in more than one colony, the Treasury would attempt once again to exert the imperial order. The Treasury, and especially James Wilson, continued to focus on colonial acts which were (a) sloppily drafted (for example, did not state the capital of the bank), (b) unduly favourable to debtors, or (c) apparently directed against British investors.[21]

This does not, however, explain how the CBR were enforced after 1862. As it happened, limited liability was not the only privilege gained by those who incorporated on terms consistent with the CBR: (a) in the early years such an incorporation, most importantly by royal charter but also by act of a colonial legislature, permitted the bank to operate in a specific area which, if it included more than one colony, might be exercised without further formality in each political jurisdiction,[22] and (b) the Treasury had ruled that only banks whose charter or articles incorporated the terms of the CBR could hold government funds or have their banknotes received at the Treasury, two potentially important activities.[23] These privileges were heavily hedged, however, the note issue being, as noted above, a subject in itself. Host governments could and did tax the banks' note issue and the Treasury decided not to interfere.[24] Even the deposit of government funds in a bank had to be carefully considered and limited since it was recognized that any withdrawal from an endangered bank would be likely to actually precipitate its collapse.[25] On the other hand, a colonial government attempting to make its own regulations so that a non-CBR bank could meet the revised basic requirements was quickly overruled.[26] The banks initially incorporated under the 1862 legislation could not subsequently revise their articles to include the CBR in a manner acceptable to the Treasury; that is, in a form which could never subsequently be reversed by the same Board or body of shareholders: hence those banks which valued government business and/or the note issue retained their former charters; new banks wishing to exercise the old privileges then still had to seek a royal charter or its equivalent.[27] Eventually a certain prestige came in consequence of the charter, giving it continuing value!

The Treasury, which was beginning to question its ability to regulate an Empire-wide banking system, found itself still responsible for chartered banks.[28] Although chartered banks continued into the present century, there was further erosion of the universality of the CBR when territories (a) enacted their own banking legislation and required even chartered banks to register locally[29] and (b) took over the issue of their own paper currency, for example Ceylon and the Straits Settlements.[30] In the case of the former, the privilege of universal operation had already been eroded as territories gained responsible governments: the Treasury would consult with each government before granting a charter, thus, as it were, obtaining permission for the chartered bank to operate in a particular colony before, rather than after that bank's incorporation.[31] Indeed, the Treasury went so far as to write to the Colonial Office in 1863 that it had agreed not to grant charters to colonial banks without the sanction of the Colonies, the East India Company or Australia.[32] Finally, there would be simple attrition as chartered banks faced banking crises.[33] Where they survived but had to be reconstituted, the Treasury did not renew or revise their charter, and the bank came either under local general banking legislation or under the British Act of 1862.[34]

Perhaps it is helpful to remember that a bank with a charter subsequently registering under a general companies or banking Act without forced restructuring did not thereby free itself from the restrictions of the charter – nor from the privileges which might go with it. Thus the Agra Bank, registering under the 1862 general Act as a 7&8 [1844] Vict. *c.* 113 bank, retained its charter until and unless released and consequently retained the right for its notes to be accepted in the Hong Kong Treasury;[35] the Hongkong and Shanghai Banking Corporation more recently added 'Limited' to its name in consequence of its 1990 registration in Hong Kong but still remains subject to the terms of its 'charter' or Hong Kong ordinance of incorporation as revised. This remains true although, as a consequence of a reverse take-over, the Hongkong Bank is now a subsidiary of one of its former subsidiaries, HSBC Holdings, plc, incorporated in the United Kingdom.

The aversion to permitting banks to incorporate with limited liability rested on the view, expressed by James Wilson of the Treasury as late as 1857, that whereas the liabilities of manufacturing companies would probably be covered by shareholders' funds, banks accepted deposits and their liabilities could thus exceed shareholders' funds.

> Banks differ from other joint stock companies in as much as they are not only Trustees for money deposited with them, but are also dealers in money deposited and the money with which they deal is to a great extent the property of others.[36]

Hence, if there were to be limited liability at all, it was thought necessary to make it a double liability; that is, as capital was fully paid up, shareholders were liable to lose this, plus being required to pay in an amount equal to the nominal value of their shares.[37] This would be ineffective in a financial crisis; too many shareholders would be without the necessary resources.[38] Nevertheless, it is not too strong to conclude that limited liability was the cornerstone of the banking system based on the Colonial Banking Regulations.

FACTORS IN THE FOUNDING OF 'LONDON AND X' BANKS[39]

The finance of trade

Although it is generally said that the chartered exchange banks were founded to finance trade, traders raised objections to the first exchange banks, especially in India. The large merchants who carried on their own exchange operations were concerned that a general exchange bank would provide facilities to smaller and allegedly speculative merchants causing over-trading and consequent disruption to either the commodity markets, the exchanges, or both. On the other hand smaller merchants feared that they would be powerless and at the mercy of exchange banks whose activities would deprive them of 'legitimate' profits. The exchange banks were not always reassuring.[40]

The opposition of merchants to exchange banks was minimized if the merchants themselves were instrumental in the establishment of the bank, as in the case of the Colonial Bank or the Hongkong Bank, or if merchants were reassured that they could, if they wished, set up a rival bank.[41] The Treasury's firm and continuous opposition to any form of monopoly resulting from a government policy was reassuring on this point; nevertheless, bank proposals to finance trade did flounder on the opposition of the very merchants intended as customers.[42]

Related to this problem – that is, who should handle the exchanges, the merchant or a bank – was the general question as to whether exchange operations were a legitimate activity for a bank in the first place. The question is both general and specific.

Given the compartmentalization of the London market, the general question of what constitutes legitimate banking was a natural one. The difficulty is that there was no consensus, and we find instances in which a new corporation was authorized to undertake (a) banking and (b) other activities performed by bankers. Or, in attempting to determine whether a colonial bank with an office in London was or was not engaging in banking, contrary to British law (before 1862), the Treasury ruled that it was not a question of whether a specific activity was part of banking but whether, if performed alone, it would make the particular office a 'bank'.[43] We can consider this question further when asking about exchange banks' activities in London. But the difficulty here is that regardless of whether exchange operations are or are not legitimate banking, the question of whether a banking institution should nevertheless operate in the exchanges remains unresolved – it could be that, even if exchange were not 'banking', it might be considered permissible as an activity normally engaged in by bankers! Thus the proposed Chartered Bank of Hong Kong listed its purpose as (a) business of bankers and (b) other business . . . usually practised by bankers, *and also* (c) the general business of exchange and remittance.[44]

There were several problems with banks undertaking exchange operations. First, they might control the exchanges against the interests of merchants. Secondly, if combined with the privilege of note issue, a bank might further impact on the exchange rate or might enable an increase in the money supply and hence affect economic policy.[45] This was indeed a factor in the thinking of the Birmingham School and therefore in the plans for the Bank of British North America and of Martin's proposed India banks. Thirdly, unless exchange operations were limited to a small position with all other transactions covered, there was great risk of speculative loss. This might be minimized by a clause in the articles of association calling for the winding up of the company should, say, one-third of the capital be lost, but in an extreme case a loss from exchange operations could exceed this limit before it could be controlled. In the worst case scenario, an exchange bank with limited liability could take a strong but incorrect position causing losses for which shareholders would not be fully responsible since they had obtained, in a favourite expression of the East India Company, 'exemption from personal responsibility'.[46]

There was the positive claim that exchange operations were properly the business of merchants. This can, of course, only apply to transactions involving the finance of commodities and, if allowed, would make exchange for other purposes subordinate to commodity finance. The argument was that banks undertook their exchange operations in connection with commodity finance, the instruments of credit relating directly to commodities and therefore the banks were taking on the risks involved in dealing in such commodities, risks which were properly those of the merchant. Underlying this argument is the concept of the 'ideal' merchant and the 'ideal' banker: the former understands the problems of his commodity, the latter of legitimate banking. Or, not to beg the question, the banker cannot know about commodities because dealing in the latter does not enter into any legitimate definition of banking. To this extent the objectors had a point: exchange bankers would have to learn about the commodities the trade in which their banking transactions facilitated. Furthermore, critics of exchange banking were correct in supposing that the risks would be high and that the banks, unless careful and expertly managed, would be subject to the consequences of commodity speculation. All these dire predictions proved, at one point or another and with one bank or another, to be valid. But banks have failed for many reasons. What exchange bankers would not accept was that a transaction which required financial and monetary expertise should not be a legitimate activity for those who had that expertise. In this instance, Robert Montgomery Martin's position was eventually accepted.

These considerations were of long-term impact mainly in dealings with

India. This is partly because exchange on India was particularly complex, the most profitable transactions involving China, and partly because the government had long before made institutional arrangements enshrining the separation of banking from exchange operations as well as the separation of the note issue from banks based outside India's jurisdiction and dealing in foreign exchange.[47] The difficulty in assessing the strength of the opposition to an Indian bank dealing in exchange arises from the particular cases in which the principle was tested. For example, the 1836 Bank of India was a leviathan which may have been opposed simply on the basis of size.[48] Then the Bank of Asia and the East Asian Bank were being promoted by Robert Montgomery Martin whose reputation in India was, to put it mildly, mixed. Certainly opposition would arise to any project with which he was personally connected.

Another motive for establishing a trade-oriented chartered bank would be the inadequacy of banking regulations in a particular foreign country. In the case of the abortive British and Oriental Bank at Constantinople, for example, those encouraging the formation of the bank were apparently the non-British merchants, a fact which tipped the scale against granting the charter. In expressing otherwise reluctant sympathy, the Treasury noted that the Foreign Office approved and, although noting that this was outside Her Majesty's dominions, this fact would have been of less account had the British mercantile community been wholeheartedly in support.[49]

Economic development

One of the problems in determining why a bank was founded lies in the often contradictory promises made by the promoters or in the fact that, once founded, the management or the board went their own ways, often introducing just those aspects of banking which, as promoters, they had specifically rejected – thus the Hongkong Bank's founding committee had determined the bank would not compete in the business of exchange on London; in fact this was one of the first activities of the bank.[50] The Scinde, Punjaub and Delhi Bank was at its founding to be restricted to those areas covered by the railway of the same name. Within a year its chairman reported having opened an office in Bombay to operate on the exchanges.[51] This was not deception (except possibly self-deception), but arose from the existence of the concept of what a bank should do, a luxury which an operating bank could ill afford – as witness the history of the Commercial Bank of London.[52]

We have considered the problems of banks established to finance the course of trade. One could add to this category those which financed personal or smaller movements of funds, e.g. missionaries, army officers, etc. – indeed one of the arguments for an exchange bank independent of big merchants.

Still to be considered are banks which intended to move funds to enable the development of the territory, which would respond, that is, to an alleged 'shortage of funds' to develop the vast resources, etc. of that territory. As Martin put it, 'India requires a sound and expansive monetary policy.'[53] It was precisely this category of bank which so concerned the Indian government. The idea that the supply of funds would stimulate profitable investment appeared a totally speculative view of the role of banks. Real investment incurring the risks likely in India required equity capital. Furthermore, if 'legitimate' banking facilities were needed, the capital of the three Presidency banks could be increased. One government specialist suggested that the promoters, Martin in this case, were confused as between potential and actual demand for funds and/or between projects which could legitimately be undertaken with minimal risk and those which required so heavy a risk that they were unsuitable for Western style banking.[54] The Indian exchange banking projects were initially faulted in major part on these grounds.

The concepts of the Birmingham School are reflected not only in Martin's India promotions, never realized, but also in the conceptual framework for the Bank of British North America.[55] Martin wrote the promotional literature. In this he was influenced by his father's friend, the country banker William Medley, who, with Mathias Attwood, had served on the board of the Provincial Bank of Ireland.[56]

'Central banking'

There was yet another motivation for founding a free-standing multinational bank – the need to establish a central bank. To use this term is, perhaps, ahistorical. But consider the Imperial Ottoman Bank and Martin's 1863 Imperial Bank of China scheme and its developments under the auspices of the Credit Foncier and Mobilier of England, and certainly Martin had the Bank of England in mind as a parallel.[57] There was a maverick 'Imperial Bank of Japan' promoted, similar in purpose to Martin's original Imperial Bank of China, but it did not go forward.[58] The exchange banks did perform services for government – but only as banks, not as policy-makers. Furthermore, in many places, if there were to be a bank at all, other business being limited, there had to be promised government business and perhaps the right of note issue; but, so well had Martin learned his lesson while dealing with the abortive Indian bank proposals, he denied his 'Imperial Bank' any role in the business of exchange.[59] But these activities were not exclusive; as noted, the British Treasury abhorred monopoly. In a later period the Imperial Bank of Persia would be established by royal charter to perform central banking functions, including the note issue, on an exclusive basis in that country.[60] But that exclusiveness was not in British territory. Martin's 1864 Imperial Bank of China, which was registered without articles of association, was one of several such projects – from wild schemes dreamed up by early merchants, including Augustine Heard, to the potentially fraudulent schemes of 'Count' Mitkiewicz, to the comprehensive plans of di Rudinì, Angelo Luzzatti *et al.* in the years 1895–97 – including development projects and a bank to finance them.[61] Martin even advertised that he had written the Imperial Government of China to permit the notes of his bank to be accepted in payment of customs duties.[62] This was exceptional, although the attraction of more or less government business was an important factor in the minds of bank promoters. There is no record that Martin's request, which was given no encouragement by the British Foreign Office, was ever considered by a Chinese official, much less by the Imperial Chinese government.

THE ROLE OF LONDON

Small colonial established banks might never seek a presence in London. Royally chartered banks might come to be 'free-standing' multinationals with direction in London but undertaking banking overseas (see discussion above) – and there were variations. Certain of the combinations of London activities and overseas activities were dictated by the purpose of the bank, others by the requirements of the bank's London 'clearer', and still others by the particular legal position relative to a banking company.

The first royally chartered exchange banks were forbidden to act as banks in England, but that did not mean they could not undertake an activity of the kind which a bank might undertake. The Oriental Bank, formerly the Bank of Western India, when moving its Head Office to London and re-establishing there in 1845, stated that all its banking in England would be done through Bankers and nothing was to be done to render the Oriental 'Bankers in England' or to violate the 1844 Joint Stock Bank Act.[63] In its subsequent 1851 draft charter as a royally chartered bank, it was in London to carry on the business of exchange, deposit, and remittance only but not the business of banking, one reason being that given its permission to operate agencies in India, the East India Company would object.[64]

One can easily imagine that, beginning modestly, an overseas bank might move into a grey area and finally be told that it was undertaking banking business on such a scale that it was considered to be engaged in banking contrary to the statute. Such, indeed, was the case of the Agra and United Service Bank, which first established an office in London in 1846; its activities developed to the point where in 1853 the Treasury judged it to be engaged in 'banking' contrary to 7&8 Vict. *c.* 113.[65]

Unlike the Oriental, the Agra's directors decided that they did indeed wish to undertake banking in London; accordingly they determined to move their head office from India and seek an English charter (or Letters Patent) as a joint-stock bank under the 1844 Act.[66] This the Agra achieved in 1857 before revision of the 1844 Act. Subsequently the bank became subject to the provisions of the 1857, 1858 and 1862 Acts, obtained limited liability in 1858 (except for the note issue), but was otherwise bound by the terms of its charter as submitted in 1857.[67]

As an illustration of the confusion which could arise in separate jurisdictions and different approaches to domestic and overseas bank regulation, the problem of the Agra's note issue is relevant. The Agra and United Service Bank, Ltd attempted to have its notes accepted by the Hong Kong Treasury on the grounds that it was a 'chartered bank'; that is, it operated on the basis of Letters Patent under the 1844 Act. When the Treasury discovered this, it claimed that such an incorporation was intended for English operating banks only and that it had no idea the Agra would undertake overseas business, blaming the Board of Trade for not noticing this. The Agra, however, was able to show that its negotiations had been frank and full, that the Board of Trade knew of its Indian connections, and that the bank's constitution permitted the minor revisions enabling it to meet CBR standards. The Treasury accordingly relented and the Agra's notes were accepted.[68]

The Agra Bank's history also illustrates another London factor – that of risk sharing. An exchange bank might have an office in London but its overseas offices were instructed to draw their bills on a London domestic bank with which arrangements had been made – usually involving a covered and an uncovered tranche against which the bills could be drawn. However, the Agra and United Service Bank, as an English bank, began drawing on itself.[69] Furthermore, its desire to operate fully in London caused it, at least from its 1857 incorporation, to seek membership in the London Clearing House, but the door remained closed.[70] In June, 1864, Agra, however, gained membership by taking over the business of a London banking partnership, Messrs Masterman, Peters, Mildred and Company; the bank was renamed Agra and Masterman's Bank.[71] How this might have developed must remain unknown; the new bank was strongly opposed by certain forces in the City, many customers were lost to other banks, its operations during the immediate financial crises were questioned, and bears attacked the shares.[72] Lacking support, one could argue, from another bank in a time of credit tightness (following the collapse of Overend Gurney), the Agra and Masterman's succumbed within three years, was reconstituted under the Act of 1862 as the Agra Bank, Ltd (thereby losing any automatic special status it had from its former charter) and became a standard 'London and X' bank of that period.[73]

What were the factors pulling banks founded overseas back to a London head office?

First, there was the need for a London office in any case. Clearing banks preferred to deal with an overseas bank which could be contacted in the City. Secondly, the founders of the overseas bank may well have retired from a colony at a relatively early age, say fifty-three, and returned to what was often the senior partnership of their corresponding merchant house in London. At such a time they might wish to continue their role in the bank they had founded by bringing the head office to London. This aspect of the problem may have simply influenced the timing. The fact is that a bank needed to be a personality capable of suing and being sued in the corporate name. With the problem of including colonial banks in general colonial companies ordinances, colonies were often left with the choice of a separate incorporation under the terms of the CBR – or nothing. If only CBR terms could be obtained, the promoters (or directors of an existing unincorporated bank) might choose a royal charter and London. Furthermore, if the bank flourished and needed additional capital, directors would find this more easily obtained from a London head office. But the move was made often with a sacrifice of the intimate local contacts which had characterized its early years (see below) and, as the Hongkong Bank's history indicates, there was nothing absolute.[74]

Another factor in a London incorporation might be the hostile attitude to exchange banking or to limited liability in the host territory. Jardine Matheson's *taipan* (chief executive officer), who was on the Hong Kong Legislative Council at the time, opposed a general companies ordinance which permitted limited liability to banks. Because the ordinance included banks without requiring the inclusion of CBR terms, the Treasury successfully advised its disallowance. As it happened the bank's promoters and a majority of the Legislative Council were anxious to have a local bank and were willing to agree to a special ordinance, incorporating the provisions of the CBR, for the Hongkong Bank. Had they been unwilling to so act, one would have a case where the promoters' only course would have been to seek a royal charter – no doubt with identical provisions – in London, but this would have required a London head office.[75]

Once the bank had re-established in London, it would have a new legal basis and its management would, in most instances, be comparable, after an initial period, to that of any London-founded overseas bank.

Before leaving this subject we should consider the case of a locally promoted bank whose promoters were sufficiently aware of the problems to foresee the advantages of incorporating in some way under the terms of the CBR, even though this might not be required locally. The problem here was that a colonial legislature had no jurisdiction outside its territory and the question arose, therefore, as to whether a corporation created by a colonial legislative ordinance could exist outside the territory of that particular colony. This was legally a misconception, because a host country could have such a bank register under the appropriate local Acts – as in the case of India after 1866. Nevertheless, this problem of colonial legislative 'extra-territorial' authority caused considerable but unnecessary problems for the Hongkong Bank. Specifically the problem arose when the bank's local charter called for the Treasury to approve its opening in some location outside the territory. Were the Treasury to do so, it might appear to be undermining the imperial extra-territorial policy. This too would prove surmountable.[76]

However, in the case of the Bombay-promoted Bank of China (1864), the promoters did immediately seek a royal charter, although all preliminary negotiations were carried out from a Bombay base.[77] They were aware that unlike many colonial authorities, the Indian government would not charter an exchange bank. Other promoters of Indian banks took the same course, either before or after initial operations.

AREA OF OPERATION

As a general principle in this period, the Treasury attempted to limit a bank's area of operations, the restrictions being based on assumptions relative to practicality or, later in the period, on the willingness of the proposed host area to accept the bank.[78] Furthermore, there might be limitations placed on the bank within the area designated, as, for example, branches could be established where there was a British Consul or, for China, only in the Treaty Ports. Different arguments were from time to time advanced in support of these limitations, but basically they reflect the consequences of the inadequacy of communication. A bank manager in Sydney, for example, might commit funds locally without realizing that the bank manager in Buenos Aires was in difficulties – neither head office in London nor either of the managers could have, it was feared, the key information in time; nor was it reasonable (given the communications problems and the consequences of on-the-job training, which limited full appreciation of problems in other areas) that they should.

However, when exchange operations became the focus of certain royally chartered banks (as opposed to discounting and the note issue) the bank's agents would wish to follow the trail of trade wherever it led, and the pressure for geographical dispersion would become a reality. Thus promoters of a bank desiring to operate in the Cape Colony, Ceylon and Australia argued that trade from Australia went via the Cape and that there were thus legitimate trade connections between the two areas; but ingenious as this argument was and despite support from South Africa, the Treasury declined to accept it.[79] However, in any decision many factors might influence the authorities. In this particular case two further points were in fact raised: (a) the promoters argued that a bank was required in Ceylon but appear not to have connected this with any supposed trade routes, and (b) the Colonial Office were concerned about the impact on the existing banking structure of South Africa.[80]

There was nothing absolute about this policy and, as always, the Treasury tended to favour an application from a bank already in successful operation.

In the case of the Oriental Bank, for example, its application for a royal charter which would permit operations, *inter alia*, in Hong Kong and Ceylon was granted, albeit in a circuitous way. The Oriental Bank, then established in London, sought first of all to operate in Ceylon with a colonial legislated charter for the Colombo branch alone. This was impractical and, as the Bank of Ceylon was on the verge of suspension, the Oriental thought to move, as it were, into that bank's charter while, at the same time, promoting a chartered Bank of Hong Kong.[81] Both ideas were checked in 1851 by a Treasury decision to issue a single charter for an Oriental Bank Corporation, to carry on the business of the former Oriental Bank, and with permission to operate in Ceylon, Hong Kong and China and with agencies East of the Cape of Good Hope and with further branches as sanctioned by the Treasury.[82] It was this charter which inadvertently permitted a royally chartered bank to open agencies in India without the permission of the Indian government.[83]

Another argument was the need for expert knowledge relative to the commodities being traded or the people being served. In the former case, the Treasury would not often find disagreement, if only because the promoters of the bank might be connected with a particular commodity and had no initial interest, at least, in operating on a broader basis. Banks which became management- as opposed to board-directed might take a broader view, but the area restriction was not, in principle, a major source of contention. As for dealing with the customers, the range here might be as restricted as the commodities handled. Travellers might note that British in one area differed from British subjected to the climate, local people etc. of another area, but in the rare cases of lateral transfer of high level staff this seems not to have been a major problem. As for dealing with local people, that, if done at all, was restricted or accomplished through one or another type of intermediary.[84]

That this is a necessary subject for consideration is based partly on the logical question as to whether variation in area might not have a favourable impact on risk diffusion, the failure of coffee in Ceylon, for example, being offset by a favourable development elsewhere. This obvious aspect of the problem does not seem to feature in the official documents.

The areas designated for operations were not, however, as clearly defined as might be expected given the above argumentation. For royal charters permitting operation in the East, the area designated was often simply 'Eastwards of the Cape of Good Hope'. However, this was less permissive than appears: first, although the world be round, 'Eastwards' was qualified by setting the limits at 180° longitude; secondly, because the charter would be granted on the basis of a submission which specifically stated the purpose of the bank, capital was not that readily available and its use would not be diffused by deviating from the original purpose stated; thirdly, specific locations for branches might be listed together with a clause requiring Treasury permission before opening in each. The restrictions on the opening of agencies, however, were not usually specific. But as to what constituted an 'agency' as opposed to a branch is a question to which there is no wholly satisfactory answer valid in all times and in all places. Even where the purpose of an agency was noted in the charter, there could be scope for development or creative thinking.[85]

Responsible management was often conservative and would itself question the advisability of opening in a new area, seeking some connection with the bank's ongoing operations. Thus the Hongkong Bank when considering Ceylon noted that 'it was not needed for China', confirming the Bank's primary orientation and casting doubt on the wisdom of establishing in Colombo.[86]

One esoteric point should be noted relative to India. The Hon. East India Company's 'territories' included not only India but also the Straits Settlements (until 1861) and British activities in China (until at least the mid-1840s). This last might be a legal quibble, but it enabled the Indian government to insist that Martin's proposed Bank of Asia refrain from exchange operations 'within the recognized limits of the Company's charter', and thus not only between India and London but also between India and the East (that is, Singapore and Hong Kong). In Martin's view, this made the whole scheme impractical – and the East India Company was aware of the fact.[87]

We must conclude, therefore, that Treasury policy prevented global banking, encouraged banking in connected and contiguous areas, but was otherwise inconsistent. Practical considerations reinforced Treasury policy, and boards of directors of established banks were rational in their assessment of the risks. In general, bank directors thought in terms of restricted areas and operations.

MANAGEMENT AND FAILURES

The Colonial Banking Regulations did not create banks which were immune to failure; regulatory authorities cannot prevent bad banking decisions, although they can restrict the areas in which these can take place! This was not always understood by the public.

One particular feature of the CBR was that a chartered bank should publish its accounts so that the public could judge for itself. By the end of the century there was Treasury concern that this implied that the government would take action should the accounts indicate the necessity, or would take responsibility if the accounts were misleading. Meanwhile, members of the public learned that interpretation of the accounts was difficult, especially so long as shareholders supported their directors in concealing true profits and reserves.

It was precisely the inability of regulators to prevent bank failures which led to the obsession relative to the banknote issue. Restrictions on the note issue were in part a consequence of monetary policy, and domestic regulations in part reflected this. However, overseas a paper currency was often popular as an alternative to a confused or inadequate coinage. Therefore any restriction on banknotes (before, that is, there was any government issue in the particular jurisdiction) was related to their safety and, therefore, to the soundness of the issuing bank. In general, banks established in the United Kingdom operating overseas were not, under British general banking Acts of the period, restricted in their overseas note issue (except that the notes were not covered by the limited liability provisions – shareholders had unlimited liability for the notes). Banks which had been established under the CBR – that is, banks with charters – were, however, totally controlled as to their note-issuing capabilities, including an overall limit related to the paid-up capital. This, plus the other provisions of the CBR, made the notes of such banks, it was thought, safer for the general public. This was to be demonstrated to the public by having the local government accept only the notes of banks conforming to the CBR, thus rendering it most unlikely that the note issue of any non-CBR bank would in fact circulate.

But the evolution of banknote regulation eventually reached the point where banknote holders were given priority before other debtors of the bank, and the government was protected by so ordering the holdings of the bank that, in effect, the note issue was 100 per cent covered.[88]

These provisions, however, did not solve the problem of bank failures.

Bank failures could occur as a consequence of poor management, lack of control of managers, lack of adjustment to new circumstances, changed conditions inadequately understood, natural disasters beyond control – and none of these can be the subject of provisions in the CBR or be avoided by regulatory genius. The Treasury indeed had no continuing regulatory authority. What authority it had came in part at the establishment of the bank, in part from its 'gate-keeping' opportunities, as for example when a chartered bank needed a charter revision or on the occasion when the charter was due for renewal; but, in the absence of any complex or developing overseas banking policy, once the bank had been chartered, the Treasury made little use of its authority except in the case of banknotes.

If a bank had been founded primarily in connection with a single purpose, for example, the finance of a particular commodity between 'X' and London, then the failure of that commodity or the fall in demand for it would affect the fortunes of the bank. As such a decline was usually seen as temporary or as the result of a one-time natural calamity, the bank was caught with funds committed. Meanwhile, since capital was limited, it was unlikely that the bank's board would have aggressively sought out other activities for their bank. This would be true of expansion into other areas. Here then was a source of weakness. At the founding (that is, when the

Treasury had authority to rule), the situation appeared prima-facie reasonable. Even here it was not government's business to predict success, although, when seeking reasons to oppose a banking promotion, officials came perilously close to attempting just that.

Banks founded in periods of speculation or unreasonable expectations could moreover expect short lives – the failure rate was particularly high after passage of the limited liability Acts.

In the East the problem of silver would eventually be key to the fate of even the oldest of the exchange banks – but that is after our period. Nevertheless the lack of focus of the Eastern banks – in that they were usually neither single commodity nor single territory institutions – led to problems of control. The Commercial Bank Corporation of India and the East, which obtained a royal charter in 1864, is a case in point. Setting up in Shanghai their branch manager became involved in the financing of the post-treaty land boom. The board of directors also sent an agent to San Francisco in connection with the shipment of silver bullion; he exceeded his instructions by lending against the security of mining shares. These two activities were, on their failure, sufficient to close the bank.[89]

The solution would seem to have been to find experienced, capable managers, but did they exist and if so how could they be found? The tasks were often without precedent and experience has shown that good managers, moved to a different corporate environment (especially if facing new-type problems), do not necessarily perform well. Furthermore, at crucial periods in the development of overseas banking, good managers of any background were in short supply – there was a limit to which domestic banks could be raided! This again was especially true in the period 1862–65. It was indeed the collapse of several Eastern banks which would be providential to the new Hongkong Bank – their famous Sir Thomas Jackson came from the troubled Agra and Masterman's.

Nor were managers brought together from different sources necessarily a compatible team. The eventual solution, therefore, was the establishment of a 'service' of long-term, career-oriented men, recruited from a relatively uniform social background (Scots and English differing in this), and trained together as juniors in a socialization process which permitted close co-operation and mutual understanding of each other's abilities. Brought up in the corporation, there was less likelihood that, when becoming a branch manager far from immediate head office control, the new manager would embark unpredictably in new directions. Whether or not he exercised initiative, and in what directions, would depend upon his training – that is, upon the corporate culture.[90]

To the extent that the problem was one of control of distant managers arising from the existence of geographically widely dispersed branches, a more general comment is helpful. The problem of judgement relative to the exchanges and the value of commodities is rather one personal to the manager than a question of control. The early overseas banks, to the extent that they operated to London, were nevertheless controlled in their place of origin overseas – the problem arose later, when the board moved to London. Nor did the early chartered banks necessarily have a network of branches, so a parallel with the Provincial Bank of Ireland or with Scottish banking is not immediately helpful.[91] Preferable is the Treasury concept of an overseas bank with branches being a collection of banks operating with a common capital.

The competition created by exchange banks in the field of exchange and related services lowered commissions and consequent profits per transaction; the banks then depended on turnover, especially in exchange – from which it followed that to 'lock up' funds, even under generous terms of interest, was a serious decision. One potential source of illiquidity would be loans against mortgage of land, and prohibition of this was found in the CBR – although sometimes only in a modified form in the actual charters. As a principle, control of lending against mortgages was accepted British banking, but it would prove unacceptable in Australia and other colonies where land was the most usual form of local wealth.[92] The issue required flexible handling, something difficult to achieve if the Treasury regulations were dominant; furthermore, Dutch law presented particular problems in Ceylon and South Africa, while banks in Mauritius faced the Napoleonic Code.[93] Thus the standard problem was compounded by local land laws which were unfamiliar both to London and to the new bank branch manager.

British overseas banking and India

The development of British overseas banking separately from domestic English banking arose in the first instance because of the perceived need for limited liability for the former in order to offset the increased risks to shareholders. From this it follows that such banks were joint-stock, a form whose suitability was still being debated in the England of the early 1830s. The differentiation in form led also to a differentiation in jurisdiction, with the Treasury virtually taking over from the Board of Trade and injecting a more thorough and even more theoretically based regulatory perception in dealing with the problems of banking and the note issue. Thus the different historical regulatory course of overseas and domestic banking was inevitable.

Since, indeed, English banks were not permitted limited liability until 1858, it is not surprising that overseas banks were forbidden to undertake banking in England unless they registered *de novo* under the Act of 1862, thereby losing other privileges.[94]

India appears at first glance to be an exception to the universality of the imperial banking scheme, but this must be put in perspective. By the mid-

1830s India had already had a stormy banking history; companies which had failed in the early 1830s were being replaced by new private banks. The Indian government's attitude towards limited liability was based on this experience; that government, having been in error, was anxious that such errors would not be repeated through banks chartered by the British imperial government. India wished to keep control of her own banking system, for which she was, after all, responsible.

Thus the main differences between India and, for example, an Australian colony were (a) the Indian government claim that a royal charter would not be valid in India, (b) the subsequent insistence that any bank operating branches in India should be chartered in India, (c) the existence of a developed banking system in which the note issue and exchange operations were separated, and (d) the consequent policy that the note issue and exchange operations should not be included in one banking institution, especially one with limited liability. The first difference, while invalid, was not a point of real dispute since the Treasury consulted with and accepted the view of self-governing territories in such matters as the right to open bank branches. The second proved ineffective when stated openly in those particular terms and consequently the third proved unenforceable once the barrier, the establishment of a precedent, had been broken. The third factor – that of a developed banking system incorporating certain principles – also served to establish the bona fides of the government's position and reinforced the view of the Treasury that India should not be handled arbitrarily on this issue, subject only to the overriding concern of a government-created monopoly.

All became routine once the Treasury relaxed its policy of imperial uniformity and India accepted limited liability. In 1866 India passed a general companies Act under which, for example, the Hongkong Bank registered preliminary to operating in that territory.

The real test of India's position had come with the Martin-promoted Bank of Asia and East India Bank and in that, as noted above, the Indian government was influenced by the reputation of Martin himself. In the end, however, the issue was simply whether the Indian authorities approved of a bank of issue and exchange operating in its territory; they did not. The next question was whether the imperial government would overrule them. India might put this incorrectly as a matter of legal right, but the Treasury considered it a matter of policy and as such would no more overrule the Indian government than it would that of an Australian colony – on this particular issue.

The apparent breakthrough occurred when the Oriental Bank Corporation was chartered in a form which permitted it to open agencies Eastwards of the Cape of Good Hope without further Treasury sanction, thus permitting it into India, where, indeed it had operated before moving to London and accepting a charter. By 1850 there were already private banks operating the exchanges and the issue had now become whether a chartered overseas bank could operate without formal permission. Even then the status of the Oriental's agencies did not necessarily break the barrier – the bank was not allowed a note issue in India and its agency activities were limited to business generated outside the territory. Indeed, James Wilson claimed that the East India Company had accepted this concept, and they had been so pressured since 1840 that this is possible.

Thus India may be joined to the colonial Empire in discussions of imperial banking during the period 1830–70. The underlying problems were that of limited liability, the suitability of exchange operations by a banking company, and the economic consequences of linking the note issue to exchange in the same institution. Additionally, but not considered in this chapter, was the jurisdictional problem in the event of the failure of a banking company, a problem especially acute for India.[95]

Consideration of India is important here because of its banking links with the Pacific Rim, both for trade finance and as part of the three-legged exchange operations in which India played a crucial role in the monetary relations of Europe with the East.

The Eastern exchange banks had their counterparts in the several London and South American banks, operating on similar principles and focused primarily on the economic activities of British communities and investors in the several countries of that continent. In the East the Australasian banks operated to the south; in the West there were the Canadian provincial banks operating in the north. There were banking support and connections to India. All these, regardless of the location of their founding office or current head office, had essential links to London. In California British banks operating under the 1862 legislation were establishing their own links with Eastern Exchange banks across the Pacific, and the new Hongkong and Shanghai Bank was setting up its first agency in San Francisco. British overseas banking with its network of agencies and correspondents was providing facilities for a diverse trade between diverse economies. That they could communicate and understand each other – despite the diversity of their primary areas of operation, and the diversity of the monetary and exchange problems they confronted and thus playing a key role in the economic history of the Pacific Rim – is explained in great part by consideration of their common legal and regulatory inspiration which originated in regulations initially designed to further the unity of an expanding Empire.

NOTES

1 Up to and including 180°.
2 A.S.J. Baster, *The Imperial Banks* (London: King, 1929) and *The International Banks* (London: King, 1935); Geoffrey Jones, *British Multinational Banking,*

1830–1990 (Oxford: Clarendon Press, 1993). See also my 'Structural Alternatives and Constraints in the Evolution of Exchange Banking', in Geoffrey Jones, ed. *Banks as Multinationals* (London: Routledge, 1990), pp. 85–98. For further references, see the following note.

3 In this chapter I shall be making reference to several of my own studies, including the bio-bibliography of Robert Montgomery Martin, a prophet of Empire, sometime Treasurer of Hong Kong, and an incurable and unsuccessful colonial, China and India bank promoter – *Survey our Empire!: Robert Montgomery Martin (1801?-1868), a bio-bibliography* (Hong Kong: Centre of Asian Studies, 1979), esp. Chapter 7, pp. 148–200 – henceforth abbreviated as *Survey*. See also the brief survey on India/China banks, in my *A Concise Economic History of Modern China (1840–1961)* (New York: Praeger, 1969), Chapter 3, pp. 63–74. For a full case study, see my *The History of The Hongkong and Shanghai Banking Corporation* (Cambridge, 1987–91), 4 vols, esp. Vol. I, *The Hongkong Bank in Late Imperial China, 1864–1902: On an Even Keel*. This latter will be henceforth abbreviated as *The History*.

4 The Colonial Banking Regulations, fully described as 'Regulations and Conditions for the observance of which provision should be made in charters or legislative enactments relating to the incorporation of banking companies in the colonies' (T.7/14, 16 November 1866, pp. 283–84), were finalized by the Treasury (T) for application through the Board of Trade (BT). They were revised from time to time, see, e.g. Minute of the BT dated 16 July 1830 and proposed revision of 1836 in T.1/3471 under 'Bank of India . . .'; for revision of 1846, see BT.1/462.

5 'The Lords have not referred to the Papers in their own Department.' Marginal note on a letter of the Committee of the Privy Council for Trade to the Lords of the Treasury, 24 February 1835, in T.1/3477.

6 See the memo of April 1835 relative to the charter of the Australasian Banking Co., the first under the new rules, see T.1/9764. The memo referred to was based on legal opinion as stated in T.1/3472, dated 11 November 1831. This would cause problems when the previously India-based Agra and United Service Bank in 1857 sought an English charter under 7&8 Victoria, *c.* 113 and the Board of Trade apparently failed to notice the significance of its overseas focus (see pp. 135–36).

7 See T.1/3473 on the West Indian banks, esp. the St Vincent Commercial Bank; for reaction to the Hongkong Bank's application process, see CO 1290/124, No. 341, 2 August 1867, ff. 2–20.

8 See for the Hongkong Bank, CO 403/17, 14 April 1868, and minute dated 19 March 1868, file 3055, in T.1/6773A (part 1); for the Bank of Ceylon, see T.1/4722/15748 of 1842.

9 This arose specifically in the 1838 charter application of the Bank of Guiana, which also requested (but was denied) single liability. See BT.6/274.

10 T.1/5624/25562/1850.

11 For the question of uniformity, note that the Treasury found that for the issue in Ceylon the Oriental Bank's charter provisions were satisfactory but those of the Chartered Bank of India, Australia and China were not – the latter, the Treasury said, could have their charter revised as it was reluctant to give the Oriental a monopoly (another policy problem). James Wilson, Treasury, to Colonial Office, 24 October 1885 in T.7/5, pp. 433–35. On the controversy of government versus bank issue, see W. Evan Nelson, 'The Hongkong and Shanghai Banking Corporation Factor in the Progress towards a Straits Settlements Government Note Issue, 1881–1889', in Frank H.H. King, ed. *Eastern*

Banking: essays in the history of The Hongkong and Shanghai Banking Corporation (London: Athlone, 1983).

12 The term 'London and X' banks is explained in my article on 'Structural Alternatives and Constraints in the Evolution of Exchange Banking', in Geoffrey Jones, ed. *Banks as Multinationals.*

13 This theme is repeated frequently in the files, if only because the government of India attempted to deny the rights of the Crown. See, e.g. BT.1/502/353, esp. note of 18 February 1853. The legal position must be separated from the practical policy position of the British government.

14 The history of the Hongkong Bank's incorporation provides a perfect example of these problems, see King, *The History*, Vol. I.

15 See T.7/15, 11 January 1868. Singapore had by then become part of the colony of the Straits Settlements; it was a trading city which would have benefited by any encouragement of trade through Singapore to the Dutch East Indies. This incident appears to be exceptional, however. In the case of the foreign consortium banks referred to, the authorities treated them as foreign corporations and controlled their activities within the territory accordingly.

16 See, e.g. the study of William J. Barber, *British Economic Thought and India, 1600–1858* (Oxford: Clarendon Press, 1975). In the case of the CBR, of course, India would prove a hold out.

17 *Public Proceedings and Official Correspondence relative to the 'Bank of Asia'* (London: Longmans, 1842), pp. 3–4.

18 The pre-1862 legislation was not intended for banks intending to operate overseas, but there could be confusion on this point as the history of the Agra Bank proves. See discussion on pp. 135–36, 146 n. 6.

19 See, e.g. the New Brunswick Act to incorporate the Woodstock Bank. The Treasury would not approve because of the lack of security for the issue of its banknotes; on the other hand, the Treasury indicated it would not interfere if the governor wanted to go ahead (T.7/13, p. 369, 4 November 1865). The Governor attempted to argue the case, presumably to obtain Treasury support, but the Treasury replied that it had had its say and advised him to go ahead (at his own risk) if he wished to do so (T.7/14, pp. 264–65, 22 October 1866). However, flagrant violations in the New South Wales bill relative to the renewal of a charter for the Commercial Banking Company – no limit to the charter and thus no chance for review, etc. – caused the Treasury to advise for disallowance despite the changed relationship of the Treasury and New South Wales since 1848 when the bank had first been chartered (T.7/14, pp. 462–65, 2 May 1867).

20 Paul Knapland, *James Stephen and the British Colonial System, 1813–1847* (Madison, Wis.: University of Wisconsin Press, 1953), quoting Francis Scott's 16 April 1849 contribution (p. 256) and Stephen to Lord Grey, 29 September 1846 (p. 218) from CO 323/61, f. 336.

21 Knapland, Chapter 8, 'Currency, banking and other business', pp. 201–27.

22 Without imperial sanction, which required incorporation subject to the terms of the CBR, a bank attempting to operate in another colony would be treated by the potential host as a 'foreign corporation'. See the discussion relative to New South Wales banks in T.7/4, 13 July 1854, pp. 582–89.

23 Generalizations are dangerous. In 1837, for example, the Governor of Van Diemen's Land refused to place government funds on deposit in the Bank of Australasia, a bank chartered including the CBR, precisely because it had limited liability – and also because the shareholders were not 'local' (T.1/3470, Colonial Secretary of Van Diemen's Land to Manager, Bank of Australasia, 12 April

1837). This was protested by Stephen, to whom a copy was sent, on behalf of the Colonial Office, November 1837.

24 Treasury to Colonial Office, 21 November 1866 in T.7/7/14. This would become a serious matter later in the century when certain banks were issuing additional notes against a 100 per cent specie backing. See, e.g. the discussion in my 'The Extraordinary Survival of Hong Kong's Private Note Issue: from profit making to public service', in Y.C. Jao and F.H.H. King, *Money in Hong Kong: Historical perspective and contemporary developments* (Centre of Asian Studies, University of Hong Kong, 1991), pp. 1–50.

25 This was early expounded in relations to South Australia banks, see T.7/3, 2 April 1852, pp. 8–9; Hong Kong was also an area of concern. Eligible, i.e. chartered, banks might bid for the main deposit (that is, to be the government's banker), but deposit accounts had to be divided and, where considered excessive, transferred (at the expense of the colonial government) to England – this being considered safer.

26 See the case of the Western Bank of India, T.1/5110/23448, in Hong Kong.

27 See T.7/14, 16 April 1866, pp. 46–47, or CO 129/118, Treasury to Colonial Office, same date, relative to the Bank of Hindustan, China and Japan. See also relative to this bank BT 31/654/2759. Incorporated on 12 July 1862 under the Acts of 1857 and 1858 with Articles of Association which did not conform to the terms of the CBR, the Treasury ruled that any voluntary offer by the Bank would be void precisely because of the Articles of Association. The Bank had the right to issue notes, but, the Treasury insisted, we must not assist it. In the case of the Hongkong Bank, the changes required were made subject to the Governor in Council. The real solution, the Treasury advised, was for the Colony of Hong Kong to protect itself by legislation. This it did, but only in the 1890s.

28 As late as 15 August 1853 James Wilson was writing on the subject of Colonial banks, 'The Treasury's regulations are designed to provide the public security, as far as can be done by regulations, for the proper regulation of colonial banks, and give the public opportunity to watch their progress through periodic required reports' (in T.7/4, pp. 94–97).

29 From the earliest days chartered banks had difficulties if they did not abide by local regulations in a colony with responsible government, e.g. New South Wales. In 1838 government funds were withdrawn from the Bank of Australasia because the directors would not submit reports as required by the colonial government for such depository banks – the government considered the report required by the CBR to be inadequate for the purpose. Although the Treasury considered its own report requirement sufficient, it would not interfere on behalf of the bank. After intercontinental discussion, the directors agreed to supply the reports in the form required by New South Wales (T.1/3470, 26 February 1838).

30 This was also true in New Zealand (see T.7/5, p. 265, Treasury to the Oriental Bank Corporation, 25 April 1855). Warrants to issue notes in Australia and Van Diemen's Land were issued, but no warrant for New Zealand would be effective while the government's note issue regulations were in force. If such notes were withdrawn, the Oriental could issue banknotes subject to the laws of New Zealand and the limitations of its charter. These were still the days favouring a bank issue of notes.

31 No generalization is safe. In 1857 James Wilson, referring to the granting of a charter to the Chartered Mercantile Bank of India, London and China, stated that rather than delay further he would consult with Australia after the granting

of the charter. This was possible because the right to open branches in Australia was, under the terms of the charter, to be subject to Treasury permission (T.7/7, pp. 231–32).

32 This was in connection with the Treasury's refusal to grant a supplemental charter to the Agra Bank (see T.7/12, 4 August 1863).

33 In T.7/4, with relation to the Oriental Bank's request to operate in Australia and New Zealand (31 March 1854, p. 376), and the Chartered Bank of India, Australia and China (11 February 1854, p. 316). On 13 July 1854 the Oriental was given a warrant permitting general banking business in Sydney and Melbourne (p. 510).

34 In this way the Oriental Bank Corporation became the New Oriental Bank, Ltd, and the Chartered Mercantile Bank of India, London and China became the Mercantile Bank of India, Ltd.

35 Treasury to Directors, Agra Bank, withdrawing objection to its note issue in Hong Kong provided it does what CBR banks do, i.e. publish returns of circulation and hold the appropriate reserve of specie permitting an inspection of the reserves by the government (in T.7/12, August 1863, p. 122). The charter continued in effect even after the Agra had become Agra and Masterman's Bank (see BT 31/375/1380). The Treasury decision to approve Hong Kong treasury receipt of the Agra's notes is consistent with the refusal to permit similar treatment of the notes of the Bank of Hindustan, the latter having no charter.

36 Wilson in T.7/7, pp. 211–14, 5 June 1857. The occasion was his recommendation of the disallowance of South Australia's Act No. 5 of 1856, which would have allowed limited liability for banking companies.

37 Exceptionally the Colonial Bank was permitted a single liability because of its size. The reasoning behind this decision is obscure, but it would cause the Treasury trouble since, naturally, other companies seeking a royal charter sought a similar concession. See also 'Colonial and Australian Banking Companies', parliamentary reports dated 16 December 1837, in *British Parliamentary Papers* (1838), XL, 95–114.

38 In the case of the Peninsular, West Indian, and Southern Bank, Ltd a call of £10 yielded only £2,993 9s instead of the expected £136,800. At the relevant shareholders' meeting there were only two shareholders present, both of whom were admitted defaulters (Report of 21 January 1867 in 1868 edn of the *Banker's Almanac and Directory*).

39 As noted previously, the term 'London and X' banks is explained in my article on 'Structural Alternatives and Constraints in the Evolution of Exchange Banking', in Geoffrey Jones, ed. *Banks as Multinationals.*

40 Robert Montgomery Martin, the promoter of the Bank of Asia and the East India Bank, for example, admitted in his promotional correspondence that merchants would, as a result of competition, have to quit exchange banking and its consequent profits, but, he advised, this loss would be more than offset by the bank's liberating merchants to do what they did best – trading. See R.M. Martin, 'Colonial Banking, Bank of Asia', *Colonial Magazine* 1: 180–82 (1840) and *passim.*

41 The principle is frequently affirmed, see, e.g., BT to CO, 24 November 1837, in T.1/3474. The charter of the Colonial Bank can be found in T.1/3/3473. See also 'Colonial and Australian Banking Companies', parliamentary reports dated 16 December 1837, in *British Parliamentary Papers* (1838), XL, 95–114.

42 The spirit of this sentiment is found in T.28/110 in dealings with the India Office (23 May 1855, p. 76). Monopoly was, in any case, prohibited under 21 James I, c. 3, except in the case of new inventions.

In another example, the Chartered Bank of Asia expressed its wish to open branches in India – with a prohibition against issuing banknotes. James Wilson replied that the government did not intend to grant this privilege unless the East India Company were to agree. He then adds significantly that were the East India Company to agree, then similar privileges would have to be offered to the other banks, i.e. the Oriental and the Chartered Bank of India, Australia and China (ibid.).

The West Indies Bank obtained permission to have its notes received in the colonial treasuries. The Colonial Bank protested, arguing that it had done a sound job and implying that there was no justification for this new competition. The protest was dated 3 June 1840 in BT.1/365/9949. This cry for monopoly was rejected.

43 BT.1/516/1753, file dated 25 September 1854.

44 T.64/381/A, 'Proposed charter of Bank of Hong Kong'.

45 See, for example, the protest of Sir R.A. Alleyne and 169 other Barbados residents relative to the granting of a charter to the Colonial Bank (T.1/3473, 14 December 1838).

46 See 'Bank of Asia', *British Parliamentary Papers* (1843), XXV, 85–125, esp. 87–89. See especially the letter of the East India Company directors to the Board to Trade, 30 April 1840, summarized in King, *Survey*, p. 157.

47 Ibid. See also 'Points relative to the "East India Bank" ', filed in T.1/4845, bundle 4.

48 For the Bank of India, see T.1/4917 and T.1/3471 and University of London MS 172. For a discussion, see Blair B. Kling, *Partner in Empire: Dwarkanath Tagore and the Age of Enterprise in Eastern India* (Berkeley, Calif.: University of California Press, 1976), pp. 201–2, and King, *Survey*, pp. 155–56.

49 BT.1/529/1458, file dated 17 September 1855. The Treasury also noted that the promoters were seeking single liability – this would not have been granted, despite the provision in the charter of the Colonial Bank.

50 See King, *The History*, Vol. I.

51 As reported in *Banker's Magazine*, 23: 956–57 (1863). Or consider the prospectus of the Hongkong and Shanghae [*sic*] Banking Co. Ltd which stressed inter-port finance rather than competition with established exchange banks; within months a London agency had been set up and the Hongkong Bank was involved in the Hong Kong/India/London exchange business. See the Prospectus reprinted in my *The Hongkong Bank in Late Imperial China, 1864–1902* (Cambridge: Cambridge University Press, 1987), p. 73, and subsequent discussion.

52 Banking was a developing, almost experimental industry and, as the examples cited in note 51 indicate, new banks were often founded for specific and 'exclusive' reasons or were committed to following specified principles. Sound though these may have been, if they were followed too rigidly, sound and profitable business might be excluded which, in a competitive environment, could put them at serious disadvantage over institutions with more pragmatic management. The Commercial Bank of London was influenced by the views of E.S. Cayley, the Attwoods, and W. Medley, with R. Montgomery Martin probably adding thoughts on Indian business. The Bank limited its business accordingly. In consequence it had difficulty competing successfully. See *Reasons for Establishing the Commercial Bank of London . . .*, n.d., but circa 1840. For a discussion, see King, *Survey*, p. 152, and references on p. 309 (nos. 166–68).

53 Martin, *The Monetary System of British India* (pamphlet, 1840), reprinted from *Colonial Magazine* 3: 67–81 (1840).

54 An excellent statement of this position is made by C.E. Trevelyan, Secretary to the Treasury, in a printed minute, found in T.1/4845, bundle 4 (1843), relative to the East Asia Bank. This is quoted in King, *Survey*, pp. 174–75.

55 This bank, with its head office in London, had originally been incorporated by an 1838 Act of the Lower Canada legislature, but the directors decided to ask for a repeal and reincorporation by charter including the terms of the CBR in England (CO to T, 11 March 1839, in T.1/3475).

56 For Martin's role, see King, *Survey*, p. 121.

57 For the Credit Foncier, see BT 31/1011/1617c; for the Imperial Bank of China, see BT 31/793/492c. This was aborted in favour of the Imperial Bank of China, India and Japan, Ltd (for which see BT.31/9371205c). Martin's dreams were once again shattered by this change – and indeed all was abandoned in favour of a (subsequently disallowed) take-over by the Bank of Hindustan, which latter bank promptly failed. See the discussion in King, *Survey*, pp. 189–98.

58 The file is BT 31/938/1211c.

59 Some places, however, might be *too* small. The Treasury, for example, doubted that Labuan, today a part of the Malaysian state of Sabah, then part of the Colony of the Straits Settlements, was big enough for a bank of its own and urged that the promoters instead seek to encourage a well-established bank to locate a branch there (T.7/15, pp. 354–55, letter dated 2 July 1868). In the present century, the British colonial authorities in Kuala Lumpur encouraged the Mercantile Bank of India, Ltd to establish agencies in the capitals of the east coast states with assignments of premises (or land for such) and promises of business. But the logic of the situation proved this was not an invitation to monopoly. See Stuart Muirhead, 'The Mercantile Bank of India on the East Coast of Malaya', in King, ed. *Eastern Banking* (London: Athlone Press, 1983).

Although Martin wrote the Foreign Office promising that his note-issuing Imperial Bank would not also engage in the exchanges, its successor, the Imperial Bank of China and Japan, over which Martin had little or no control, stated as its object: 'the business of banking in the United Kingdom, China, India, Japan, and Australia and in any other places in the East and in any other countries with which there may be commercial relations, the business of banking in all its branches and discounting and dealing in exchanges, in specie and securities . . .' Promoters were learning, in the absence of the restraints of the CBR, to be all-inclusive (BT 31/937/1205c).

60 For a history of the Imperial Bank of Persia (now the British Bank of the Middle East), see Geoffrey Jones's two-volume study: *Banking and Empire in Iran* and *Banking and Oil* (Cambridge: Cambridge University Press, 1986, 1987).

61 References to the Mitkiewicz scheme, which was fully covered in the local Shanghai press, e.g. the *North-China Herald*, can be found in Volume I of King, *The History*. The di Rudinì–Luzzatti scheme, which eventually led to the Pekin [*sic*] Syndicate, is referred to in King, 'Joint Venture in China: the experience of the Pekin Syndicate, 1897–1961', in William J. Hausman, ed. *Papers Presented at the Thirty-Sixth Annual Meeting of the Business History Conference*, a special issue of *Business and Economic History*, second series, 19: 113–22 (1990).

62 Section V of the draft prospectus read: 'The authorization of the Government at Pekin [*sic*] has been solicited, by which the Specie Notes of the Imperial Bank of China will be receivable in payment of Customs Duties and at the Tax Offices throughout the Empire.' See Martin to Layard, 19 July 1863, FO 17/402, ff. 70–71, and the Foreign Office's comments.

63 Petition in T.1/5376/15425, dated 15 May 1845 and T.1/5624/25562/1850.

For earlier comments on this bank, critical of the London move, see 'Aristides', pseud., *A Letter to the Shareholders in the Bank of Western India* (London: Pelham Richardson, 1842).

64 See T.1/5624/25562/1850 and the file in T.64/381/A, 1851.

65 The Agra was cited for permitting customers to write cheques payable to bearer on demand on their current accounts. See letter of Treasury to Board of Trade, 27 February 1854, and opinion of 30 March 1854 in BT.1/516/1753.

66 For the Agra's cap. 113 charter, see copy in T.64/381/A.

67 Treasury to Governor of Hong Kong, 1 August 1865, in CO 129/108. For the 1857 registration see T.41/7 (30); for limited liability see BT 31/375/1380, and for the general file see BT.1/556/2041/61.

68 See correspondence in BT.1/556/2041/61; also Agra to Treasury, 23 January 1863 (in CO 129/95 of 1863), Colonial Office to Governor, Hong Kong, 27 December 1862 (in CO 403/12).

69 *London and China Express* (16 June 1866).

70 *Bankers' Magazine* 23: 573–74 (1963).

71 BT 31/375/1380. Agra and Masterman's was wound up 23 June 1866.

72 W.T.C. King, *A History of the London Discount Market* (1936), p. 244. Apparently false cables were sent reporting that the bank had failed overseas. The bank, some contemporaries thought, was brought down needlessly by lack of last-minute support. This would seem to confirm the danger of being 'alone' (that is, providing one's own credit – not having the support of a major London clearer).

73 The reconstituted bank took over the Indian business; confidence had never been lost in India where the Agra had been first established in 1833. The Agra Bank had cross-directorships with the British and Californian Banking Co., Ltd; British banking now flourished on both edges and across the Pacific (*London and China Express*, 17, 20 and 26 October 1866). If a bank were suspect, of course, their correspondent bank in London might in any case refuse to accept their bills and so cause a suspension – as in the case of the Commercial Banking Corporation of India and the East in dealing with the London Joint Stock Bank in 1866 (see C26/135). For the reconstituted Agra Bank, Ltd, see BT 31/1306/3347.

74 These comments arise from the discussions in King, *The History*, Vol. I. The particular factor in Hong Kong/China in the early years of the Hongkong Bank is that the decision-makers remained in the East. When senior partners retired to England they might work with the London correspondent, but power was often retained in Hong Kong. Hence the different history of the Hongkong Bank.

75 King, *The History*, Vol. I. Full references may be found there.

76 See the article by Peter Wesley-Smith in King, ed. *Eastern Banking* (London: Athlone Press, 1983) and the discussion based on this in King, *The History*, Vol. I. Reference also should be made to T.1/7371A/8742, files dated 26 September 1873 and 3 February 1874.

77 For a history of this promotion, see King, 'The Bank of China is Dead', *Journal of Oriental Studies* 7: 37–62 (1969).

78 The general principle agreed between the Treasury and the Board of Trade was that it would be inexpedient to connect under the same establishment banks in colonies at a great distance from, and having no natural connection with, each other (T.1/9764, 25 May 1835).

79 This attempt of the Bank of Australasia provoked a key policy letter, dated 24 February 1835, from the Office of the Committee of the Privy Council for

Trade to the Lords of the Treasury. It was not well received by the latter for bureaucratic reasons. It reads in part: 'The Lords of this committee have no information before them to induce them to think it desirable to connect together, and under one and the same Responsibility, the Banking Establishments of Colonies having no natural connection with, and being situated some thousand miles distant from each other. As a general principle their Lordships would consider this to be objectionable [here there is a Treasury check mark in the margin] and such a plan has all the appearance of adventure and Hazard at variance with the solidity and security which are so desirable in banking establishments. No person trusting a bank at the Cape of Good Hope could have any means of Judging of the Degree of Credit due to an Establishment of such wide and unconnected Responsibilities. The different branches would be directed necessarily with an Ignorance of the whole mass of their affairs and should any interruption at any time occur to the perfect credit of any of the Establishments (a danger much increased by such a system) it might most inconveniently disturb at the same time the interests of so many colonies. For these reasons the Lords of the Committee would be adverse to holding out in any shape to this Company an expectation that any such system of one extensive banking company dispersed through colonies at a Distance from each other, would be sanctioned by the Government.'

80 This bank, originally promoted from Tasmania, was first designated 'Australasiatic and South African Banking Company'. In May 1833 it was to be the 'Royal Bank of Australasia and South Africa' (see T.1/3469). For the trade argument, see T.1/9764/33, letter registered 25 May 1835. For support of the project, see T.1/3477, 6 January 1835. See also Colonial Office to the promoter, the Hon. J. Stewart, dated 15 November 1833, in T.1/9764/33. The argument about Ceylon's requirements is in T.1/3477, dated 6 January 1835.

For a note on a Bank of South Africa seeking a charter similar to that of the Bank of Australasia, see 23 April 1836 in T.1/3477.

81 The draft charter for the Bank of Hong Kong is in T.64/381/A. For the Oriental Bank see T.1/5624/25562 of 1850. For the Bank of Ceylon's charter, see the Chancery Rolls, C.66/4608 and 4672.

82 The progress of these negotiations may be followed in T.64/381/A.

83 The Indian government argued that it operated in trust for the Crown and that therefore a royal charter purporting to permit operations in India was invalid to this extent. Any case brought by India on this basis was overturned; the Crown had the authority but the Board of Trade and the Treasury accepted that the responsibility lay with India. In this case, however, the Treasury neglected to notice that by authorizing agencies to be opened Eastwards of the Cape of Good Hope, they had included India without consulting that government. Branches had still to be sanctioned by the Treasury, which would lead to consultation with India. Given the basic opposition to monopoly, the Treasury then had no choice but to permit other chartered banks to establish agencies in India despite the latter's objections.

84 Reference is made here to the compradores and to the guarantee shroffs of Ceylon, matters discussed in King, ed. *Eastern Banking* and King, *The History.*

85 For a preliminary discussion, see King, 'Structural Alternatives and Constraints in the Evolution of Exchange Banking', p. 88. As noted there, the one agreed activity forbidden to agencies was the note issue, but even here there was at least one exception, that of the Bank of Ceylon – see notes 8 and 81 above.

86 The Hongkong Bank did in fact open in Colombo. Nevertheless management too accepted the need to restrict geographical coverage, see discussion on

pp. 138–40. The history of the development of the Colombo branch is found in King, *The History*, Vol. II.

87 As reported by Martin to the Bank of Asia's provisional board of directors. See their minute, dated 3 December 1840, in Martin, ed. *Public Proceedings and Official Correspondence relative to the 'Bank of Asia'* (London: Longmans, 1842), p. lviii. See discussion in King, *Survey*, pp. 168–77.

88 For this development and the stages in the history of the Hong Kong banknote issue, see my 'The Extraordinary Survival of Hong Kong's Private Note Issue: from profit making to public service'.

89 As noted above, the final factor was the refusal of the London Joint Stock Bank to accept the bank's bills. The bank's charter is discussed in T.1/6509c/6227; see C.26/135–44 for some nine volumes of papers relative to the winding up of this bank. This is actually a complicated story. The Shanghai manager and his San Francisco agent transferred funds of the old India-based company, the Commercial Bank of India. The wind-up proceedings of the royally chartered successor, which occupies several volumes of papers and testimony, included arguments that these funds should not be considered on the grounds that they belonged to 'another' bank. However, it is clear that neither manifestation of the Commercial Bank actually established a branch or an agency in San Francisco. They had an 'agent' in the most limited sense of that term.

90 See Frank H.H. King, 'Does the corporation's history matter? Hongkong Bank/HSBC Holdings: A case study', in Westall and Godley, eds, *Business History and Business Culture* (Manchester University Press, 1996), pp. 116–38. The evolution of the culture is described in King, *The History*.

91 The founder of the Hongkong Bank was inspired by the Scottish example as portrayed in a journal article. The actual working of the bank, however, was so influenced by the CBR and by British banking traditions and its own development that the Scottish claim is not helpful. See discussion in King, *The History*, Vol. I.

92 On this see, e.g., Wilson to Merivale relative to the Victoria Bank Act for the Bank of Victoria, 2 February 1855, in T.7/5, pp. 136–37.

93 The directors of the Mauritius Bank were examined for lending on the security of land (see Stephen to Trevelyan, 26 February 1847, in T.1/5252/9130). For Ceylon see the branch archives in the Hongkong Bank collection, Group Archives, HSBC Holdings, Midland Bank Archives, London. See also the history of the Ceylon branch in King, *The History*, Vol. II.

94 Registration under the 1844 Act for an English bank intending to operate overseas would be in error, see the case of the Agra on p. 136.

95 The Commercial Bank Company of India and the East is a prime example. The problem arose when a locally established and apparently profitable bank transferred its business to a royally chartered bank with its head office in London. When it failed, as often happened, the Indian creditors claimed that they were neglected and that the assets were subject to judgements in London, where they were inadequately represented. For the Commercial Bank see references in note 89 above.

9

THE RECONSTRUCTION OF HONG KONG NINETEENTH-CENTURY PACIFIC TRADE STATISTICS

The emergence of Asian dynamism

A.J.H. Latham

In the last few years there has been a surge in interest in the origins of economic dynamism in Asia. This began with papers presented at the International Economic History Congress at Bern in 1986 (Fischer *et al.* 1986) and continued through the Leuven Congress in 1990 (Latham and Kawakatsu, 1994b) to the Milan Congress of 1994 (Latham and Kawakatsu, 1994a). Japanese scholars like Hamashita, Kawakatsu and Sugihara have contributed to this and there have also been contributions from scholars like Ho Chuimei, and also Shi Zhihong and Mi-Rucheng of the Chinese Academy of Social Sciences in Beijing. This chapter hopes to contribute to the discussion by examining the trade of one of the great redistribution centres of Asia, the British Colony of Hong Kong, and assessing its role in the emergence of Asian dynamism in the late nineteenth century.

It might be assumed that because Hong Kong was a British colony, its function was to distribute British exports to East Asia. But it is clear its real importance lay in re-distributing Asian goods within Asia, and more particularly Chinese goods within China. Trade with Britain was of minor significance, and one is forced to the conclusion that really Hong Kong was just a port of Southern China, which happened to be administered by the British (Latham, 1993, p. 83).

A major problem in examining the trade of Hong Kong in this period stems from the fact that there are no trade figures for the Colony until after the First World War. It is said that they were not collected because the Governor-General believed they would only be misinterpreted by scholars in later generations! So at first sight, it seems there is an unfillable gap in the material for understanding the mesh of trade in East Asia. But on further examination, an opportunity presents itself for reconstructing the trade figures – or at least making a rough sketch of them in that the trade figures of many of Hong Kong's trading partners exist. By using these, we can assemble at least a skeleton set of figures. For example, we have details of Japan's exports to Hong Kong, and these must be roughly equivalent to Hong Kong's imports from Japan. Conversely, Japan's imports from Hong Kong must be equivalent to Hong Kong's exports to Japan. Of course there are problems like insurance and freight to be taken account of, and in this provisional exercise these matters will be conveniently ignored. But by assembling the figures for Hong Kong's major trading partners from a variety of sometimes rather obscure sources, a picture begins to emerge. Other specialists will see better ways of tackling this problem, but at least this effort can be seen as a first attempt. But even this presents considerable problems, as figures for trading partners like Bangkok, French Indo-

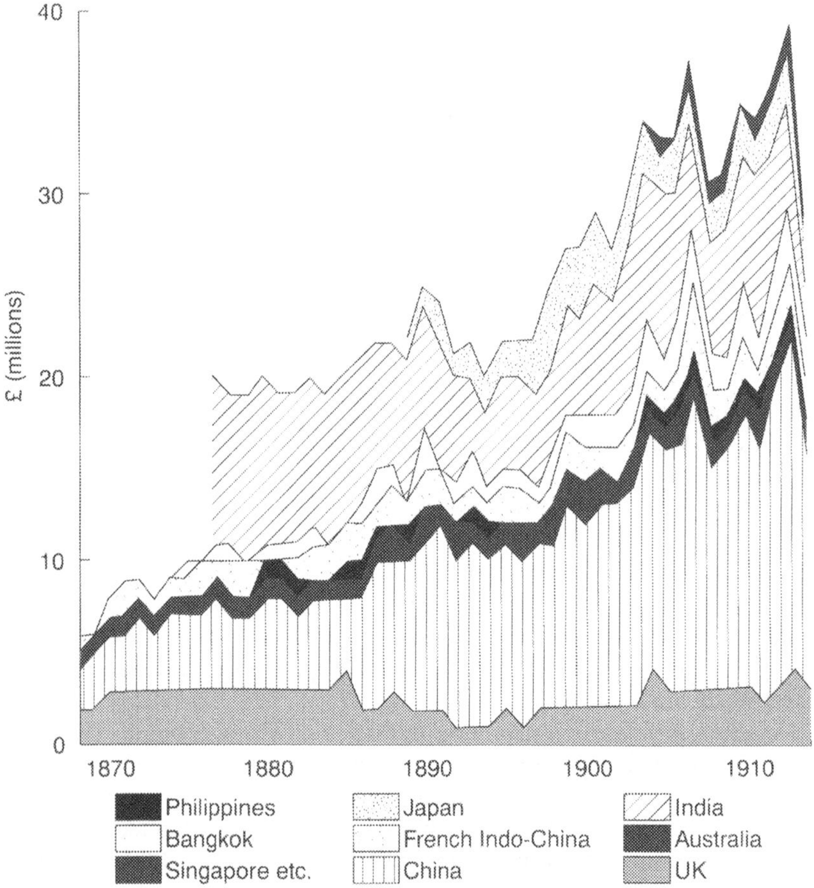

Figure 9.1 Imports to Hong Kong
Source: Appendix I (see pp. 165–67)

China, and the Philippines were difficult to find. When the figures were eventually unearthed, they then had to be converted into pounds sterling, raising the problem of accurate exchange values. In the case of French Indo-China, figures exist only for rice exports to Hong Kong, but because rice was the major commodity traded from French Indo-China to Hong Kong, these figures serve reasonably well as a proxy.

Figure 9.1 shows a graph of Hong Kong's imports, calculated as outlined above. As suggested earlier, Britain was only a minor supplier of Hong Kong's imports, despite the fact that Hong Kong was a British Colony. What is more, imports grew very little over the period. Proportionately they contributed nearly 18 per cent in 1877, the first year for which there is a reasonably full set of figures, and just less than 12 per cent in 1913. Table 9.1 lays out the percentage of imports from the various countries, and Table 9.2 the rate of growth of trade with each country. Given the state of the information, and the irregularity of some of the flows, too much reliance must not be put upon these growth rates. That for British imports, for example, is frankly meaningless. China emerges as the main source of Hong Kong's imports, with 22 per cent of the total in 1877 and 45 per cent of a much larger total in 1913, and imports from there were growing strongly at an annualized rate of 4.37 per cent. Hong Kong's other major trading partner was British India, but, by contrast with China, imports from India suffered a big decline: 43 per cent of the Colony's imports came from British India in 1877 but by 1913 the figure was less than 14 per cent, and the growth rate, or rate of decline, was negative at −1.41 per cent. Decrease in the opium trade was a major reason for this, as opium was India's main export to China in general (Latham, 1978, pp. 75, 81, 88–90). The decline in the trade from India reduced the pace of the overall growth of Hong Kong's imports after 1877, and in particular offset the positive surge of imports from mainland China, the overall growth rate coming down to 1.78 per cent per annum. The growth of imports from China requires some explanation. One might assume that these imports were based upon imports of food, especially rice from the mainland, but as will be discussed later, this is not the case. China was an importer of rice, not an exporter, and indeed it was the fact that Hong Kong was a major distributor of overseas rice to mainland China which explains the growth of imports of rice from Bangkok and French Indo-China. Many observers reported that the major trade of Hong Kong was rice, and although the leading destination was mainland China, she also re-distributed it to Japan, Hawaii and even California (Latham, 1986a, p. 647; British Parliamentary Papers, 1895, 1896, 1900, 1902a). It was the rice trade which was largely responsible for the substantial growth of imports from French Indo-China, at 5.31 per cent per annum, and from Bangkok at 3.42 per cent per annum. These were Hong Kong's two leading suppliers of rice, and by 1913 they were supplying nearly 13 per cent of Hong Kong's imports. Singapore,

Table 9.1 Imports to Hong Kong

	*1877** (%)	*1880** (%)	*1890*† (%)	*1900* (%)	*1910* (%)	*1913* (%)
UK	17.63	19.40	10.57	10.78	10.73	11.66
China	22.13	23.55	32.92	36.22	40.98	45.28
Singapore, etc.	3.89	4.68	6.72	5.91	3.24	3.96
Australia	0.85	1.26	1.59	1.41	1.94	2.19
French Indo-China	8.06	4.52	7.68	7.25	5.23	5.42
Bangkok	4.16	2.49	6.44	4.23	8.17	7.30
India	43.24	44.06	27.95	19.69	22.08	13.78
Japan	—	—	6.09	14.46	6.96	8.74
Philippines	—	—	—	—	0.63	1.62
Total	99.96	99.96	99.96	99.95	99.96	99.95

Source: Appendix II (see p. 168–69)
Notes: * Excluding Japan and Philippines
† Excluding Philippines

Table 9.2 Growth rates of Hong Kong imports and exports, 1868–1913

	Imports	*Exports*
UK	1.52	2.36
China	4.37	3.98
Singapore	1.23	4.07
Australia	4.44	1.62
French Indo-China	5.31	—
Bangkok (from 1870)	3.42	2.91
India (from 1877)	−1.41	−3.45
Japan (from 1889)	4.70	−6.77
Philippines (from 1903)	7.91	2.63
Total from 1877 (not including Japan and Philippines)	1.47	2.26
Total from 1877 (including Japan and Philippines)	1.78	2.28

Sources: Appendix I, Appendix II

herself a major redistribution centre in Asian trade, and also a British colony, was a fairly unimportant source of Hong Kong's imports, and they did not grow much. But trade with Japan reveals some important characteristics, particularly in respect to the emergence of Asian dynamism. Japanese exports to Hong Kong, as apart from China, are not recorded before 1889, and in 1880 only accounted for about 6 per cent of her imports. But they grew strongly at an annualized figure of 4.70 per cent, and by 1913 were contributing nearly 9 per cent of the total. Japan was rapidly becoming an important centre of Asian dynamism, although even in 1913 she supplied less than Britain to the Hong Kong market.

The overwhelming importance of rice in Hong Kong's imports has already been commented upon. Apart from rice her various suppliers contributed sugar, flour, cotton piece-goods and yarn, beans, hemp, kerosene, lead, opium, rattan, sandalwood, sulphur, tea, timber and general merchandise. There was also a large transit trade which is difficult to evaluate, but clearly played an important part in Hong Kong's role as a provider of shipping services (British Parliamentary Papers, 1902b).

As has been stressed, Hong Kong was a major Asian redistribution centre, so much of what she imported was subsequently re-exported. Figure 9.2 shows the details of her exports to various countries. At a glance it can be seen that the main destination for Hong Kong's exports was

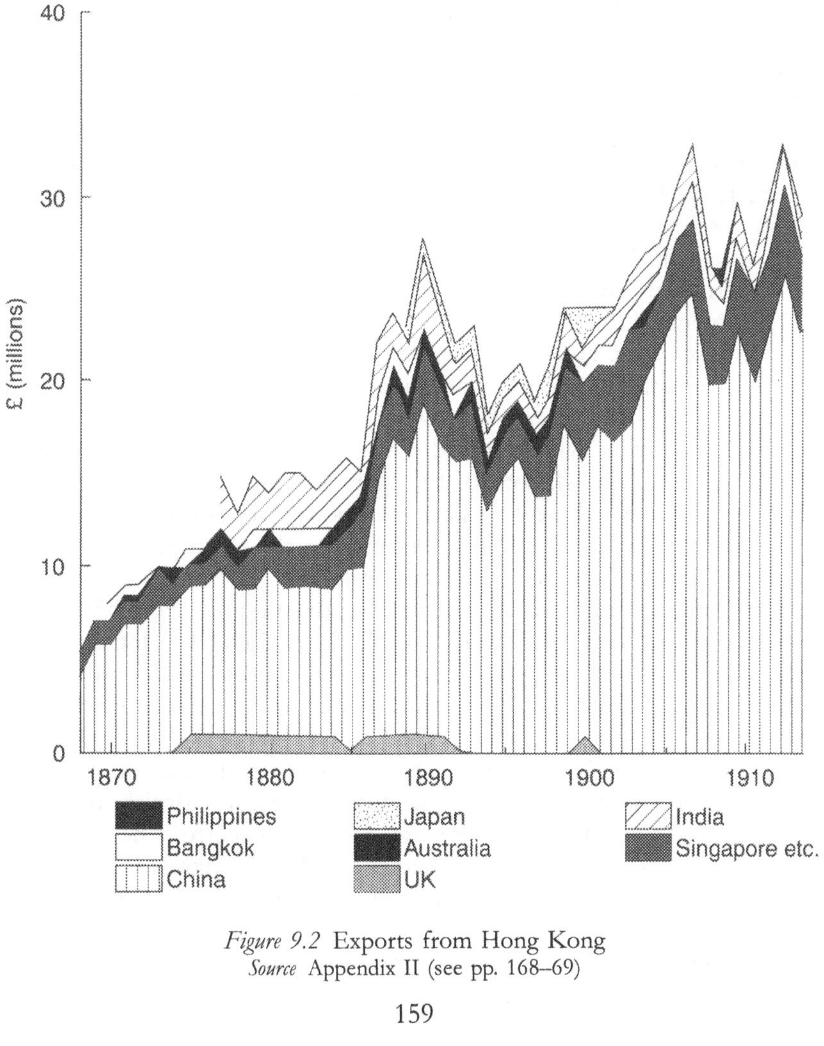

Figure 9.2 Exports from Hong Kong
Source Appendix II (see pp. 168–69)

China. If the main source of imports to Hong Kong was China, and the main destination of exports from Hong Kong was China, then it seems clear that Hong Kong was first and foremost a redistribution centre for the domestic trade of China. Goods must have arrived there from some Chinese ports to be redirected to other Chinese ports. Hence the suggestion made above that Hong Kong was really just a port of Southern China which happened to be administered by the British. But this cannot have been Hong Kong's only task, because we know that less than half her imports came from China. Clearly some of the exports to China originated elsewhere. Rice from Siam and French Indo-China has already been mentioned, and so has opium from India. What was Hong Kong sending in return for this rice to Siam and Indo-China? We do not have details of the Colony's exports to French Indo-China, and the French operated a protectionist import policy. However, in neighbouring Siam the British Consul noted that the imports from Hong Kong were cotton piece-goods, earthenware, brass ware, silk piece-goods, other silk goods, tea, paper, American flour, vegetables, matches, liquid sugar and molasses. As most of Bangkok's external trade was with Hong Kong and Singapore, it was through these ports that British manufactures were imported (British Parliamentary Papers, 1892, 1897). But obviously few of these exports to Siam were of British origin, with the exception of cotton piece-goods. This bears out the point that British goods were relatively unimportant in Hong Kong's import structure, and that Hong Kong was more a redistributor of Asian goods in general (Latham, 1993, 1994b). Items such as silks, tea, earthenware, brass ware, and even possibly sugar, probably came from China, and went to supply the substantial Chinese community there with the kinds of items they liked. They were distributed by the network of Chinese merchants who were widely spread throughout Asia. Similar goods would have gone to Saigon–Cholon for the same reason, and also to Singapore. We can only ponder the extent Japanese goods were also re-distributed to Asian countries from Hong Kong, but the fact that even in 1913 Japanese imports to Hong Kong were less than British imports suggests that they were not large. Exports to China from Hong Kong grew from 55 per cent to 76 per cent of the total from 1877 to 1913 (see Table 9.3), increasing at a rate of 3.98 per cent per annum. In contrast, exports to Britain declined from just under 13 per cent to about 2 per cent of the total, again underlining the relative unimportance of the Colonial power as a trading partner.

Perhaps surprisingly, the second most important destination for Hong Kong's exports after China was not Britain, or even British India, but Singapore and the Straits Settlements. Exports rose from nearly 11 per cent to more than 14 per cent, at an annualized rate of increase of 4.07 per cent, the highest rate of growth of exports to any of her trading partners. The absolute size of this trade however was a long way behind that to China. Again, as there is no convenient Consular report or similar material,

Table 9.3 Exports from Hong Kong

	*1877** (%)	*1880** (%)	*1890*† (%)	*1990*† (%)	*1910* (%)	*1913* (%)
UK	12.55	8.51	4.28	4.43	1.94	1.98
China	54.85	59.63	65.32	64.73	75.28	76.15
Singapore, etc.	10.72	11.48	8.84	15.87	12.62	14.51
Australia	2.25	3.07	2.43	1.17	0.79	1.07
Bangkok	1.98	2.18	2.71	2.84	3.74	3.27
India	17.62	15.09	13.16	6.44	4.99	2.30
Japan	—	—	3.24	4.48	0.22	0.38
Philippines	—	—	—	—	0.38	0.31
Total	99.97	99.96	99.98	99.96	99.96	99.97

Source: Appendix II
Notes: * Excluding Japan and Philippines
† Excluding Philippines

we can only assume that much of this trade was in goods for the substantial Chinese immigrant community both in urban Singapore, and in the mines and rubber plantations of the Malayan Peninsula and the Dutch East Indian possessions of Java and Sumatra (Latham, 1986b). Singapore itself, of course, was a major Asian redistribution centre (Latham, 1994b). Besides being the fastest-growing destination for Hong Kong exports, she also seems to have provided Hong Kong with a substantial surplus. In 1913 exports to Singapore and the Straits were worth £4,939,638 but imports only £1,550,341, a surplus of £3,389,297. British India was a very different story, taking nearly 18 per cent of Hong Kong's exports in 1877 but barely more than 2 per cent in 1913. One can only assume that this was due to the big decline in India's trade in opium to Hong Kong, and the consequent fall in India's ability to make purchases from Hong Kong.

Other markets for the Colony's exports were of minor importance, although some mention must be made of the Japanese market. Although imports to Hong Kong from Japan grew strongly at 4.70 per cent per annum, Hong Kong's exports to Japan actually declined significantly at a negative rate of −6.77 per annum. In 1913 Hong Kong imported £3,367,639 worth of goods from Japan, but sent to Japan in return goods worth a mere £88,653, giving Japan a substantial surplus of £3,278,986. Clearly Japan was getting a big source of earnings for her economic development and industrialization from this trade link and with one of the ways she tied into the Asian market was through Hong Kong. Her sales there were much larger than her sales to Singapore for example (Latham, 1994b). The benefits to Japan from her sales to Hong Kong and China has recently been discussed by Sakae Tsunoyama (Tsunoyama, 1994) and also Peter Schran (Schran, 1994). Japanese sales to Hong Kong, however, and her surplus there were vastly overshadowed by her sales to China proper, which were much larger and grew rapidly from about 1899. Her surpluses in relation to both Hong Kong and China were very important for Japan, as she suffered a deficit on her Asian trade at large because of heavy deficits with British India throughout the period. This seems to have been due largely to purchases of raw cotton. From 1898 she also ran up a deficit with the Dutch East Indies due to sugar purchases, and also had smaller deficits with Siam, French Indo-China, and even the Philippines from the 1890s. Japan was also in deficit with Europe, and in particular Britain and Germany due to purchases of machinery and equipment for modernization, although she had surpluses with France and Italy from the 1870s. She also enjoyed a surplus with Russia from 1894. But it was with North America in the years 1873 to 1914, and in particular of course the United States, that Japan earned her biggest surpluses due to silk sales. These surpluses were a vital input to the modernization and economic development of Japan. To emphasize this point, it must be noted that despite her large American surplus she was in overall deficit in most years, apart from good years in the 1880s, and the exceptional years of 1906 and 1909. This means that the surplus with Hong Kong was all the more welcome. On the other hand, Japan's deficits with so many Asian countries clearly helped the development of those countries' export trades. Japanese imports included rice from Siam and French Indo-China, sugar from the Dutch East Indies, and hemp and sugar from the Philippines (Ishibashi, 1935). One further point about the trade of Hong Kong is that although the trade with Australia was relatively small, imports from there grew quickly but exports slowly, although they did not decline as in the case of Japan.

Bearing in mind the fragile quality of the figures, a cautious examination of Hong Kong's overall balance of trade is worthwhile. From the figures we have, Hong Kong seems to have had an overall trade deficit between 1877 and 1913, her exports in 1913 being £34,032,063 and her imports £39,054,905, a deficit of £5,022,842. But she was normally in surplus with her major trading partner, China, and also usually in surplus with Singapore and the Straits Settlements. Her major deficits came from her trade with Britain and India, and she had smaller deficits with Siam, Japan, Australia and the Philippines. There are no figures for Hong Kong's exports to French Indo-China, and she probably had a deficit here as well as her trade there was similar to that with Siam, consisting mainly of rice purchases, and the French also had a protectionist policy with regards to imports from non-French territories. The fact that imports from French Indo-China are included in the total but not exports to French Indo-China does of course falsely increase the total deficit. But the overall outline is still probably true. So it appears that Hong Kong was in deficit in general, and in particular with London. The fact that these conclusions are very tentative is reinforced by the fact that although Hong Kong had a substantial trade with Germany there are no figures for the trade. This is because the German statistics lump Hong Kong and China together, as do those of the United States. This may be a major omission. From the numbers of ships listed as visiting Hong Kong in the early years of the new century, we know that Germany was the second most important shipping nation in terms of steamships, usually sending about half the number that Britain sent. The Japanese sent about half as many as the Germans. Shipping from the United States was negligible, with about fifty ships a year in comparison with Britain's 2,000 (British Parliamentary Papers, 1903, 1904). The United States China trade in general was of little importance (Schran, 1986). The lack of German figures is the most serious omission from this exercise, and it is not possible at the moment to make an informed guess of the features of the German trade. All we can say is that it seems to have been about half the British trade in general, and as already noted, the British trade was itself relatively small. The other omission is that of the Dutch East Indies, and this is due to the fact that there is no handy statistical source. Figures do exist, but they are broken down by item and country for each year. It would be necessary to list each item going to every country for the years from 1874 to 1914, and then summarize them year by year. This is a perfectly feasible task, but not practical for the purposes of this chapter (*Statistiek*, 1877–). There may have been significant trade with Hong Kong as the majority of the exports of sugar and other goods from the Dutch East Indies were consumed within Asia, rather than in the Netherlands (Kano, 1986). That, of course, is why Japan had its deficit with the Dutch East Indies.

Certain inferences may be drawn from this study of Hong Kong's trade. Clearly there was a dynamism in her trade, particularly with China with whom she seems to have enjoyed a parasitic relationship. This was a phenomenon generated within Asia and, indeed, within China. Her trade with Britain, her colonial power, was weak, and showed little growth. Even her trade with India, the major market in the British Empire, was in decline. Hong Kong's trade was growing because she was a redistribution centre within the Chinese economy. Unlike Singapore, that other dynamic Asian entrepôt, she did not have a hinterland producing goods in massive demand in the West like tin and rubber. So why was the trade of China growing?

It has often been assumed that the Chinese economy was in some difficulties in this period. There were massive imports of rice into her southern provinces, and it has in the past seemed reasonable to assume that this was an indication of an economy in such crisis it could not even feed itself. Hong Kong was a major actor in this rice trade, drawing in supplies from Siam and Indo-China which were then shipped onwards into China. But it has been recently argued that these rice imports indicate quite the contrary. Rice was a preferred grain amongst ancient foods like millet, barley, and pulses such as soya beans, broad beans and peas, and even newer crops like maize, potatoes and sweet potatoes. The increased purchases of rice in China took place because incomes were rising there. As people became better off, they chose to enjoy some of their improved prosperity by consuming luxuries, one of which was rice (Latham, 1994a).

What seems to have been happening in this period is that new cash crops were being introduced, like tobacco, sugar, cotton, and mulberry leaves for silk worms, and peasants were increasingly specializing in these (Liu, 1989, 1990; Shi, 1989, 1990). As they did so, they gave up some of their food production, whether it was rice or inferior grains. They had calculated that they would be better off by this specialization, and would be able to buy food to replace the home-grown food they had lost turning to cash crops. With their new wealth they were able to buy that most prized luxury item, rice. The increased flow of rice into China reflected this surge of income growth. In reality, the preferred kind of rice in China was from the lower Yangtze region, but supplies were also brought in from Siam and Indo-China. It was no more difficult to bring rice from there by sea than it was to bring it by sea from the lower Yangtze. It has been argued in this chapter that Hong Kong was really just a port in the internal trade of China, and the rice trade bears this out. In China long-distance bulk cargoes travelled by water where feasible rather than by land, in the absence of adequate road or rail facilities. So the coastal trade was the highway of domestic commerce. A recent paper by Hajime Kose has examined in detail the inter-port trade of China (Kose, 1994). In this he makes clear that the two most important trade centres were Shanghai, for Northern and Middle China, and Hong Kong for Southern China. Domestic trade between Shanghai and Hong Kong showed steady growth, as did trade between Canton and Hong Kong. There was a considerable trade in rice from the Yangtze to Southern China.

So it is clear that fundamental changes were taking place in China. The steady growth of internal trade there was reflected in the growth of her trade with Hong Kong, and informs us that the Chinese economy was growing steadily. Even away from the great industrial city of Shanghai fundamental changes were taking place. Great technological change was not necessary for this. The economic benefits of increased specialization of function and exchange were making themselves felt. The increased specialization of agriculture which took place as cash crops were adopted is a clear example of precisely this type of economic process. If some of the increased income gained in this way enabled the peasants to purchase a luxury like rice, part of their income also could be spent on other luxuries like tobacco, sugar, silk, and both handloom- and factory-made cotton goods. The reciprocal gain between the agricultural sector and nascent industrial sector, which is a necessary process of industrialization, had begun.

Appendix I: Hong Kong imports

Indo-China	1 *UK exports* (£)	2 *China exports* (£)	3 *Straits Settlements exports* (£)	4 *Australia exports* (£)	5 *French Indo-China exports* (£)	6 *Bangkok exports* (£)	7 *India exports* (£)	8 *Japan exports* (£)	9 *Philippine exports* (£)
1868	2,305,009	2,575,061	893,724	121,096	206,319	–			
1869	2,254,608	3,662,505	645,299	136,044	94,968	–			
1870	3,570,733	3,365,323	794,815	105,632	431,563	670,157			
1871	3,024,084	3,629,925	1,009,847	120,593	1,469,218	787,644	Statistics include some China figures to 1876	Hong Kong figures included in China before 1889	Hong Kong figures included in China before 1903
1872	3,099,244	4,015,301	1,100,629	148,116	1,167,423	–			
1873	3,610,265	2,511,222	1,101,036	168,722	626,142	357,218			
1874	3,909,246	3,584,498	1,270,887	210,716	306,815	463,413			
1875	3,839,136	3,940,097	969,793	201,502	895,494	704,540			
1876	3,261,805	4,306,907	872,802	150,707	1,602,435	732,335			
1877	3,645,068	4,576,800	804,851	177,634	1,668,067	861,798	8,904,944		
1878	3,041,329	4,462,244	861,778	156,323	1,704,851	900,095	8,445,834		
1879	3,128,227	4,601,041	992,215	239,480	1,104,166	654,691	8,685,626		
1880	3,967,792	4,818,270	958,274	259,418	924,869	510,685	9,011,798		
1881	3,800,189	4,892,097	1,082,570	318,658	870,577	572,736	7,834,541		
1882	3,143,674	4,705,675	1,082,862	303,580	1,691,872	600,643	8,086,754		
1883	3,047,470	5,282,330	1,202,241	314,645	1,745,936	575,767	7,953,914		
1884	3,587,487	4,811,684	1,216,750	351,206	1,042,092	640,184	7,656,221		
1885	4,062,182	4,197,615	1,610,771	352,369	1,939,682	725,709	7,269,941		
1886	2,559,766	5,649,526	1,396,587	444,677	2,726,386	971,632	7,797,446		
1887	2,803,561	7,619,081	1,374,681	348,659	1,661,849	1,484,064	7,297,020		
1888	3,003,379	7,878,009	1,364,489	365,025	1,451,988	1,168,330	7,506,443		
1889	2,378,197	8,318,206	1,000,569	402,273	961,687	794,544	7,485,458	1,113,704	
1890	2,741,404	8,539,008	1,743,829	413,948	1,993,919	1,671,992	7,248,277	1,580,112	
1891	2,732,157	9,268,626	1,121,777	458,986	1,544,979	711,103	6,416,091	2,022,654	

Appendix I cont.

Indo-China	1 *UK exports* (£)	2 *China exports* (£)	3 *Straits Settlements exports* (£)	4 *Australia exports* (£)	5 *French Indo-China exports* (£)	6 *Bangkok exports* (£)	7 *India exports* (£)	8 *Japan exports* (£)	9 *Philippine exports* (£)
1892	1,972,935	8,860,607	1,282,690	431,427	1,264,055	495,571	5,775,262	1,909,563	
1893	1,935,419	9,503,472	1,162,604	558,303	1,363,745	2,061,248	3,985,722	2,006,607	
1894	1,980,277	8,116,881	1,144,616	786,892	1,173,669	963,494	4,435,166	1,700,945	
1895	2,044,616	8,955,549	1,155,925	305,115	1,810,282	1,157,254	4,748,056	1,935,439	
1896	1,959,209	9,005,229	1,229,566	313,512	1,765,939	1,392,438	5,059,716	2,162,306	
1897	2,079,951	8,993,857	1,334,958	291,117*	539,021	971,646	5,255,415	2,579,653	
1898	2,347,689	8,952,512	1,763,205	350,385	1,227,123	1,713,988	5,568,134	3,185,158	
1899	2,862,345	10,812,823	1,569,789	434,222	1,656,347	1,363,550	5,605,637	3,514,859	
1900	2,956,262	9,926,902	1,621,434	388,362	1,987,021‡	1,161,324	5,397,882	3,964,758	
1901	2,797,978	10,579,523	1,674,452	413,711	1,176,385	1,703,708	6,700,818	4,245,523	
1902	2,274,217	10,745,410	1,348,982	390,178	1,566,245	2,117,898	6,474,510	2,652,296	
1903	2,891,710	11,764,952	1,589,426	390,564	1,270,010	1,851,136	7,500,937	3,031,918	296,737
1904	4,574,767	12,446,751	1,913,914	595,769	1,287,501	2,692,425	7,816,482	2,838,538	353,529
1905	3,841,735	12,250,531	1,501,864	796,539	926,956	2,322,426	9,027,706	2,053,852	560,810
1906	3,220,498	13,610,730	1,647,616	726,094	997,078	2,806,145	7,405,169	2,760,255	607,848
1907	3,355,403	15,799,225	1,462,917	859,946	4,099,873	2,575,931	5,953,867	2,487,245	464,983
1908	3,088,340	12,277,996	1,185,339	756,779	2,351,123	2,010,938	6,013,166	1,890,951	517,421
1909	3,713,852	12,589,778	1,242,128	569,933	974,832	2,613,333	6,996,116	2,210,914	432,817
1910	3,834,005	14,634,115	1,159,185	693,751	1,868,606	2,918,774	7,884,389	2,485,126	226,574
1911	2,985,812	13,922,881	1,433,047	730,924	1,575,455§	1,934,891	8,885,617	2,491,433	201,799
1912	3,761,337	15,776,398	1,476,274	856,313	1,760,444	1,908,386	7,338,260	2,928,716	321,294
1913	4,554,590	17,686,479	1,550,431	855,903	2,118,790	2,854,334	5,382,693	3,415,992	635,783
1914	3,710,016	12,880,115	1,124,973	452,114†	1,845,962	2,108,344	2,889,267	3,367,639	405,183

Notes:

Column 1. *Annual Statements of the Trade of the United Kingdom.*

Column 2. Hsiao, Liang-Lin, *China's Foreign Trade Statistics 1864–1949* (Cambridge; Mass.: Harvard University Press, 1974), pp. 148–51, 190–1.

Column 3. *Statistical Abstract for British Colonies.* These figures have been adjusted for the fall in the value of silver.

Column 4. * Includes Tasmania from this date. † Six months ended 30 June. *Statistical Abstract for British Colonies.*

Column 5. ‡ Cochin China only before this date. § Official valuation after this date. Albert Coquerel, *Paddys et Riz De Cochin Chine* (Lyon: Imprimerie A. Ray, 1911), p. 203 etc. (Appendices) *Bulletin Economique de L'Indochine* 4 (1902) – 17(1915). Exchange rate from Hsiao p. 190–1. *Note*: Figures are for rice only. The quantity for the year is multiplied by the average price. From 1900 the figures are for all Indo-China. But the same method is employed as the official valuation uses a constant Franc conversion figure. From 1911 this official figure is used in the absence of reliable average values. Rice was the main item of trade with Hong Kong.

Column 6. Siam, Dept. of Customs, Statistical Office, *Foreign Trade and Navigation of Port of Bangkok 1910–1912* (Bangkok 1911–23). *British Parliamentary Papers*, Diplomatic and Consular reports on the Trade and Commerce of Bangkok (from 1870). Exchange rate from Owen, see Philippines (col 9).

Column 7. *Statistical Abstract for British Colonies.* Exchange rate from G.F. Shirras, *Indian Finance and Banking* (London: Macmillan, 1919), p. 466.

Column 8. Tanzan Ishibashi (ed.), *Foreign Trade of Japan: A Statistical Survey* (Tokyo: Oriental Economist, 1935), p. 349. Exchange rate. Govt of Japan, Dept. of Finance, *Finance and Economic Annual of Japan*, Vol. I (Tokyo 1902), 108–9, Vol. VII (Tokyo 1907), 154–5, Vol. XV (Tokyo 1915), 148–9.

Column 9. *Statistical Bulletin of the Philippine Islands*, No. 2 (1919), pp. 99–100 (Manila), No. 3 (1921) p. 128–9 (Manila). N.G. Owen, *Prosperity without Progress: Manila Hemp and Material Life in the Colonial Philippines* (Berkeley: University of California Press, 1984), pp. 264–5, 277; Hsiao, pp. 190–1 (see col. 2).

Appendix II: Hong Kong exports

	1 *UK imports* (£)	2 *China imports* (£)	3 *Straits Settlements imports* (£)	4 *Australian imports* (£)	5 *Bangkok imports* (£)	6 *India imports* (£)	7 *Japan imports* (£)	8 *Philippine imports* (£)
1868	235,804	4,473,876	819,619	177,075	—			
1869	281,932	6,375,914	747,934	201,228	—			
1870	281,159	6,350,760	1,167,589	170,228	324,108			
1871	367,944	7,394,400	1,060,659	219,235	230,766	Statistics	Hong Kong	Hong Kong
1872	833,764	6,951,949	1,140,819	188,337	286,630	include	figures	figures
1873	783,457	8,005,884	1,398,635	319,927	196,748	some China	included in	included in
1874	747,291	7,504,805	1,634,401	325,745	224,644	figures to	China before	China before
1875	1,154,910	8,507,977	1,033,436	292,411	297,709	1876	1889	1903
1876	1,356,850	8,143,170	1,333,821	333,171	316,202			
1877	1,895,310	8,280,600	1,618,422	340,408	300,357	2,661,037		
1878	1,174,469	8,175,865	1,438,127	355,785	337,761	2,508,954		
1879	1,327,085	8,314,300	1,869,218	412,328	262,665	3,756,946		
1880	1,253,541	8,776,395	1,690,348	452,685	322,252	2,220,849		
1881	1,015,716	8,639,630	1,668,959	538,797	323,252	3,114,989		
1882	1,429,749	8,294,580	1,718,807	556,348	307,780	3,175,463		
1883	1,171,986	8,151,298	2,151,649	503,079	225,969	2,599,924		
1884	1,052,302	8,587,907	2,138,479	890,826	277,395	2,252,561		
1885	968,414	9,328,386	2,132,098	670,753	293,435	2,842,267		
1886	1,556,062	8,739,945	2,204,308	608,981	341,314	2,484,555		
1887	1,409,241	14,018,594	2,735,778	625,021	453,989	2,822,124		
1888	1,296,690	16,398,666	3,224,187	769,501	509,263	2,208,202		

1889	1,129,190	14,980,904	2,595,212	948,006	417,799	2,319,369	634,022	
1890	1,225,064	18,684,380	2,528,596	697,800	775,845	3,764,813	927,160	
1891	1,101,702	16,752,744	2,642,572	588,344	389,555	3,437,125	818,408	
1892	836,705	15,199,160	2,232,169	617,876	300,440	2,103,803	1,003,848	
1893	885,634	15,919,348	2,258,856	440,513	652,156	2,131.657	1,057,486	
1894	630,818	13,171,355	1,843,908	377,520	376,000	1,205,274	944,970	
1895	759,441	14,419,228	1,924,147	417,256	498,702	1,156,146	851,441	
1896	797,158	15,220,076	2,308,472	307,548	544,056	1,120,222	989,188	
1897	606,314	13,419,761	2,193,442	369,534*	593,733	1,405,886	1,221,963	
1898	726,637	14,018,258	2,305,203	328,852	773,307	1,381,363	1,609,532	
1899	883,126	17,773,448	3,060,042	302,453	719,265	1,326,137	752,191	
1900	1,066,048	15,565,054	3,816,431	282,042	684,074	1,550,691	1,078,777	
1901	602,841	17,820,873	3,118,101	285,010	637,886	1,273,990	1,132,005	
1902	610,398	17,358,120	3,178,013	320,385	786,280	1,931,379	251,625	
1903	582,764	18,006,988	5,049,256	309,555	1,007,104	1,428,990	177,452	81,606
1904	466,811	20,217,480	3,213,118	379,320	1,049,328	1,726,017	251,537	49,346
1905	386,440	22,269,878	3,042,838	277,038	927,175	1,413,207	114,665	45,299
1906	638,507	23,842,136	3,606,756	230,311	1,213,209	1,974,800	69,843	62,830
1907	600,109	25,291,825	3,763,690	260,792	1,584,468	1,991,283	83,702	75,390
1908	510,495	20,028,591	2,964,594	247,689	1,351,252	1,325,374	113,784	84,762
1909	455,674	19,546,182	3,214,934	241,533	1,150,887	1,358,341	64,097	88,039
1910	596,402	23,079,323	3,869,878	244,724	1,149,522	1,530,498	68,544	117,972
1911	734,628	19,909,840	4,389,033	302,762	660,183	859,260	71,285	165,068
1912	841,616	22,554,432	4,247,562	331,007	108,826	1,145,967	89,918	166,324
1913	675,276	25,917,036	4,939,638	365,607	1,114,111	782,958	131,546	105,891
1914	598,876	22,914,381	3,538,270	155,667†	1,157,092	662,558	88,653	59,429

Sources: As for Appendix I

BIBLIOGRAPHY

British Parliamentary Papers (1892) Accounts and Papers, *LXXXIV* No. 938 (35–).

British Parliamentary Papers (1895) Accounts and Papers, *C* No. 1520 (329–).

British Parliamentary Papers (1896) Accounts and Papers, *LXXXVIII* No. 1653 (483–).

British Parliamentary Papers (1897) Accounts and Papers, *XCIII* No. 1787 (295–).

British Parliamentary Papers (1900) Accounts and Papers, *LIV* cd 3–5 (487–).

British Parliamentary Papers (1902a) Accounts and Papers, *LXV* cd 788–10 (1–).

British Parliamentary Papers (1902b) Accounts and Papers, *LXV* cd 788–39.

British Parliamentary Papers (1903) Accounts and Papers, *XLIII* cd 1388–17 (251–).

British Parliamentary Papers (1904) Accounts and Papers, *LVI* cd 1768–26 (467–).

Fischer, Wolfram, R. Marvin McInnis and Jurgen Schneider (Eds) (1986) *The Emergence of a World Economy 1500–1914*, Weisbaden: Franz Steiner Verlag.

Hayami, Akira and Yoshihiro Tsubouchi (eds) (1989) *Economic and Demographic Development in Rice Producing Societies: Some Aspects of East Asian Economic History, 1500–1900*, Tokyo, pp. 119–41.

Hayami, Akira and Yoshihiro Tsubouchi (eds) (1900) *Economic and Demographic Development in Rice Producing Societies*, Leuven: Leuven University Press, pp. 50–68.

Ishibashi, Tanzan (ed.) (1935) *Foreign Trade of Japan. A Statistical Survey*, Tokyo: Oriental Economist, pp. 22–3, 349–68.

Kano, Hiroyoshi (1986) Javanese Sugar Industry in the 1920s: A Historical Case of 'Dependent' Industrial Development, Unpublished paper presented at Workshop 34 on Development Theory and Comparative Approaches to the Economic History of the Third World, Berne, Switzerland.

Kose, Hajime (1994) Chinese Merchants and the Chinese Inter-Port Trade, in Latham and Kawakatsu (1994b).

Latham, A.J.H. (1978, 1983) *The International Economy and the Undeveloped World, 1865–1914*, London: Croom Helm; Totowa J.J.: Rowman & Littlefield.

Latham, A.J.H. (1986a) *The International Market in Rice and Wheat, 1968–1914*, in Fischer, McInnis and Schneider, p. 647.

Latham, A.J.H. (1986b) Migration in South East Asia: A Preliminary Survey, 1800–1914, in Luigi de Rosa and Ira A. Glazier (eds) *Migration Across Time and Nations: Population Mobility in Historical Contexts*, New York: Holmes & Meier.

Latham, A.J.H. (1993) *Decline and Recovery in Britain's Overseas Trade*, London: Macmillan, pp. 77–89.

Latham, A.J.H. (1994a) Rice Moves To Areas Where Incomes Are Rising: A Reinterpretation of Asian Economic History since 1800, in Latham and Kawakatsu (1994a).

Latham, A.J.H. (1994b) The Dynamics of Intra-Asian Trade, 1868–1913: The Great Entrepôts of Singapore and Hong Kong, in Latham and Kawakatsu (1994b).

Latham, A.J.H. and Heita Kawakatsu (eds) (1994a) *The Evolving Structure of the East Asian Economic System since 1700: A Comparative Analysis*, Milan: Universita Bocconi.

Latham, A.J.H. and Heita Kawakatsu (eds) (1994b) *Japanese Industrialisation and the Asian Economy*, London: Routledge.

Liu, Ts'su-jung (1989, 1990) Rice Culture in Southern China, 1500–1900: Adjustment and Limitation in Historical Perspective, in Hayami and Tsubouchi, pp. 119–41; also (1990), pp. 50–68.

Schran, Peter (1986) The Minor Significance of Commercial Relations between the United States and China, 1850–1931, in Ernest R. May and John K. Fairbank (1986) *America's China Trade in Historical Perspective: The Chinese and American Performance*, Cambridge, Mass.: Harvard University Press, pp. 237–58.

Schran, Peter (1994) Japan's East Asia Market, 1870–1940, in Latham and Kawakatsu (1994b).

Shi, Zhihong (1989, 1990) The Development and Underdevelopment of Agriculture During the Early Qing Period (1644–1840), in Hayami and Tsubouchi (1989), pp. 154–91; also (1990), pp. 69–88.

Statistiek van den handel, de scheepvaart en de in-en uitvoerrechten in Nederlandsche Indie over het jaar 1874 . . . 1908, 1909 . . . 1914, Batavia, 1877–1909; 1910–15.

Tsunoyama, Sakae (1994) Sino-Japanese Trade and Japanese Industrialisation, in Latham and Kawakatsu (1994b).

10

CHINESE VIEWS OF THE MONEY SUPPLY AND FOREIGN TRADE, 1400–1850

R. Bin Wong

CHINESE FOREIGN TRADE: CONVENTIONAL VIEWS AND REALITY

Scholars often consider the late imperial Chinese state's negative attitude toward foreign trade to be a factor explaining the country's failure to develop a modern economy before the twentieth century. By European standards, China experienced a precocious commercial revolution in the eleventh and twelfth centuries through which increasing amounts of grain and cash crops entered commercial networks to support growing numbers of urban dwellers. In the early fifteenth century several fleets of large Chinese ships sailed as far as Africa and the Middle East. Yet despite these signs of dynamism, China did not enjoy continued economic advance. Domestic commerce's failure to continue expanding is often blamed on state interference. Foreign commerce was also discouraged when government-sponsored naval expeditions were halted after 1433. This was one sign that the Chinese had turned introspective; changes in philosophical attitudes also attest that the Chinese had lost their curiosity about the outside world and their desire to engage with it. These more general intellectual conditions diminished the attractiveness of foreign trade for Chinese officials. Since in European experience foreign trade was a key component of broader economic development, we are told that this lack of state enthusiasm also hampered Chinese development (Elvin 1973: 203–34; Hall 1985: 45–54; Jones 1988: 73–84; McNeil 1982: 24–62, especially 42–9).

There are several difficulties with this conventional view of late imperial Chinese foreign trade. In a country as large as China the relative importance of foreign trade will always be far less than in smaller countries. Foreign trade and domestic trade are similar in terms of their immediate economic advantages except when foreign trade makes available hitherto unknown goods and exposes a country to new techniques and ideas. Then the benefits from trade exceed those measured directly by the market. But before the nineteenth century it is not clear that there were any crucial technological techniques exploited by Europeans that were not known to the Chinese. Government policy toward foreign trade was not uniformly negative. Indeed, one Chinese scholar has argued that government opposition to foreign trade was relatively rare through China's two thousand years of imperial history (Shen 1985). Even in the sixteenth century when officials expressed concern over possible problems of local unrest when large numbers of ships gathered along the coast, others recognized that trade was beneficial to those living there (Lin 1987: 77–84). Even if official policy from the sixteenth century usually stressed government surveillance of foreign trade, the government lacked the capacity to enforce its restrictions. Government opposition simply turned foreign trade into "smuggling."

Much suggests that foreign trade was important in late imperial times. Sixteenth-century Chinese merchants from the southeast coast were heirs to five centuries of Chinese sea trading experience. During the thirteenth and fourteenth centuries these Fujian merchants traded with what are now Cambodia, Sumatra and Java; some of them conducted their business as short-term dwellers in Southeast Asian ports. Traditions developed along the southeast China coast made possible the famous voyages of Zheng He to Africa and the Middle East in the early fifteenth century. These seafaring practices did not stop in the sixteenth and seventeenth centuries just because government-sponsored expeditions were halted. Indeed Chinese merchants become an ever larger presence in Southeast and Northeast Asian trading networks, with a growing presence in Manila after the 1570s and in Nagasaki after 1600 (Wang Gungwu 1990). While some trade in the seventeenth and eighteenth centuries was clearly channeled through the tribute system, private trade also flourished with government acceptance; south China and Southeast Asia formed a regional trading network within which rice shipments into China became an important component (Liu 1993; Kikuchi 1993).

Another second indicator of the importance of foreign trade in late imperial times comes from the large amount of silver imported into China between the sixteenth and eighteenth centuries. Estimates of silver imports into Asia, let alone China specifically, vary considerably; the data are not conclusive. Ward Barrett has estimated silver flows into Asia as part of a larger study of world silver flows in the early modern period. His figures for Asia, as he himself notes, undercount total silver imports because they are based on estimates of Dutch East India Company and English East India Company imports alone. This limitation notwithstanding, they indicate large imports that grow through the eighteenth century from an average of 20 tons annually (1651–1675) to 101 tons annually a century later (1751–1775) (Barrett 1990). Flynn and Giráldez (1995) suggest even higher figures. Whatever future research shows, it is safe to assume that silver imports to China were large enough to cause major changes in the domestic economy. A "second commercial revolution" spread over parts of the empire that had not experienced the eleventh- and twelfth-century changes. Two major groups of merchants, from Shanxi and Huizhou, established networks across different areas of the empire to build up local and long-distance trade (Terada 1972; Fuji 1953–1954; Fu [1956] 1980). Silver imports were used to provide the monetary basis for this commercial expansion. For the government, increased commerce made possible a gradual commutation of land taxes into money form (Huang 1974). Chinese foreign trade between the sixteenth and eighteenth centuries was important, not only to those merchants engaged in foreign trade but also to those who participated in the domestic market economy. It was also important to the state. Perhaps China would have experienced this commercial expansion if silver imports had not taken place, but it seems unlikely. The provision of large amounts of silver for the domestic economy was a significant consequence of foreign trade. What, then, did Chinese officials and educated observers of these centuries think of silver imports?

CHINESE ATTITUDES TOWARD SILVER AND THE MONEY SUPPLY

Sixteenth-century Chinese officials had a long tradition of monetary policy stretching back more than 1,500 years. A variety of materials had been used as money in different parts of the empire through the dynasties, including copper, iron, cowries, paper, and silver. Given the importance that silver came to enjoy in China's trading and fiscal systems, it is surprising, from a modern Western point of view, to discover that officials do not seem to have specified clear and effective policies regarding silver imports. Between 1500 and 1850 they debated the relative virtues of relying upon silver imports or promoting domestic copper coin production. There seems to have been less government concern about silver during the periods when it flowed freely into the country; occasionally someone would question the wisdom of goods leaving China to finance silver imports. But generally officials did little to promote or hinder silver inflows. However, when silver imports were lacking – or worse, when silver was leaving the country – officials expressed great concern. Two periods in particular were times of anxiety over silver supplies. The first was in the mid-seventeenth century when the late Ming political collapse and the formation of the Qing empire reduced silver imports. The second was in the early nineteenth century when growing opium imports began to cause silver outflows from China.

Late Ming and early Qing officials and observers reacted in several ways to the decline of silver circulating in the Chinese economy. All began from a recognition that silver had become the crucial medium for long-distance trade which made it basic to commerce. Policy positions ranged from those seeking to increase silver in circulation to those arguing for a reduced reliance on silver in favour of other currencies. Believers in the importance of increasing silver supplies argued for increased domestic production as well as efforts to import additional silver; some of them believed that rich individuals were hoarding silver to drive up its value. Many analysts believed that a lack of silver in circulation caused price deflation which made it difficult for goods to circulate. Under these conditions demand for handicrafts and cash crops fell; artisans then experienced unemployment and peasants a drop in their cash incomes. Other observers argued that the way to break reliance on scarce silver was not to increase silver volumes as this was difficult to achieve through government policy. Rather, the government should aim to reduce the importance of silver to the monetary system by promoting the use of alternatives. Some argued for expanded circulation of copper coins which were already in use, maintaining that they should be used along with silver to form a bi-metallic monetary system. Silver dominated long-distance trade transactions and copper the local exchange; for some analysts it was clear that pressing for copper rather than silver meant promoting local exchange over long-distance trade. Yet others argued for the reintroduction of paper currencies which had had a chequered history in earlier centuries, their use usually suspended after inflation wiped out their nominal face value (Kishimoto 1984; Xiao 1987: 279–93).

Anxieties over the price deflation of the late seventeenth century and the depression that accompanied the early decades of Qing rule were ultimately alleviated by the resumption of foreign trade and silver imports, a process largely outside government policy control. During the eighteenth century, China's domestic economy expanded dramatically. With population more than doubling from 150 million to 350 million people, large amounts of new land were opened within the interior and along the frontiers. Domestic trade continued to expand on local and regional scales as well as across great distances. The state played a considerable role in promoting economic expansion, especially in frontier areas, by building up transportation infrastructure and giving subsidies to peasants and soldiers opening new lands (Peng Yuxin 1990; Wang Yuquan *et al.* 1991; Lin and Wang 1991; Wang Xilong 1990; Wang and Wei 1989; Lee 1982; Shepherd 1993). A mix of private and state initiatives propelled the expansion of China's economy in the eighteenth century. Prices in general rose during the course of the century. At mid-century there was concern over rising grain prices, and the Qianlong emperor instructed his provincial governors to report to him on the reasons for this. No reports have been found that argue that price inflation was due to increased amounts of silver flowing into the country (Wong 1983: 124–36). Chinese officials and observers do not seem to have expressed any great concern over silver supplies during this century of economic expansion. In short, increasing silver inflows were not an object of government policy; they were simply in the background and not worthy of serious policy discussion so long as sufficient silver was available to facilitate domestic trade.

By the 1820s, foreign trade relations had dramatically shifted from the norm that had characterized China's trade with European powers between the sixteenth and eighteenth centuries. Whereas China had previously been a net importer of silver, except in periods of disrupted trade, the country now became a net exporter of silver to fund the ever larger amounts of opium brought from India by the British. Chinese opposition to the opium trade had two major components. Moral outrage existed over another country presuming to permit, let alone promote, commercial imports of a dangerous drug with unambiguously detrimental consequences for Chinese society. Of immediate concern in this chapter, there were Chinese anxieties over the economic implications of the silver outflow for the domestic economy. Most observers understood that a shrinking money supply and price deflation threatened to hamper commercial exchange. They also realized that it would be difficult to reverse the flow of silver back to China's favor. They aimed instead to reduce the outflow of silver and to reduce reliance on silver as a medium of exchange. To stem the outflow many officials argued that opium imports had to be prohibited since opium purchases were the principal sources of silver payments; others argued that China's foreign trade should be done on a barter basis so that no silver was involved. As in the situation of some 150 years earlier, some analysts called for reduced use of silver with either copper or paper notes taking on greater roles in the monetary system (Xiao 1987: 308–58). For their part, merchants expanded the circulation of privately issued paper to facilitate transactions.

Contrary to at least some scholars' suppositions, Chinese observers in the late imperial period did care about foreign trade. They were acutely aware of how foreign trade could affect the economy. But their priorities and concerns did not lead to a set of policies toward international trade and silver supplies similar to those adopted by European countries. Thus it is difficult for Western observers to understand how the Chinese approached these issues because of Western concepts invoked to judge the level of interest Chinese officials showed in foreign trade and silver supplies. Chinese interests were very different and thus are difficult to assess from European experiences.

CHINESE AND EUROPEAN VIEWS OF FOREIGN TRADE: EXPECTATIONS AND RESULTS

Mercantilist states of the early modern period conceived themselves to be engaged in a competition with the governments and merchants of other European countries for wealth and power. This perspective led them to stress the importance of amassing silver at the expense of other governments and merchants. For many European merchants engaged in overseas adventures, amassing large sums of money often involved them in state chartered companies and various types of monopoly arrangements for the purchase and sale of scarce goods, like spices and teas. For European governments, foreign trade was a source of revenue for the warmaking that was so central to early modern absolutist state making; in addition, the merchants engaged in foreign trade were often important political supporters of the regimes seeking to expand and stabilize their power, both domestically and in competition with other European states. As part of these concerns, European governments and merchants developed new banking and credit institutions as well as elaborate new forms of merchant companies which together promoted new channels to accumulate capital for private commerce and for government expenditures. This political economy of commercial capitalism is a distinctly European phenomenon during the early modern period.

Chinese political economy during late imperial times was centered on the promotion of an agrarian economy founded upon the labours of myriads of peasant households each of which ideally combined some amount of handicraft production with agricultural cultivation. The state recognized and even promoted commercial exchange according to supply and demand conditions. Merchants played a positive social function by moving goods over short and long distances according to market prices. Chinese political economy focused its greatest attention on domestic economic issues, at the center of which was the increase in the number of small-scale households engaged in market exchange. The state took an active interest in both production and distribution. The state monitored and on some occasions even managed water control projects for both paddy production and transportation; officials also maintained adequate food supplies for distribution in the lean spring season, especially in years of bad harvests. Officials favored commercial exchange according to market prices, but routinely opposed hoarding and market control exercised by merchants. In contrast to European governments, the Chinese government did not depend either economically or politically on the support of rich merchants for its fiscal security or its political power and legitimacy. Foreign trade and the merchants who engaged in it were peripheral to dominant state concerns. The late imperial Chinese state did aim to regulate foreign trade. Where it succeeded in the eighteenth century, the Chinese merchants who were the authorized agents with whom foreign merchants were expected to deal became extremely wealthy. But the general logic linking government policy to merchant activities was fundamentally different in China and Europe.

The Chinese political economy of an agrarian empire and the European political economy of mercantilist competition produced different priorities and promoted the development of different political and economic capacities. Chinese and European officials aimed for different goals. Chinese officials aimed to tax lightly and support the government without burdening the people whose economic welfare was conceived to be basic to the state's political stability; merchants, especially the many of modest scale, had a socially useful function, but they had no political importance as a group. European governments aimed to amass ever larger resources to compete with each other in an era of aggressive state building and economic expansion; merchants, in particular those of great wealth and privilege, played an important political role as well as an economically crucial one.

Chinese policies are often imagined to be lacking a forward-looking and positive function because these policies did not contribute to the arc of historical change familiar in the West. But this perspective is problematic. As already suggested, it measures significance according to standards derived from European experiences and this creates a danger that priorities beyond European experience will not be recognized.

Despite European countries' professed desire to amass as much silver bullion as possible in their competition with others, massive amounts of bullion ended up in the Middle East, South Asia and East Asia. Not only were European desires not achieved, but their objects were challenged in the seventeenth century, and by Adam Smith in the late eighteenth century (Appleby 1992). After Adam Smith, the measure of a country's success in international trade was not its bullion stocks but its levels of consumption; international trade, like trade within a nation's borders, could be beneficial to all parties, rather than be a zero-sum competition for bullion. On the Chinese side there was no policy imperative to amass ever larger sums of bullion; only in times of silver shortage did officials call for changes to reduce the impact of short silver supplies on commercial exchange. Chinese policies differed from those in Europe, but their consequences were equally limited. Silver imports promoted domestic commercial development, even though the state did little to encourage these changes, and shortages of silver imports created domestic commercial problems that government policies were unable to solve easily or swiftly.

To return to international trade and consider its economic and political components, Chinese merchants competed successfully in Southeast Asia between the sixteenth and eighteenth centuries, except when European military power created monopolies over certain goods for European merchants; thus, economic competition in the Asian trading world was first settled in Europe's favor because coercion was introduced. Advantages so gained provided the conditions under which European institutions of commercial capitalism combined the search for wealth and power in a manner distinctive from the political economy of late imperial agrarian China. These differences in institutions and ideology help to explain the different arcs of historical change in the political economies of China and Europe. Foreign trade and money supply were two components of this picture. These concerns deserve further attention in future scholarship.

BIBLIOGRAPHY

Appleby, J. (1992) *Liberalism and Republicanism in the Historical Imagination*, Cambridge, Mass.: Harvard University Press.

Barrett, W. (1990) "World Bullion Flows, 1450–1880," in J.D. Tracy (ed.) *The Rise of Merchant Empires*, New York: Cambridge University Press.

Elvin, M. (1973) *The Pattern of the Chinese Past*, Stanford: Stanford University Press.

Flynn, D.O. and Giráldez, A. (1995) "Born with a 'Silver Spoon': The Origin of World Trade in 1571," *Journal of World History* 6, 2: 201–21.

Fu Yiling ([1956] 1980) *Ming Qing shidai shangren ji shangye ziben* (Ming Qing period merchants and their merchant capital), Renmin chuban she.

Fuji Hiroshi (1953–1954) "Shinan shōnin no kenkyū" (Research on Hsinan merchants), *Tōyōgakuho* 36.1–4: 1–44, 32–60, 65–118, 115–45.

Hall, J.A. (1985) *Powers and Liberties*, London: Penguin.

Huang, R. (1974) *Taxation and Governmental Finance in Sixteenth-Century Ming China*, Cambridge: Cambridge University Press.

Jones, E.L. (1988) *Growth Recurring: Economic Change in World History*, Oxford: Oxford University Press.

Kikuchi Michiki (1993) "Tōnan Ajia to Chūgoku" (Southeast Asia and China), in Mizoguchi Yuzo, Hamashita Takeshi, Hiraishi Naoaki and Miyajima Hiroshi (eds), *Chiiki shisutemu*, Vol. 2 of *Ajia kara kangaeru*, University of Tokyo Press.

Kishimoto Mio (1984) "The Kangxi Depression and Early Qing Local Markets," *Modern China* 10, 2: 227–55.

Lee, J. (1982) "China's Southwestern Frontier: State Policy and Economic Development, 1250–1850," Unpublished University of Chicago Ph.D. dissertation, University of Chicago.

Lin Renchuan (1987) *Mingmo Qingchu siren haishang maoyi* (Late Ming and early Qing private maritime trade), Shanghai: Huadong shifan daxue chubanshe.

Lin Yonggui and Wang Xi (1991) *Qingdai Xibei minzu maoyishi* (A history of Qing dynasty northwest China trade), Zhongyang minzu xueyuan chuban she.

Liu Xufeng (1993) "Junana hasseki no Chūgoku to Tō Ajia" (17th–18th century China and East Asia), in Mizoguchi Yūzō, Hamashita Takeshi, Hiraishi Naoaki and Miyajima Hiroshi (eds), *Chiiki shisutemu*, Vol. 2 of *Ajia kara kangaeru*, University of Tokyo Press.

Ma Ruheng and Ma Dazheng (1990) *Qingdai bianjiang kaifa yanjiu* (Studies on Qing dynasty border development), Zhongguo shehui kexueyuan chuban she.

McNeill, W. (1982) *The Pursuit of Power*, Chicago: University of Chicago Press.

Peng Xinwei (1958) *Zhongguo huobishi* (A history of Chinese currency), Shanghai renmin chubanshe.

Peng Yuxin (1990) *Qingdai tudi kaikenshi* (A history of Qing dynasty land clearance), Nongye chuban she.

Shen Guangyao (1985) *Zhongguo gudai duiwai maoyishi* (A history of Chinese foreign trade), Guangdong renmin chubanshe.

Shepherd, J. (1993) *Statecraft and Political Economy on the Taiwan Frontier, 1600–1800*, Stanford: Stanford University Press.

Terada Takanobu (1972) *Sansei shōnin no kenkyū* (Studies of Shanxi merchants), Dohosha.

Wang Gungwu (1990) "Merchants Without Empire: The Hokkien Sojourning Communities," in James D. Tracy (ed.), *The Rise of Merchant Empires: Long-distance trade in the early modern world, 1350–1750*, Cambridge: Cambridge University Press.

Wang Xilong (1990) *Qingdai xibei tuntian yanjiu* (Studies of Qing dynasty northwestern land colonies), Lanzhou daxue chubanshe.

Wang Yuquan, Liu Zhongri, Guo Songyi and Lin Yonggui (1991) *Zhongguo tunken shi* (A history of Chinese land clearance), Vol. 3, Nongye chubanshe.

Wang Zhizhong and Wei Liying (1989) *Ming Qing xiebei shehui jingjishi yanjiu* (Studies of northwestern social-economic history in the Ming Qing period), Sanqin chubanshe.

Will, P.-E. and Bin Wong, R. (1991) *Nourish the People: The State Civilian Granary System in China, 1650–1850*, University of Michigan Center for Chinese Studies.

Wong, R. Bin (1983) "The Political Economy of Food Supplies in Qing China," Unpublished Harvard University Ph.D. dissertation, Harvard University.

Xiao Qing (1987) *Zhongguo gudai huobi sixiangshi* (A history of traditional Chinese monetary thought), Renmin chubanshe.

11

THE DEVELOPMENT OF THE COAL MINING INDUSTRY IN TAIWAN DURING THE JAPANESE COLONIAL OCCUPATION, 1895–1945

Tsu-yu Chen

INTRODUCTION

The growth of the coal mining industry in Taiwan during the Japanese occupation was an important phenomenon. Coal mining in Taiwan has a long history, but there were no attempts at large-scale production until the 1870s. These attempts bore little fruit in the late Qing period and the early Japanese occupation. During the First World War, Japanese *zaibatsu* and several Taiwanese capitalists invested in coal mining enterprises in Taiwan under the guidance of the Japanese colonial government, and the golden age of Taiwan's coal mining industry (1916–1927) occurred. Because modern industry as a whole in Taiwan was still in its infancy, demand for coal was small. Consequently coal owners began to seek overseas markets. The main export markets were Southern China, Hong Kong and the Southeast Asian colonies of Great Britain and France. So the international economic and political situation influenced the development of coal mining in Taiwan. In this way, although Taiwan was a Japanese colony, the coal industry was connected to the world economy.

This chapter examines the coal industry in Taiwan between 1895 and 1945. The main external factors which influenced its development are considered, then the structure of production and distribution, in order to reveal the power of the *zaibatsu*. Finally, the role of Taiwan's coal mining in the entire Japanese coal industry is appraised, for Japan did not need coal from Taiwan.

THE DEVELOPMENT OF THE COAL INDUSTRY

Coal was the most important fuel for industry and transport before petroleum or gas came into use. Taiwan's industrial development and the formation of its transport networks may be understood through an examination of the development of the coal industry. As a colonial product, the development of coal mining was closely linked both with the economy of Japan and with the world situation.

The initial stage: 1895–1915

Although coal could be used for cooking, most people in Taiwan used wood as fuel before modern times. In the seventeenth century, the Spanish and the Dutch, who then occupied Taiwan, excavated coal in order to smelt iron with it and to export it. After 1662, when Taiwan became Chinese territory, the government discouraged people from digging for coal because of traditional Chinese beliefs in the spiritual properties of the earth. The British vessels which frequented East Asia in the late nineteenth century needed coal as fuel. They bought coal from the Taiwanese, and the Taiwanese provincial authorities began to attempt large-scale coal mining operations in Jilong (north Taiwan) from the 1870s. This attempt at government-operated coal mines was not very successful (Chen 1992: 621–656). Taiwan became a Japanese colony in 1895. Both Japanese and Taiwanese citizens were permitted to develop coal mines, but the growth of coal production was slow during the period 1895–1905 for several reasons (Fujita 1925: 17–29):

In Japan, the scale of coal mining was larger and more capital intensive. In Taiwan, however, coal miners still used primitive methods, and people without much capital or experience could easily get started. As a result, some Japanese citizens who could not get loans from Japanese banks to start a coal mine at home, came to Taiwan to try their luck. This lack of capital and expertise limited the development of coal mining in Taiwan. Another problem was the fact that the Sijiauting area of Jilong county, the richest coalfield in Taiwan, was designated as a supplier to the navy by the colonial government. Local people were only allowed to exploit inferior coal mines and so produced very little. Even when a few better coal mines were established, proprietors could not overcome the difficulties posed by Taiwan's rugged natural environment with traditional methods of excavation. Most of the mines were very small operations and could not afford equipment for deep excavation. Miners often illegally worked adjoining outcrops, causing many disputes.

The main coal mines were located in northern Taiwan, while the sugar factories which used coal were located in the South. Transport became a big problem. Southern Taiwan imported coal from abroad before the railway from the North was finished in 1908. Even then, when the demand by the sugar factories and other industries for coal grew, domestic coal contributed little due to low productivity.

Growth: 1916–1927

The First World War stimulated Taiwan's coal mining industry. The main coal-producing nations (that is, Great Britain, Germany and the United States) reduced their output of coal because of shortages of labour and transport. Total output was reduced from 1.37 billion tonnes in 1913 to 1.1 billion tonnes in 1916 (Takemoto 1921: 17). The shortage of shipping and the naval warfare quickly reduced sea transport capacity. Europe, which had supplied capital goods to the world, needed military supplies and other industrial products. The increase in demand and the crippling of the European shipping industry pushed freight rates up. As a result, Japanese shipping companies made tremendous profits and expanded their fleets. The demand for steel and for coal thus increased. Backward linkages from the shipping industry upgraded Japan's engineering industries. The chemical industry also grew vigorously owing to the growth of textile exports to other Asian areas (Nakamura 1988: 83–95). To meet the growing demand for coal, Japanese authorities and *zaibatsu* were keen to import coal from her colonies as well as increasing domestic production. As Table 11.1 shows, Taiwanese coal was exported to Japan even after the end of the war. The table also reveals that the overseas market for Taiwanese coal in other areas, including Hong Kong, Southern China and Southeast Asia was larger than the Japanese market. These areas were the main export destinations for Taiwanese coal before 1916. As Table 11.2 shows, Hong Kong, a transit port, was one of the largest coal markets in Eastern Asia. Coal imports decreased significantly after the beginning of the war due to shortage of shipping and the decline in Japanese coal exports (Takemoto 1921: 71). Imports of coal in 1918 were only 47 percent of the 1914 figure. Shipments of coal from Japan and Fushun in northeastern China sharply decreased, while those from Taiwan increased. In other words, coal from Taiwan filled a void left by the fall in exports from "the Greater Japanese Empire." Japanese coal, including Taiwanese coal, thus accounted for 71.2 percent of the Hong Kong coal market, while coal from China only accounted for 16.5 percent.

Fujian and Guangdong were also important markets for Taiwanese coal. Fuzhou, the capital of Fujian, had imported coal from Japan and Taiwan, but depended on the supply from Taiwan during and after the war (TNS 1907: 2871.2; TNS 1919: 6906.6). Before the war, the quantity of Chinese coal in the Amoy market equalled foreign coal, including that from Japan and Taiwan, but after the war Taiwanese coal made up 62 percent of imports (Takemoto 1921: 67; TNS 1908: 2903.2, 2904.2). Taiwanese coal replaced Japanese coal in Guangdong supplying the steamships and silk factories there (Takemoto 1921: 67–70; TNS 1924: 8599.5; TNS 1926: 9318.4). Another new market was Southeast Asia. The flow of coal from Japan and China to this area was stopped by China's civil disorder, Japan's

Table 11.1 Taiwan output and sales volume of coal in metric tonnes, 1912–45

Year	Output (A)	Sales Volume								Storeage	C/B (%)	F/B (%)	D/C (%)	E/C (%)	G/F (%)
			Domestic consumption			Exportation									
		Total (B)	Sum (C)	Local (D)	Steamship (E)	Sum (F)	Japan (G)	Other areas (H)							
1912	276,246	419,810	390,484	249,998	140,486	29,326	2	29,324		11,478	93.01	6.99	64.02	35.98	0.01
1913	319,371	466,690	444,386	279,006	165,380	22,304	—	22,304		18,611	95.22	4.78	62.78	37.22	—
1914	342,787	526,856	483,679	275,235	208,444	43,177	1,614	41,563		12,634	91.80	8.20	56.90	43.10	3.74
1915	379,368	524,837	487,453	278,038	209,415	37,384	—	37,384		17,472	92.88	7.12	57.04	42.96	—
1916	517,581	511,543	422,724	266,506	156,218	88,819	10,549	78,270		47,957	82.64	17.36	63.04	36.96	11.88
1917	673,008	767,300	499,281	344,249	155,032	268,019	15,030	252,989		54,089	65.07	34.93	68.95	31.05	5.61
1918	801,520	820,296	529,942	376,696	153,246	290,354	8,268	282,086		128,506	64.60	35.40	71.08	28.92	2.85
1919	1,086,907	1,184,495	649,575	404,778	244,797	534,920	57,571	477,349		95,057	54.84	45.16	62.31	37.69	10.76
1920	1,139,358	1,258,755	710,383	487,863	222,520	548,372	90,295	458,077		103,060	56.44	43.56	68.68	31.32	16.47
1921	1,029,410	1,322,187	811,506	499,760	311,746	510,681	56,092	454,589		78,559	61.38	38.62	61.58	38.42	10.98
1922	1,347,449	1,375,426	717,919	518,158	199,761	657,507	188,794	468,713		45,242	52.20	47.80	72.17	27.83	28.71
1923	1,444,921	1,473,807	807,806	519,355	288,451	666,001	181,088	484,913		150,873	54.81	45.19	64.29	35.71	27.19
1924	1,506,451	1,685,712	813,858	485,736	328,122	871,854	198,618	673,236		80,353	48.28	51.72	59.68	40.32	22.78
1925	1,704,581	1,780,764	890,477	526,931	363,546	890,287	189,694	700,593		106,812	50.01	49.99	59.17	40.83	21.31
1926	1,794,511	1,881,412	991,662	608,962	382,700	889,750	136,497	753,253		83,023	52.71	47.29	61.41	38.59	15.34

1927	1,857,257	1,752,599	1,062,412	782,093	280,319	690,187	129,797	560,390	146,201	60.62	39.38	73.61	26.39	18.81
1928	1,583,598	1,397,102	953,160	657,235	295,925	443,942	79,147	364,795	198,339	68.22	31.78	68.95	31.05	17.83
1929	1,530,025	1,608,699	1,219,752	715,590	504,162	388,947	42,860	346,087	110,942	75.82	24.18	58.67	41.33	11.02
1930	1,598,728	1,520,667	1,136,875	640,641	496,234	383,792	41,633	342,159	145,716	74.76	25.24	56.35	43.65	10.85
1931	1,421,544	1,419,287	1,045,874	597,902	447,972	373,413	64,094	309,319	133,114	73.69	26.31	57.17	42.83	17.16
1932	1,354,995	1,407,351	1,174,532	622,321	552,211	232,819	61,830	170,989	80,520	83.46	16.54	52.98	47.02	26.56
1933	1,533,103	1,584,572	1,251,107	658,611	592,496	333,465	146,515	186,950	70,036	78.96	21.04	52.64	47.36	43.94
1934	1,520,926	1,570,513	1,303,126	681,341	621,785	267,387	105,350	162,037	74,762	82.97	17.03	52.29	47.71	39.40
1935	1,596,672	1,706,301	1,477,325	701,224	776,101	228,976	81,526	147,450	121,120	86.58	13.42	47.47	52.53	35.60
1936	1,743,777	1,976,904	1,735,394	895,105	840,289	241,510	114,134	127,376	152,637	87.78	12.22	51.58	48.42	47.26
1937	1,953,346	2,269,729	1,861,814	858,206	1,003,608	407,915	270,159	137,756	133,054	82.03	17.97	46.10	53.90	66.23
1938	2,198,542	2,369,038	1,782,288	885,478	896,810	586,750	439,544	147,206	132,187	75.23	24.77	49.68	50.32	74.91
1939	2,618,877	2,667,964	2,100,036	1,105,706	994,330	567,928	276,258	291,670	190,988	78.71	21.29	52.65	47.35	48.64
1940	2,841,414	2,706,635	2,038,758	1,169,476	869,282	667,877	284,703	383,174	242,006	75.32	24.68	57.36	42.64	42.63
1941	2,853,832	2,617,000	2,139,000	1,452,000	687,000	478,000	86,000	392,000	531,000	81.73	18.27	67.88	32.12	17.99
1942	2,356,313	2,519,000	2,104,000	1,755,000	349,000	415,000	146,000	269,000	363,000	83.53	16.47	83.41	16.59	35.18
1943	2,237,725	2,312,000	1,978,000	1,623,000	355,000	334,000	37,000	297,000	272,000	85.55	14.45	82.05	17.95	11.08
1944	1,913,937	1,941,763	1,807,023	1,426,316	380,707	134,740	—	134,740	225,822	93.06	6.94	78.93	21.07	—
1945	794,558	745,104	705,470	675,244	30,226	39,634	—	39,634	140,663	94.68	5.32	95.72	4.28	—

Source: *Taiwan Kuangyeshi*, pp. 1262–1263

Table 11.2 Origins of coal exported to Hong Kong in tonnes, 1912–19

	Japanese Empire				*China*			*Other areas*		*Percentage*			
Year	*Taiwan*	*Japan*	*Yaeyama*	*Sum*	*Kaiping*	*Fushun*	*Sum*	*Sum*	*Total*	*Japan*	*China*	*Others*	*Taiwan*
1912	—	906,857	—	906,857	59,000	102,337	161,337	170,950	1,239,144	73.2	13.0	13.8	—
1913	117	1,023,647	—	1,023,764	123,794	125,608	249,402	214,584	1,487,750	68.8	16.8	14.4	0.008
1914	8,164	994,056	5,764	1,007,984	260,975	83,890	344,865	260,262	1,163,111	62.6	21.3	16.1	0.5
1915	2,550	722,026	9,310	733,886	167,875	63,147	231,022	87,962	1,052,870	69.7	21.9	8.4	0.2
1916	15,889	740,129	24,797	780,815	137,478	73,975	211,453	80,764	1,073,032	72.8	19.7	7.5	1.5
1917	125,376	674,508	54,708	854,592	165,466	52,345	217,811	118,103	1,190,506	71.8	18.3	9.9	10.5
1918	129,384	422,690	35,246	587,320	120,318	16,190	136,508	101,087	824,915	71.2	16.5	12.3	15.7
1919	71,800	125,904	13,391	211,095	19,445	859	20,304	42,041	273,440	77.2	7.4	15.4	26.3

Source: Takedo Takemoto, *Taiwan Tangyoron*, pp. 71–72

increasing domestic demand, and the unavailability of transport. Taiwanese coal filled the gap (Sotokufu 1935: 169–170). Exports grew quickly from 1917 as shown in Table 11.1.

According to a survey in the 1920s, the total output of coal in Southern China (Hong Kong, Fujian and Guangdong) and Southeast Asia was about 2 million tonnes, while the demand for coal was 4.5 million tonnes (TNS 1921: 7643.3). Japan could not increase its exports of coal to Asia, so Taiwan, with its favorable geographical position, increased its exports to the Indian Ocean area with the cooperation of the Japanese colonial authorities and Japanese companies. The development of these overseas markets stimulated a thriving coal industry in Taiwan. The old companies improved their equipment and carried out activities on a larger scale. In addition, new investors entered the field. The mining area was expanded from Northern Taiwan to Central Taiwan and Penghu, an island located to the southwest of Taiwan. Japanese *zaibatsu* played an important role in that expansion. Because Taiwanese coal was inferior to Japanese coal, the Japanese believed it might be subject to spontaneous combustion and could not be carried long distances or used as fuel for steamships. As a result, they did not invest in Taiwanese mines before the First World War but did so after 1917, realizing that the possibilities for increasing coal production in Japan were limited. Some of them operated jointly with Taiwanese, others independently. Most of the new companies were joint-stock companies unlike the smaller enterprises of early times (Fujita 1925: 42–53). Among these companies, the Jilong Coal Mining Co. and the Taipei Coal Mining Co. were established by the Yen Family of Jilong in 1918, in cooperation with the Mitsui *zaibatsu* and Fujitakumi. Two years later, Fujitakumi withdrew from the Taipei Coal Mining Co., which was later renamed the Taiyang Mining Company (Chen 1992: 632–633).

After the First World War, depression in Japan led to a glut of Taiwanese coal and a fall in its price. Many coal mines were closed, while a few mechanized mines continued due to their lower production costs. The depression, however, induced owners to improve their management. They reduced the number of miners, cut wages, and improved equipment to cut expenditure and raise the quality of coal (Fujita 1925: 61–69). But as shown in Table 11.1, annual output continued to increase. From late 1921, economic recovery brought renewed demand. The industry in Taiwan grew steadily and reached its peak in 1927. Consumption increased to 1.88 million tonnes in 1926 due to a boycott in Southern China against British-owned Kaiping coal in the north of China (Sotokufu 1935: 171). Demand for exports and steam coal for bunkering became the most important forces controlling Taiwan's coal mining industry, and these markets were affected by the world economic and political situation.

Stagnation: 1928–1935

The international political and economic situation caused a slump in the Taiwanese coal mining industry from 1928 to 1935. First, the Jinan Incident, in which the Japanese army attacked Jinan in Northern China, caused a Chinese boycott against Japanese goods. As a result, Taiwanese coal, which was seen as a Japanese product, was not imported by Southern China, and Indian coal was purchased instead (Sotokufu 1935: 172). The export of Taiwanese coal in 1928 dropped to only 64 percent of the previous year and 50 percent of the peak year (1926). Nearly two-thirds of the mines in Taiwan shut down (*Taiwan Jihpo* 1929: 10–11). The worldwide economic depression hit Japan and Taiwan in the following years, and exports of Taiwanese coal declined further. After Japan took control of Manchuria in northeastern China in 1931, a great quantity of good quality Fushun coal flooded into Japan and Taiwan. So the Taiwanese mining faced a crisis in the domestic market as well as a drop in exports. The president of the Taiyang Mining Co. went to Japan to present a petition asking Japan to limit the imports of Fushun coal and give priority to Taiwanese coal. He took advantage of his close relationships with the powerful *zaibatsu* and his connections in high-level political circles. The Japanese government, recognizing that there might be difficulties in depending on Fushun coal, given the anti-Japanese sentiment in China, agreed (Taiyang Mining Co. 1978: 49). We can see from Table 11.1 that the export of Taiwanese coal to Japan increased in 1933. Domestic consumption also increased. The main reasons were the rising demand for fuel to power the sugar factories, the increasing demands of power stations, the development of domestic industry, and the higher living standards of the people who now used coal instead of wood at home (Sotokufu 1935: 174–175). The big coal companies were able to reduce their costs, increase output and improve quality by mechanizing and improving transportation (Chen 1992: 635–638). In this way they laid a foundation for greater production in the future.

Transformation: 1936–1945

The years from 1936 to 1945 might be called the period of centralized control in the Taiwanese coal industry. Centralization was started by the president of the Taiyang Mining Co., and continued by the colonial government. The main goals of the Taiwanese Coal Mining Industry Association, founded in 1933, were to control production and prices so as to strengthen the international competitiveness of Taiwanese coal. The Association also planned to improve the mining industry and increase profits. Following the establishment of national control of mines in Japan, the Japanese colonial government gradually intervened in Taiwan and reinforced the Association's control over the Taiwanese industry by setting up some additional regulations (Taiyang Mining Co. 1978: 50; Society of Mining in Taiwan Province 1969: 839). In this way, the authorities controlled the production and marketing of Taiwanese coal. Owing to the continued development of heavy industry in Japan, a prosperous ocean shipping industry, and the growth of industrialization in Taiwan, the consumption of coal in Taiwan amounted to more than 2 million tonnes in 1937. Meanwhile, the output reached 1.95 million tonnes, which was greater than at the peak of the growth phase ten years earlier. The outbreak of the Sino-Japanese war in July 1937 increased Japan's demand for coal; and projects for producing more coal in Taiwan were implemented. This resulted in a rise in the amount of Taiwanese coal exported to Japan and Southeast Asia, and sold to the navy. The Taiwan Coal Company was founded that year by the colonial government in order to increase production, maintain stable price and control distribution. Both the output and sales volume of Taiwan's coal industry were more than 2 million tonnes during 1938–1943. After 1944, output fell due to shortages of capital and labor, and exports stopped because of lack of shipping. The coal industry came to a halt in 1944/45 because of bombing by American planes, which destroyed mines and processing works (Bank of Taiwan 1950: 9).

PRODUCTION AND MARKETING STRUCTURE

To further its colonial interests, the Japanese government encouraged Japanese *zaibatsu* to monopolize the production and marketing of Taiwan's coal. Although some Taiwanese entrepreneurs emerged, most of them were linked to the *zaibatsu* through joint ventures.

The management of mining companies

In the early part of the colonial period, most mines were individually owned. The government established a mining area, and granted mining rights of that area to the first applicant. To begin with Japanese adventurers were the ones who got the mining rights. The existence of many small mining areas hindered the mechanization of coal mines. Mines operated by joint-stock companies were established during the period 1916–1927. All the large companies were financed by Japanese investors, except the Taiyang Mining Co. Ltd. which was founded by the Yen family of Jilong, who were Taiwanese. The output of this company with that of the Jilong Coal Mining Co., founded by the Yen family and the Mitsui *zaibatsu*, made up nearly two-thirds of coal production in Taiwan (Yusekai 1924: 51–52). Sixty percent of the stock of the Jilong Coal Mining Co. belonged to Mitsui (Fujita 1925: 50–51). The Taiyang Mining Co. entrusted the Jilong Coal Mining Co. with the management of its mines, the output of which was sold by Mitsui Bussan Co. (Nagahama 1939: 21–22). So the Mitsui *zaibatsu* controlled the production and marketing of the mines of the Yen family, and thus controlled Taiwan's coal mining industry. In addition to the mines owned by publicly quoted companies, there were many mines owned by individuals. Table 11.3 shows a comparison of the output of these two types of organizations. We can see that the output from publicly owned companies comprised 80 percent of total production during 1928–34. Thereafter, production greatly increased under a system of intense administrative control and in response to external demand. Output from individually owned companies increased faster than that from public companies. Because market forces no longer operated under the controlled economy, and because production and sale functions were controlled by the authorities (who adjusted supply and demand and laid down prices), the small individually owned companies were in a good position to increase production with steady prices and good profits. During the period from 1936 to 1945,

Table 11.3 Taiwan output of mines, public and private ownership ('000 metric tonnes)

Year	*Public companies*		*Private companies*	
	Output	*Percent*	*Output*	*Percent*
1928	1,289	81	294	19
1929	1,202	79	328	21
1930	1,201	82	271	18
1931	1,185	81	255	19
1932	1,112	82	242	18
1933	1,452	79	381	21
1934	1,185	78	334	22
1935	—	—	—	—
1936	1,314	75	428	25
1937	1,464	75	489	25
1938	1,557	71	640	29
1939	1,720	66	898	34

Source: Bank of Taiwan (1950: 10)

Table 11.4 Taiwan numbers of mines, classified by output (metric tonnes)

Year	*Over 100,000*	*50,000–100,000*	*30,000–50,000*	*10,000–30,000*	*5,000–10,000*	*Below 5,000*	*Total*
1936	3	4	8	30	16	17	78
1937	4	3	5	33	24	19	88
1938	3	5	7	43	20	19	97
1939	3	5	9	59	30	25	131
1948	—	4	4	41	43	32	124

Source: Bank of Taiwan (1950: 11)

numerous small and medium-sized mines sprang up, as Table 11.4 shows. The smaller mines, with up to 30,000 tonnes production accounted for 80 percent of output in 1935, and this increased up to 87 percent from 1936 to 1939. Especially noticeable was the increase during 1939. The sharp increase in the output of individually owned companies, as shown in Table 11.3, was due to the appearance of new small and medium-sized mines. It is possible that the large companies had reached their productivity limits, and that the increasing output from 1940 (see Table 11.1) reflects more production by small and medium-sized companies.

The marketing structure

Various markets for Taiwanese coal were available during the colonial period. It was used in Taiwan itself for sugar factories, locomotives and household purposes and for producing coke. It was also used for both foreign and domestic steamships, and it was exported to Shanghai, Fujian, Guangdong, Hong Kong, Japan and Southeast Asia. The international political and economic situation influenced both the export and domestic market. As a Japanese colony, Taiwan was linked to the world economic system. Its economic development was dominated by Japan and strongly influenced by the world economy. As Table 11.1 shows, the output of Taiwan's coal mines was always less than the sales (including exports) before 1940, except in the period 1927–1931. Japanese and Fushun (Chinese) coals were imported to make up the shortage. After 1930, Japanese coal was no longer imported (Bank of Taiwan 1950: 39). During the period 1916–1927, output rose by 27.87 percent; sales, on the other hand, rose by 29.19 percent, and the exports greatly increased – especially to areas other than Japan. This indicates that the authorities and managers of the mining industry had worked hard to develop overseas markets in addition to increasing supplies for domestic production. The increasing quantity of coal used in Taiwan indicated Taiwan's gradual industrialization. The amount of coal used for steamships also increased. Both were closely related to the growth of merchandise exports from Taiwan (Zhou 1957: 33–40). Japan was not an important market for Taiwanese coal by the Second World War. The amount of coal exported to Japan accounted for less than 20 percent of total exports before 1931 except for the period from 1922 to 1925. Instead of using Taiwanese coal (which was inferior to Japanese coal) as a domestic Japanese fuel resource, the Japanese government wanted Taiwan to be self-sufficient in industrial fuel. They also planned to export Taiwanese coal to Southern China and Southeast Asia in order to make up shortfalls which the Japanese coal industry could not supply. Japan also intended to coordinate the development of the coal industries in Japan and Taiwan, to fulfill the demands of the Japanese navy invading Southeast Asia. Sales inside the country were conducted differently from exports. Mines could compete with one another for the domestic market, while *zaibatsu*, especially Mitsui Bussan, controlled exports up to 1940. Mitsui Bussan merely imported Japanese coal to Taiwan in the early colonial period. After the Russo-Japanese war (1904–1905), Mitsui Bussan became interested in exporting Taiwanese coal, which was controlled by Taiwanese and other Japanese at that time. Mitsui Bussan defeated these rivals and began to sell coal to two Japanese steamship companies, Osaka Shosen Kaisha and Nihon Yusen Kaisha. It also supplied fuel to the Taiwanese railway, to Taiwan's monopoly enterprises and to sugar factories, and it exported coal to Hong Kong and South China. Mitsui Bussan sold the coal produced by the Jilong Coal Mining Co. and the Taiyang Mining Co. Mitsui Bussan established its dominant position in the field of selling Taiwanese coal through the cooperation of the Yen family. In 1920, Taiwanese coal sold by Mitsui reached 830,000 tonnes, 72 percent of the total output (Fujita 1925: 282–295). Although competition from Ōkura, Suzuki Shōten and Mitsubishi appeared afterward, Mitsui constantly controlled more than 70 percent of the total output (Fujita 1925: 295–306).

The Taiwan Coal Company Ltd. was founded in order to control the production and marketing of Taiwan's coal in 1941. The marketing process is shown in Figure 11.1. The Taiwan Coal Company, being responsible for sales, accepted consumers' applications for coal, planned the distribution, and then reported to the Industry and Mining Bureau of the government. After getting approval from the bureau, the Taiwan Coal Company permitted the coal merchants to make deals and told the producers to deliver the coal. First the mines delivered the coal according to the company's instruction, then they squared the accounts. The wholesale dealers were appointed by area and kind of industry. To prevent manipulation by merchants, the authorities strictly examined the quality of the coal, controlled prices, and stipulated the commission that wholesale dealers should get (Bank of Taiwan 1950: 29; Society of Mining in Taiwan Province 1969: 822–823; Zhou 1958: 182). The committee members of this company were appointed by the Bureau of Colonial Production of the Taiwan Governor-General's Office. All twelve members were Japanese industrialists except

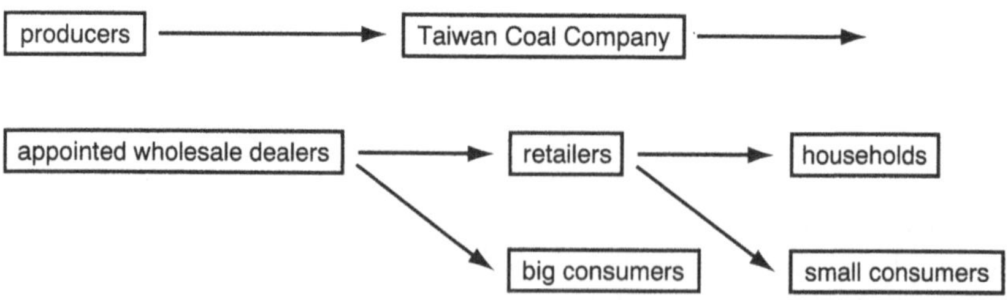

Figure 11.1 Marketing process of the Taiwan Coal Company

Yen Qin-xian, who was president of Taiyang Company at the time. The investors in the Taiwan Coal Company were as follows: the coal industry union, 2.5 million yen; the coal merchants' union, 1.5 million yen; a steamship company and Taiwan Takushoku Company, (Taiwan Development Company), 2 million yen; Taiwan Power Company, 0.5 million yen; sugar industry interests, 0.3 million yen; the Bank of Taiwan, 0.2 million yen (*Taiwan Kogyokaiho* 1941: 203). This company thus combined the production, distribution, and consumption of coal under official supervision.

THE POSITION OF TAIWAN WITHIN THE GREATER JAPANESE COAL MINING EMPIRE

Economic development in Japan was characterized by rapid industrialization. Coal gradually shifted from being an important export before the twentieth century to being an important import from the 1960s. Here only the period before the Second World War will be examined. Domestic demand for Japanese coal in the late nineteenth and early twentieth centuries was for factories (63 percent), ships (24 percent), and railways (13 percent). After the First World War, the proportion used by ships increased to 27 percent, while that of factories and railways decreased to 61 percent and 12 percent respectively. The foreign markets for Japanese coal were Shanghai, Hong Kong and Singapore (Umemura and Yamamoto 1989: 210–216). In the three decades around the turn of the century, the total volume of coal produced sharply increased (Takemoto 1921: 50–60). The average growth rate of coal production from 1885–1915 was 9.6 percent, exceeding the 7.5 percent growth rate of fiber production (Nishigawa 1990: 22). Japan also imported bituminous coal for naval use, mainly from Great Britain and Fushun (Takemoto 1921: 47), and a small amount of coal from its colonies Korea and Taiwan. However, it is not correct to define these colonies as suppliers of food and materials to Japan, and as export markets for Japan's industrial products. Such a role for its colonies would suggest that Japan had inadequate resources and limited markets, a situation similar to that of Britain. Although Taiwan and Korea were important sources of food for Japan, they were not important suppliers of other raw materials and accounted for only 7–9 percent of Japan's mining needs (Yamazawa 1988: 18; Nakamura 1988: 240–248). While Taiwan and Korea imported 40 percent of Japan's heavy industrial products, such heavy industrial products accounted for only 11–12 percent of Japan's total output on the eve of the Second World War (Yamazawa 1988: 24). The colonies were poor, and so could not purchase much from Japan.

As for the coal industry, Japan not only controlled the industry in Taiwan, but also invested in China. Japanese investments reached 56.7 percent of the value of China's coal mining industry. During the Second World War, Japan occupied most of China, and the output of coal from Japanese-controlled mines amounted to 88 percent of the coal produced in China (Yen 1955: 126, 132–133). The colonies became important sources of raw materials and semi-manufactured goods for Japan. This helped the development of heavy industrialization in Japan and also increased demand for the final products of the iron and steel industries. Japanese *zaibatsu* also invested in Korea's coal mining industry in order to supply the iron industries and the railways there. If they had not, Korea would have depended on coal from Manchuria, Japan and Taiwan (Takemoto 1921: 62). Japan worked toward making Taiwan self-sufficient in coal by the early twentieth century. Taiwanese coal had to expand its market overseas subsequently because of overproduction. One of the main reasons for overproduction was the limited demand for coal in Taiwan. This was the result of the colonial policies of Japan. Japan only encouraged the development of agricultural production such as rice and sugar. Coal had to find an overseas market beyond supplying Taiwan's sugar factories, railways and steamships. In this situation, where *zaibatsu* monopolized coal exports, Taiwanese coal exports were coordinated with the coal production of Japan and Manchuria. As a result, the main overseas markets for Taiwanese coal were South China and Southeast Asia. This distribution structure of Japan's coal mining empire remained unchanged during the Second World War. For example, in 1940, the total output of the empire was 93.84 million tonnes of coal. While Japan produced 57.31 million tonnes (61 percent), and Manchuria supplied 21.13 million tonnes (22 percent), Taiwan only produced 2.84 million tons (3 percent) (Yamamoto 1992: 124–125). Due to the limitations of Taiwan's natural environment and Japan's successful policy of an "agricultural Taiwan," the island's industrialization fell behind that of Korea and Manchuria. Taiwan, being unable to supply raw materials and resources to its monopolist, became a relay station in Japan's economic and political invasion of Southeast Asia.

CONCLUSION

The mining industry in Taiwan was subject to rising cost. The coalfields in Taiwan were shallow and occurred in small deposits, so the coal mining industry was unstable (Bank of Taiwan 1950: 3, 24). After the beginning of the First World War, Japanese *zaibatsu* and several Taiwanese capitalists invested in coal mining enterprises in Taiwan under the guidance of the colonial government. Because industry as a whole in Taiwan was still in its infancy, the demand for coal as fuel was small. Consequently, coal investors, faced with the problem of overproduction, began to try to expand their overseas markets. The international economic and political situation influenced the development of the coal mining industry. Moreover, the Mitsui and Mitsubishi *zaibatsu* monopolized the coal export business. Meanwhile, the principal coal mining operations of these *zaibatsu* were in Japan, and even the output from mines in Manchuria (northeast China) and Korea was larger than that from Taiwan. Taiwan's native investors could not develop foreign markets on their own, and due to the island's late industrialization, domestic demand for coal could not increase as fast as production. Under such circumstances, the development of the coal mining industry in Taiwan was limited. Expansion of coal production in Taiwan depended directly on exports, which were restricted in the period under study because of the low profile of Taiwan in the multi-regional production structure managed by the *zaibatsu.*

BIBLIOGRAPHY

The Bank of Taiwan (1950) *Taiwan Zhi Mei* (The Coal in Taiwan), Taipei: The Bank of Taiwan.

Chen, Tsu-yu (1992) 'The Yen Family of Keelung and Taiwan's Mining Industry during the Japanese Colonial Occupation' (in Chinese, *Family Process and Political Process in Modern Chinese History*), Taipei: Institute of Modern History, Academia Sinica, 621–656.

Fujita, Kiichi (1925) *Taiwan Tankoshi* (The Gazetteer of Taiwan's Coal Mining), Taipei: Mitsui Bussan Co., Taipei Branch.

Nagahama, Minoru (ed.) (1939) *Gan Koku-nian Kun Shoden* (A Biography of Mr Yen Guonian), Jilong: Shoyukai.

Nakamura, Takahide (ed.) (1988) *Niju Ko zo* (The Dual Structure), Tokyo: Iwanami Shoten.

Nishigawa, Toshisaku (ed.) (1990) *Sangyōka no Jidai* (The Epoch of Industrialization) Vol. 1, Tokyo: Iwanami Shoten.

The Society of Mining in Taiwan Province (ed.) (1969) *Taiwan Kuangyeshi* (The History of Mining in Taiwan), Taipei: The Society of Mining in Taiwan Province.

Sotokufu Shosankyoku (Taiwan Governor-General's Office, Bureau of Colonial Production) (1935) *Taiwan No Kogyo* (The Mining Industry in Taiwan), Taipei: Taiwan Sotokufu.

Takemoto, Takedo (1921) *Taiwan Tangyoron* (A Discourse on Taiwan's Coal Mining), Taipei: Nanpo Keizai Kenkyusha.

Taiwan Jihpo (*Taiwan Times*) (1929) 'The Unusual Depression of Coal Mining Industry in This Island,' August.

Taiwan Kogyokaiho (The Newsletter of the Association of Mining Industries in Taiwan) (1941) 'Taiwan Sekitan Kabushiki Kaisha Setsuritsu Keika' (The Process of Founding the Taiwan Coal Company), No. 203, Taipei, April 30.

Taiwan Nichinichi Shinpo (hereafter *TNS*) (*Taiwan Daily News*) (1907) 'Taiwan's Coal and Fuzhou', No. 2871, Nov. 27.

TNS (1908) 'Amoy and Taiwan Coal', Nos. 2903, 2904, Jan. 7, 8.

TNS (1919) 'The Negotiations of Coal Merchants', No. 6906, Sept. 6.

TNS (1921) 'The Coal in Southern China and South-east Asia', No. 7643, Sept. 12.

TNS (1924) 'The Sharp Increase of Taiwan Coal Exportation', No. 8599, April 25.

TNS (1926) 'The Prosperous Exportation of Coal', No. 9318, April 14.

Taiyang Mining Co. (ed.) (1978) *Taiyang Gongsi Liushinian Zhi* (in Chinese, *The Sixty-Years History of Taiyang Mining Company*), Taipei: Taiyang Mining Co.

Umemura, Yūji and Yamamoto, Yuzo (eds) (1989) *Kaiko to Ishin* (Port-opening and Restoration), Tokyo: Iwanami Shoten.

Yamamoto, Yuzo (1992) *Nihon Shokuminchi Keizaishi Kenkyu* (The Research on the Economic History of Japanese Colonies), Nagoya: Nagoya Daigaku Shuppankai.
Yamazawa, Ikuhei (1988) *Nihon No Kezaihakten To Koksaibungyo* (Japan's Economic Development and International Division of Labor), Tokyo: Tokyo Shinposha.
Yen, Zhong-ping (1955) *Zhong-guo Jindai Jingjishi Tongji Ziliao Xuanji* (The Selected Works of Statistical Materials of Modern Chinese Economic History), Beijing: Ke-xue Chubanshe.
Yusekai (ed). (1924) *Gan un-nen Ko Shoden* (A Biography of Mr Yen Yun-nian), Jilong: Yusekai.
Zhou, Xian-wen (1957) 'Riju Shidai Taiwan Zhi Duiwai Maoyi' (Taiwan's Foreign Trade in the Japanese Colonial Period), *Taiwan Yinhang Jikan* (Quarterly Journal of the Bank of Taiwan) 9: 1, Taipei, June.
Zhou, Xian-wen (1958) *Riju Shidai Taiwan Jingjishi* (Taiwan's Economic History in the Japanese Colonial Period), Taipei: The Bank of Taiwan.

12

TRADE, INSTITUTIONS, AND LAW

The experience of Mexican California

Karen Clay

California was bound by trade to the Pacific Rim. Already in the first half of the nineteenth century, California's products, such as hides, tallow, furs, horses, and lumber, reached markets in the Pacific ports of Latin America, Mexico, Hawaii, and China, and goods from or transshipped through those ports found a market in California. Reflecting its importance, trade is a recurring theme in this volume. Trade across the Pacific predated California's active participation in it (Chapter 2). The French presence in California was tied in part to trade (Chapter 7), and almost as soon as the New Almaden mine was recognized as a source for quicksilver it became an important item in trade (Chapter 13). An open question, however, is how this trade was organized.

This chapter examines the organization of trade in Mexican California between 1830 and 1846. Although historians have studied the hide and tallow trade and the activities of individual merchants, little is understood about the institutions within which trade was conducted. What is known is that the central figures in Californian trade were the merchants. In the late 1820s and early 1830s, these merchants, who were primarily American or British by birth, began to act as intermediaries between the ships' captains and supercargoes, who represented California's links to the Pacific Rim and the Atlantic, and the Spanish-speaking residents in towns along the coast. A complex system of trade began to develop at this time among the larger merchants.

Trade in Mexican California prospered under conditions that appear to have been less than hospitable. The economy labored under the burden of the lack of state enforcement of contracts, a persistent scarcity of specie, an absence of banks, uncertain arrival of ships, and continuing political unrest. Although California had a legal system, the judicial officer, the *alcalde*, did not enforce his decisions in civil cases (Langum 1987). In contrast, in modern economies the legal systems facilitate trade by enforcing valid contracts, if necessary by sending an agent of the state such as a sheriff out to seize property or conduct a sale of assets to meet the obligation. As a result of the scarcity of both specie and banks, most Californian trade involved the exchange of hides and tallow for goods rather than the exchange of either for money. The unpredictable arrival of ships and the regional political climate led to uncertainty about the supply of goods, prices, and tariffs, as well as the future of trade more broadly.

Credit was a central feature of trade. At all levels of trade, credit eased the restrictions that barter, with its simultaneous exchange of goods, would have imposed. For example, extending goods on credit to merchants permitted ships' captains to unload their cargoes prior to loading hides and tallow for the return trip. The credit that merchants received enabled them to sell to their retail customers on a year-round basis. Merchants often engaged in trade with their counterparts in other towns to address problems of over- and under-supply caused by the uncertain arrival of ships, and to sell regionally produced domestic goods. The use of credit for inter-merchant trade meant that goods could be shipped unaccompanied and payment made when mutually convenient.

From an economist's vantage point, the fact that trade in Mexican California progressed beyond barter to a credit-based system is noteworthy. The extension of goods on credit and the fact that the legal system did not enforce credit contracts opened the possibility that individuals would not pay their debts. The successful use of credit throughout the period suggests that the threat of some type of sanction made these debt contracts self-enforcing; that is, individuals who received credit had some incentive to pay their debts. The norms that individuals adhere to, together with the punishments imposed by community members for violating these norms, are often referred to by economists as private-order institutions to differentiate them from legal institutions, which are characterized by state enforcement of a legal norm.

A private-order institution enabled California merchants to trade with one another on credit. The merchants' ability to support the use of credit in trade with one another is of particular interest because the merchants were neither dependent on other merchants, as they were on ships' captains and supercargoes, for supplies, nor did they have the advantage of proximity, social ties, or kinship ties, as was often the case with their retail customers. Surviving business correspondence, descriptions of trade in the accounts published by American and British visitors, and court records make it possible to study the private-order institution that supported trade: the coalition.

The results of this research are of interest to both economists and historians. For economists, they shed light on the operation and evolution of private-order institutions, which are not well understood in enabling the expansion of trade despite their historical importance. For historians, they shed light on the merchants' trade with one another, trade in California more generally, and the political role that the merchants' played in California.

BACKGROUND

Three nations governed California during the nineteenth century. Spain ruled until Mexican independence in 1821. California continued as a part of Mexico until 1846, when it was annexed by the United States. This annexation was formalized in the Treaty of Guadalupe-Hidalgo in 1848, and California became a state in 1850. During the Spanish and Mexican periods, California was a thinly settled frontier. By 1846 a trickle of overland migration had become a small stream of settlers. The discovery of gold at Sutter's Mill on January 24, 1848, however, kicked off an unparalleled movement of persons, animals, and equipment to California. The arrival of 250,000 people over four years, 1848–1852, ended its frontier status.

Trade in California during the Mexican period can be divided into two phases. The first ended in the early 1830s and was characterized by the commercial dominance of the Roman Catholic missions, which controlled most of the coastal land between San Francisco and San Diego. The mission priests traded directly with the ships' captains and supercargoes who brought goods to the coast. This trade, which centered on the exchange of cattle products for luxury food items such as chocolate, sugar, and tea, as well as cloth for the Mission Indians and religious items, was almost universally based on credit. Despite opposition by the missions, the Mexican government offered land grants to individuals for the purpose of ranching. The cumulative effect of these grants created a new class of producers. Thus, by 1830 the relative importance of the Catholic missions in trade had already begun to diminish. Their secularization in the mid-1830s, which reduced them to the status of parish churches and returned their land to the government, abruptly ended their dominance.

The second phase lasted from the early 1830s to 1846. It was associated with the dominance of individual producers and the rise of merchants as intermediaries. Spain had made fewer than twenty-five grants of land up to 1821. Mexico was considerably more liberal, and the pace at which land was granted accelerated even further after secularization. With the exception of a few in the interior, such as John Sutter's New Helvetia, grants were made near the coast out of former mission lands. Most encompassed between 4,000 and 40,000 acres and could support hundreds of head of cattle. The cattle were slaughtered beginning in the early summer, and the next few months were taken up with drying the hides and rendering the fat. Ranchers then took the hides and tallow to the nearest coastal town, where they used them to pay debts and buy goods. The products eventually passed to the ships' captains, whose crew would salt the hides and prepare the tallow and other goods for shipment.

The move from a small number of large producers (missions) to a large number of smaller producers (ranchers) led to a change in the organization of trade. Resident merchants, who were, like many of the ships' captains and supercargoes, predominantly British or American by birth, began to act as intermediaries. The presence of Anglo-American merchants and wholesalers in California reflects the expansion of British and American traders throughout Latin America in the first half of the nineteenth century. Many merchants had arrived in the 1820s and early 1830s as ships' captains or supercargoes and had settled in the larger towns. They had assimilated by learning Spanish, and, with few exceptions, by converting to Catholicism, becoming Mexican citizens, and marrying into local families. The size and scope of their enterprises varied significantly. Petty and small merchants were itinerant or operated shops, whereas larger more prosperous merchants owned branch stores, ranches, flour mills, and other businesses in addition to their retail establishments.

MERCHANTS

The largest merchants, who are the subject of this chapter, frequently used one another as agents. An agent would typically sell goods and collect debts for another merchant or a partnership of merchants. For example, in 1842 John C. Jones, a Santa Barbara merchant, left Thomas Larkin, a Monterey merchant, rum to sell for him on consignment (Larkin 1951–1968, 3: 78). Nathan Spear, a Monterey merchant, asked Abel Stearns, a Los Angeles merchant, in a letter dated November 2, 1837, to act as his agent to collect a debt: "I take the liberty of enclosing to you a bill against Juan B. Leandry . . . You will do me a favor to use your influence to try to collect it" (Stearns). Henry Fitch, a San Diego merchant, acted as an agent for a number of different partnerships, which involved both buying goods abroad and selling them on the coast between 1839 and 1842 (Ogden 1981; Miller 1972). Merchants acting as agents regularly handled several hundred and often thousands of dollars' worth of goods. A contract defined the precise nature of their agency relationship. In a debt contract, the agent agreed to repay a fixed amount, whereas in consignment and partnership contracts he agreed to provide trade-related services in return for a share of the profits. In partnership contracts, unlike in the other two cases, the agent also usually supplied capital on an equal footing with the other partners.

By employing one another as agents, the California merchants confronted the complexities of trade on the coast in a cost-reducing manner. Such an arrangement enabled merchants to respond to supply and demand shocks in their local markets by buying or selling goods on credit or consignment. Hiring another merchant to collect debts owed by residents of his town and to transact business in that locale limited the time a merchant spent away from his store as well as the costs of travel. Further, by employing an agent to conduct business in distant towns, a merchant made efficient use of another merchant's knowledge of and influence within his local market. Finally, partnership agreements to purchase goods abroad ensured a supply of appropriate goods at reasonable prices, and partially diversified the risks that the merchants faced.

Hiring an agent was in many cases cost-reducing, but the provision of goods on credit or investment in a partnership also opened up the possibility that the agent would act opportunistically. The potential gains to cheating were often large. For instance, Abel Stearns's trial balance for 1846 listed David Alexander and John Temple as owing him $1,077 and investments in excess of $3,000 in the *Ninfa* voyage (California Historical Documents). According to an account current between Nathan Spear and William Hinckley, dated July 1836, Hinckley owed Spear $16,945.77½, one of the largest debts of the period (Spear). Merchants were extending and receiving credit that was large, both in absolute value and relative to their wealth. In absolute value, these sums frequently represented three or more years' worth of wages for a semi-skilled worker (Larkin 1951–1968, 1: 217; Spear: Leese to Spear, October 27, 1837). In relative terms, they represented a sizable fraction of the net worths, $38,000 and $55,000 in the mid-1840s, of Thomas Larkin and Abel Stearns, respectively, the two largest merchants of the day, and an even larger fraction of the net worth of smaller merchants (Bancroft 1874–1890, 4: 706; California Historical Documents, Trial Balance).

Despite the agents' ability to engage in opportunistic behavior, the interaction among the California merchants was characterized by trust and a relatively low level of conflict. Complaints regarding the quality of goods, discussion of merchants' behavior, and commentary on current disputes appeared in letters moderately frequently, but the number of disputes in which action is taken beyond complaint to a request for compensation or arbitration is quite small. In the ninety-eight letters in the Larkin Collection, written between Thomas Larkin and other California merchants during the years 1839 to 1842, reference is made to two minor and two major disputes. The collection of a debt and the interest on a loan were the subject of the two minor disputes. The two major disputes, which were resolved in one case through arbitration and in the other through settlement, arose because the parties did not provide the agreed-upon quality and quantity of goods (Larkin 1951–1968, 1: letters between Larkin and Hinckley, Jones, Paty, and Temple).

The trust did not arise because the merchants were innately honest or because the Mexican legal system in California provided contract enforcement. The merchants explicitly identified themselves as self-interested. James Forbes, a San Francisco merchant, wrote to Thomas Larkin in 1845, "Self interest is the predominant passion in the human breast and that in California, this passion is mingled with that of bitter enmity wherever those interests clash" (Larkin 1951–1968, 3: 113). John C. Jones, a Santa Barbara merchant, had, just a couple of weeks earlier, addressed this point when he succinctly wrote, "There is no friendship in trade" (Larkin 1951–1968, 3: 78–9). The legal system did not provide state enforcement of contracts. In civil cases, the judicial officer, the *alcalde*, relied on community pressure rather than force to induce the parties to comply with his decision. Furthermore, complex jurisdictional problems and the *alcaldes'* limited powers of enforcement made the resolution of disputes between individuals who did not live in the same town all but impossible. The merchants' profound distrust of the courts inspired by these problems, and the courts' use of civil rather than common law, prompted settlement of disputes outside the legal system (Langum 1987).

In their studies of trust and order, social scientists have identified four types of sanctions that support norms and, by extension, cooperation (Landa 1994). The first three (religious, physical, and social sanctions), do not appear to have played a significant role in supporting the norms that facilitated cooperation among the California merchants. Although most of the merchants were nominally Roman Catholic, there is no indication that they shared common religious beliefs or that religious sanctions were used. Their letters reveal few references to God, and none imply that merchants' misdeeds will be punished in the afterlife. Similarly, there is no evidence that physical sanctions played a role in contract enforcement. Individual merchants did not, like the fictional Zorro, demand their payments at sword point or engage in other means of violent self-help. The fact that the merchants lived in different towns and were therefore difficult to punish through social sanctions suggests that these played at most a secondary role. In some instances merchants were related by blood or marriage, which may have made such sanctions more effective. Their letters, however, offer little indication that these ties constrained them.

The elimination of three of the four types leaves economic sanctions as the remaining one, and the type that in all likelihood supported norms among the merchants. In light of studies of merchants in other settings, which have shown that economic sanctions played an important role in supporting cooperation, the fact that merchants in California would use them is not entirely surprising. Merchants punished individuals who violated group norms by cutting off credit, refusing to pay debts, and otherwise reducing economic interaction with them. That the merchants used economic sanctions does not, however, answer the question of how trust was maintained, because it does not tell us how these sanctions were actually used to support trade. In particular, this fact does not identify the private-order institution that enabled the merchants to trust one another.

Two kinds of private-order institutions, both of which impose economic sanctions for cheating, could have supported cooperation among merchants in California.. The first is based on interaction between pairs of merchants. Cooperation is profitable for both parties, so the cessation of cooperation is the economic sanction. For instance, a merchant might hire another merchant as his agent at a wage that is higher than the agent would otherwise receive, with the explicit promise that the agent will always be rehired as long as he has been honest. By paying the agent a high enough wage, the merchant can make it more appealing for the agent to be honest and continue his employment than to cheat. Economic theory has demonstrated that cooperation (honesty) is feasible if a principal, the merchant, can perfectly monitor the agent's behavior and even in some cases where he can only imperfectly monitor the agent's behavior (Fudenberg and Tirole 1991). Under many circumstances, however, a merchant may not be able to commit to rehire an agent.

The second kind of private-order institution is based on interaction among groups of merchants. These institutions may be able to support cooperation, even if merchants are only able to hire other merchants for periods of short duration. A familiar example of such an institution would be a guild or club (Greif *et al.* 1994). Both guilds and clubs are formal institutions in which a central authority identifies cheating and organizes punishment. A less familiar example would be a coalition (Greif 1989, 1993). A coalition is composed of a small number of individuals who interact frequently and are linked by an information network. The information network, by providing market information and reports on merchants' behavior in distant towns, allows the coalition to limit a merchant's ability to misrepresent his profits. By making the hiring of merchants as agents contingent on the agents' past behavior and paying them a sufficiently large wage, coalition members collectively provide agents with incentives for honesty. Unlike a guild or club, a coalition is decentralized in the sense that individual merchants identify and punish cheating.

THE COALITION

Evidence from the historical record supports the hypotheses that a coalition supported cooperation among the merchants in California. The merchants' letters document the existence of the characteristic components of a coalition: an information network that linked the California merchants, norms that specified appropriate behavior and the importance of reputation in the hiring of other merchants as agents. If the institution were based on interaction between pairs of merchants, one would expect to see long-lasting, frequent interaction between pairs of merchants. In fact, merchants often interacted infrequently and for a single task. If the institution were a club or guild, rather than a coalition, one would expect to find evidence of a central organization such as membership lists or printed rules. In particular, one would expect to see centralized determination of cheating. Surviving letters and other business materials from the California collections do not include membership lists, rules, directives to punish cheating, or any other indications of centralization.

The information network furnished the merchants with vital market news, informed them when merchants failed to adhere to standards of appropriate conduct, and kept them apprised of the subsequent events in these disputes. Henry Fitch's September 7, 1839, letter of inquiry to Abel Stearns demonstrates the importance that the merchants attached to the information that they received through the network. Fitch wrote, "I have not received the news I expected from the North, therefore I hope you will write me by the next post without fail . . . I wish in particular to know about what time I may expect the Catalina along, and in fact any news that you will have the goodness to communicate will be thankfully received" (Stearns). The network also provided merchants with information regarding the activities of other merchants. In an 1845 letter, John C. Jones, a Santa Barbara merchant, revealed detailed knowledge of market conditions in Monterey, which he had doubtless acquired from the information network. He wrote to Talbot Green, Thomas Larkin's clerk, stating, "I presume from the *very low* price for which you appear to have sold it [the rum], that it was of course for cash . . . I shall say nothing of 3 arrobas of rancid butter for $37.4, but the *9 Gallon keg at 4* Dollars is rather too outrageous" (Larkin 1951–1968, 3: 78).[1]

Norms set common standards of behavior for merchants in their economic interaction with each other and permitted misconduct to be identified as such by other merchants. Their letters referred to these norms frequently. Common law and prevailing practice formed the basis for the norms, which covered contractual issues such as failure to provide goods of customary or agreed upon quality and defined liability in instances such as when a merchant refused to pay a bill of exchange that had been transferred to a third party (Langum 1987: 183). Deviations were a source of dispute. William Hinckley outlined in an October 10, 1839, letter to Abel Stearns the reasons why James McKinley should pay a debt owed by Charles Hall: "McKinley has proved himself to be a partner in the business with Hall, by having paid debts of his"; "McKinley has paid all the other debts on the same footing with mine"; and "McKinley's alleged reason for not paying was, that it was a gambling debt which the acct proves to be false" (Stearns).

California merchants implicitly referred to the importance of reputation in their correspondence. When he wrote to Nathan Spear on February 13, 1836, William Hinckley linked past behavior and future interaction: "I have begged hard of Thompson to let me have 5 or 10 casks [of brandy] for you but he is not inclined to accommodate and I hope you will remember it when he is on the coast" (Spear). An 1839 letter from Thomas Larkin to John Temple shows that Larkin also conditioned future interaction on past behavior: "I thought you would be willing to take good flour at a fair price, in order to continue trade between us . . . It seems not!" (Larkin 1951–1968, 1: 18). Another example of this link is found in a November 28, 1840, letter by Henry Fitch to Abel Stearns: "He [Williams] acted very sharpley [*sic*] with me about the dried beef . . . I shall know how to deal with him another time" (Stearns).

Reputation played the twin roles of preventing misconduct in situations where merchants had an opportunity to act dishonestly and of spurring resolution of disagreements that arose. Thomas Larkin alluded to the importance of a merchant's reputation in preventing misconduct in an April 21, 1844, letter to Monsieur Gauden, the owner of the French ship *Ganges*: "I cautioned him [the captain] about his crew and with trading with People on shore who had no character to sustain as merchants, as for their own profit they would ill advise him" (Larkin 1951–1968, 2: 102). Often the California merchants arranged for an impartial survey of goods that arrived damaged. In 1840 Isaac William reported to Thomas Larkin that he had had several merchants known to both of them examine Larkin's flour and that Larkin could appoint additional individuals if he so desired (Larkin 1951–1968, 1: 61, 138). When disagreements arose, most letters expressed a desire for an amicable resolution to the problem (Larkin 1951–1968, 1: 66, 190; Stearns: Larkin to Stearns, January 7, 1834).

A dispute that arose between Nathan Spear and William Hinckley provides additional evidence of the importance of reputation. While Nathan Spear was away, William Hinckley made out their account current, which showed that Spear owed him $10,657.50. News traveled quickly, for Stephen Reynolds reported to Spear from the Hawaiian Islands in a letter dated May 1, 1838, "Letters have been received here stating your a/c current with W.S. Hinckley makes him quite in funds, say 11,000 dollars, some were almost frantic with joy" (Spear). On May 5th, in a scathing letter to Hinckley regarding the inaccuracy of the account current, Spear referred to the relationship between reputation and credit and the fact that the California merchants refused to extend additional credit to Hinckley: "It was also told me that you had got in your hands a document (the a/c [account] current) which you meant to show as you went down the coast to show what had become of your property and by that means reestablish your credit" (Spear).

As Hinckley's experience suggests, the California merchants appear to have punished those with bad reputations by refusing to grant them further credit. Hinckley's problems with his reputation are worthy of further investigation. On December 12, 1837, Stephen Reynolds hinted in a letter to Nathan Spear from the Hawaiian Islands at these problems: "If one tenth of the Reports concerning WSH are true I shall feel very sorry as it would seem he pays little regard to his word, and less to his obligation" (Spear). Reynolds may have been referring to Hinckley's agreement with Thomas

Larkin and James Watson to exchange hides for cash in which he took the cash and then failed to produce the hides (Larkin 1951–1968, 4: 15).[2] The results of his actions were that the California merchants refused to extend him further credit. Some Hawaiian merchants went further and refused to pay him the money they owed (Spear: Reynolds to Spear, May 1, 1838).

In 1845 and 1846 Alpheus Thompson, a Santa Barbara merchant, had similar problems. In 1845 Thomas Larkin received concerned letters from two firms in Mazatlan, which had extended credit to Thompson, inquiring about his ability to pay (Larkin 1951–1968, 3: 163–4, 166–8). In reply, Larkin stated that he believed that Thompson's credit was good, although Thompson had a reputation for being slow to pay (Larkin 1951–1968, 3: 263). In 1846 Thompson complained to Larkin that a supercargo, who had unsuccessfully tried to collect a debt, "is determined to injure us as far as talk goes" (Larkin 1951–1968, 1: 203). By that time his credit problems were not limited to the supercargo. His hunters discovered that Thompson's credit was not good in Monterey when they attempted to obtain supplies there (Nidever 1937: 61, cited in Langum 1987: 205).

The economic punishment that the merchants did impose was sufficiently severe that it eventually led individuals to resolve the problem rather than face continuing punishment. The problems associated with a business in which Charles Hall and James McKinley had allegedly been partners first arose in late 1837, when McKinley refused to pay debts owed by Hall after Hall left the business. The dispute wore on through 1838 and into 1839. On November 1, 1839, William Hinckley finally reported to Abel Stearns, "After some trouble I am happy to be able to say that McKinley has settled the affair by consenting to pay in full of all claims, and also to go to Monterey to adjust the affairs of the Don Quixote" (Stearns).

The merchants' norms, together with the economic sanctions that they imposed, constituted a private-order institution: the merchant coalition. The norms defined appropriate conduct. Economic sanctions were applied for violation of the norms. Community, rather than pairwise, application of these sanctions enabled merchants to support cooperation even though they could not necessarily commit to rehire another merchant in the future. Because the coalition provided incentives for honesty by tying past conduct to future interaction through the use of reputation, punishment was seldom necessary. The result was trust and cooperation among the merchants.

The coalition lasted until the gold rush of 1848–9. The two primary factors in the decline in the merchant coalition appear to have been the chaos induced by the changes that the gold rush brought and the opportunities that these changes offered to a number of the most prominent merchants. The radical shift of trading activity northward to San Francisco and the vast number of new merchants in the region made the orderly assimilation of these merchants into the coalition and the maintenance of the information network all but impossible. Further, the flooding of San

Francisco with goods, and the lack of transportation along the coast because of the desertion of virtually all crews in San Francisco, limited the need for and ability to conduct inter-merchant trade. With the waves of migration into California in the 1840s and 1850s came the opportunity to make fortunes in land speculation and ranching; it is these opportunities that prominent merchants such as Abel Stearns, Thomas Larkin, and David Spence seized. Thus, the decline in merchants' need and ability to hire agents, the rise of outside opportunities for some members, and possibly strains on the information network precipitated the dissolution of the merchant coalition.

CONCLUSION

In California during the 1830s and 1840s, trade among the merchants was organized through a coalition. Prior to the 1830s, the Catholic missions had been a powerful economic as well as social and religious force in California because they controlled nearly all of the agricultural land along the coast. With the rise of individual producers and the secularization of the missions, merchants began to act as intermediaries between ships' captains and supercargoes and local residents. Gains were possible from trade with other merchants in foreign goods because of the sporadic arrival of ships, and in domestically produced goods because of regional specialization. Credit greatly facilitated this trade by allowing merchants to send goods unaccompanied and pay when it was mutually convenient. The alternative was to travel with the goods and engage in face-to-face barter. The coalition arose to enable merchants to capture the gains to trade on credit. It did so through norms that specified appropriate behavior, an information network which allowed merchants to detect deviations from these norms, and the application of economic sanctions for violation of these norms. The norms and economic sanctions for violation of the norms created incentives for merchants to be honest in their dealings with other merchants. As a result, trade based on credit flourished in the absence of state enforcement of contracts.

Answers to the question of the organization of trade among California merchants bear on two historical issues. The first is the broad organization of trade among merchants, their customers, and ships' captains and supercargoes. This chapter has addressed the central puzzle of how this trade was organized. The study of merchant interaction provides clues to how they resolved similar problems regarding the use of credit with their retail customers. Interestingly, economic relationships among the residents of towns, including the merchants, were supported by an institution that was very similar to the merchant coalition. Understanding this institution provides insight into why the firms that sent goods to the coast failed in their attempt to take over retail trade with the decline of the missions. These firms, because they lacked strong ties to the local community, experienced significant difficulties collecting debts and quickly began to sell to the merchants.

The second issue is the political role that the merchants played. A number of merchants, notably Thomas Larkin, became active in financing the California government. Their political ties arose from their economic prosperity, which enabled them to provide funds. At the same time, the continued prosperity of merchants who lent to the government and those who did not was tied to the current government. With these ties came risk. A conflict between Abel Stearns and the governor led Stearns to be expelled briefly from California. Thomas Larkin lent heavily to Micheltorena's government and encountered difficulty collecting from his successor. More significantly, the merchants were directly and indirectly responsible for transforming trade with the United States into formal political ties. Larkin wrote numerous letters to newspapers, which excited interest in California and attracted immigrants. His letters to government officials in Washington raised their awareness of California and led to his appointment as consul. Many merchants took little direct action, but their presence gradually broke down some of the cultural barriers between the United States and Mexican California.

NOTES

1 An *arroba* is 25 pounds. Emphasis is in the original.

2 The exact timing of this is uncertain, because Larkin mentioned it many years later. Larkin's description does, however, date it as occurring before August of 1842.

BIBLIOGRAPHY

Bancroft, H. (1874–1890) *History of California*, 7 vols, in *The Works of Hubert Howe Bancroft*, 39 vols., San Francisco: History Company. Reprinted (1963–1970) *History of California*, Santa Barbara: Wallace Hebberd.

California Historical Documents Collection, Henry E. Huntington Library, San Marino, California.

Fudenberg, D. and J. Tirole (1991) *Game Theory*, Cambridge, Mass.: MIT Press.

Greif, A. (1989) "Reputation and Coalitions in Medieval Trade: Evidence on the Maghribi Traders," *Journal of Economic History*, 49: 857–882.

—— (1993) "Contract Enforceability and Economic Institutions in Early Trade: The Maghribi Traders' Coalition," *American Economic Review*, 83: 525–548.

Greif, A., P. Milgrom and B.R. Weingast (1994) "Coordination, Commitment, and Enforcement: The Case of the Merchant Guild", *Journal of Political Economy*, 102: 745–776.

Landa, J. (1994) *Trust, Ethnicity, and Identity: Beyond the New Institutional Economics of Ethnic Trading Networks, Contract Law, and Gift Exchange*, Ann Arbor: University of Michigan Press.

Langum, D. (1987) *Law and Community on the Mexican California Frontier*, Norman, Okla.: University of Oklahoma Press.

Larkin, T.O. (1951–1968) *The Larkin Papers: Personal, Business, and Official Correspondence of Thomas Oliver Larkin, Merchant and United States Consul in California*, edited by G.P. Hammond, 10 vols and index, Berkeley: University of California Press.

Miller, R.L. (1972) "Henry Delano Fitch: A Yankee Trader in California, 1826–1849," Unpublished Ph.D. dissertation, University of Southern California.

Nidever, G. (1937) *The Life and Adventures of George Nidever*, edited by W.H. Ellison, Berkeley: University of California Press.

Ogden, A. (1981) "Captain Henry Fitch, San Diego Merchant, 1825–1849", *Journal of San Diego History*, 27: 238–259.

Spear, N. Spear Papers, Bancroft Library, Berkeley, California.

Stearns, A. Stearns Collection, Henry E. Huntington Library, San Marino, California.

13

CALIFORNIA QUICKSILVER IN THE PACIFIC RIM ECONOMY, 1850–90

David J. St. Clair

Did Pacific rim trade play an important role in developing the early California economy? This chapter will argue that it did. Most histories, however, emphasize the state's integration into the domestic United States economy after 1848, neglecting Pacific Rim trade and ignoring this important factor. Nowhere is this neglect more striking than in the case of California's quicksilver mining industry.

Quicksilver is mercury, a liquid metal with unique properties and uses. Historically, its most important use has been in the extraction and recovery of gold and silver from ores. The great outflow of silver from Spanish America was dependent on quicksilver from the Almaden Mine in Spain, and the Huancavelica Mine in South America.

Quicksilver was discovered in California before the Gold Rush, making it one of the first minerals mined in the region. It quickly became one of the state's largest mining industries. Until the end of the nineteenth century, quicksilver was second only to gold in value of output (California Miners' Association 1899: 430). The value of California quicksilver produced in the nineteenth century was about a quarter of the value of all gold and silver mined from Nevada's Comstock Lode. And since quicksilver was indispensable to gold and silver refining, California quicksilver played a crucial role in the California Gold Rush and the Nevada silver boom. The New Al'maden Quicksilver Mine was California's first and largest quicksilver mine. Named after the great Almaden Mine in Spain, New Almaden became the richest single mine in California history, producing a profit that rivaled the profits from all the Comstock mines combined.[1]

Recognition of quicksilver's importance in California and Nevada history has faded with the development of new methods of gold and silver recovery. This chapter seeks to remedy this, and to argue that the development of California quicksilver must be seen in a Pacific Rim context. The emphasis on domestic factors such as the Gold Rush, the Comstock boom, and the political annexation of California have all tended to obscure the role of Pacific Rim trade in the discovery and development of New Almaden. A better understanding of this Pacific Rim connection enhances our understanding of early California development.

The name "quicksilver" derives from mercury's color and liquid state throughout the normal range of climatic temperatures. It is primarily mined from cinnabar, a reddish rock containing mercury sulfide. It is readily extracted by heating cinnabar to vaporize the quicksilver, and then condensing the vapor.

Cinnabar and quicksilver have been mined since antiquity. One of the earliest uses of cinnabar was as a body paint. Later, quicksilver was used in the production of vermilion, a prized red pigment. Quicksilver has also been used in explosives, in the plating of mirrors, in scientific instruments, and in medicines.

But quicksilver's most important use was in the recovery of gold and silver from mineral ores. Quicksilver has an affinity for gold and silver that was known to ancient alchemists and miners. In 1554, the Patio Process for recovering silver and gold with quicksilver was invented in Mexico.[2] Ore was crushed, wetted, and quicksilver, salt, and copper added. The mixture was spread out in large patios and periodically mixed. The quicksilver formed an amalgam with gold and silver. The amalgam was then recovered and heated to vaporize the mercury, leaving the precious metals behind. The mercury vapor was collected and part of the mercury was recovered for further use.

In the 1860s, the Washoe Process was invented to treat silver ore from the Comstock Lode. The Washoe Process employed mercury amalgamation, improving on the Patio Process by replacing the patio with vats and adding heat to speed up and improve recovery.[3]

The dramatic outflow of silver from the New World that began in the sixteenth century was made possible by the Patio Process. There were other ways of extracting silver, such as through smelting, but these methods were usually expensive and often impractical. Mexican and Peruvian silver mines soon came to depend on mercury amalgamation to work their ores, and the quicksilver trade was placed under a crown monopoly. Silver and gold output soared.

Historically, deposits of cinnabar in exploitable concentrations have been rare. Only a handful of mines have produced the bulk of world output. A single mine, the Almaden Mine in Spain, dominated world quicksilver production for centuries. Colonial gold and silver mines in Mexico and Peru relied on quicksilver from Almaden and from another rich mine discovered in 1563 at Huancavelica, Peru. From the mid-sixteenth century to 1850, Almaden produced over 2.83 million flasks of quicksilver, or about 50.7 percent of the western world's output.[4] Huancavelica produced 1.5 million flasks, or about 26.9 percent, while mines at Idria, Slovenia, produced about 1.25 million flasks, or 22.4 percent. Almaden and Huancavelica

Table 13.1 New Almaden and California quicksilver production 1850–90 (in 76.5-pound flasks)

Year	*New Almaden*	*New Almaden % California*	*California*
1850	7,723	100.0	7,723
1851	27,779	100.0	27,779
1852	15,901	79.5	20,000
1853	22,284	100.0	22,284
1854	30,004	100.0	30,004
1855	29,142	88.3	33,000
1856	27,138	90.5	30,000
1857	28,204	100.0	28,204
1858	25,761	83.1	31,000
1859	1,294*	10.0	13,000
1860	7,061*	70.6	10,000
1861	34,429	98.4	35,000
1862	39,671	94.5	42,000
1863	32,803	80.9	40,531
1864	42,489	89.5	47,489
1865	47,194	89.0	53,000
1866	35,150	75.5	46,550
1867	24,461	52.0	47,000
1868	25,628	53.7	47,728
1869	16,898	50.0	33,811
1870	14,423	48.0	30,077
1871	18,568	58.6	31,686
1872	18,574	58.7	31,621
1873	11,042	39.9	27,642
1874	9,084	32.7	27,756
1875	13,648	27.2	50,250
1876	20,549	27.4	75,074
1877	23,996	30.2	79,396
1878	15,852	24.8	63,880
1879	20,514	27.8	73,684
1880	23,465	39.2	59,926
1881	26,060	42.8	60,851
1882	28,070	53.2	52,732
1883	29,000	62.1	46,725
1884	20,000	62.7	31,913
1885	21,400	66.7	32,073
1886	18,000	60.0	29,981
1887	20,000	59.2	33,760
1888	18,000	54.1	33,250
1889	13,100	49.5	26,464
1890	12,000	52.3	22,926
Total	916,359		1,567,770

Source: Compiled and calculated from Day (1893b: 166)
Note: * The New Almaden Mine was closed by court injunction from October 30, 1858, through January 1861. Small amounts were nonetheless produced

Table 13.2 European quicksilver production, 1850–88 (in 76.07-pound flasks)*

Year	*Almaden and Idria (combined)*	*Almaden*	*Idria*	*Italy*
1850–54	101,517			
1855–59	110,058			
1860–64	122,117			
1865–69	153,224			
1870–74	165,608			
1875–79	208,200			
1880		41,640	12,358	
1881		50,353	11,333	
1882		46,591	11,663	
1883		46,143	13,152	6,065
1884		43,099	13,967	7,850
1885		46,739	13,503	6,965
1886		51,199	14,496	7,375
1887		53,276	14,676	7,500
1888		51,872	n/a	n/a

Source: Compiled from Day (1890: 105–6)
Note: * Flasks here are smaller than the 76.5-pound flasks used in the United States at this time

were usually able to meet the demands of the Mexican and Peruvian mines, but the threat of quicksilver shortages and high quicksilver prices were constant concerns. At times, colonial officials had to import quicksilver from Idria, and even tried unsuccessfully to import quicksilver from China (Bakewell 1971: 150–80).

By the early nineteenth century, Huancavelica was exhausted and quicksilver production in the western world was essentially confined to Almaden and Idria. However, by 1835, Almaden and Idria had both been acquired by the Rothschild family, giving them a monopoly in quicksilver production.

NEW ALMADEN AND CALIFORNIA QUICKSILVER

Quicksilver was discovered in a cave in the hills south of San Jose, California, in 1845. The cave was across the Santa Cruz Mountains from Monterey, the Mexican capital of Alta California. Originally called the Santa Clara Mine, its name was changed to New Almaden after ore assays revealed quicksilver concentrations even higher than those found at the great Spanish mine.

Sporadic production at New Almaden occurred between 1846 and 1848, with some quicksilver being shipped to Mazatlan, Mexico (Splitter 1947: 41). But full production did not begin until 1850. New Almaden's production is shown in Table 13.1, while European quicksilver output is shown in Table 13.2. New Almaden output quickly surpassed Almaden and Idria and prompted the discovery of other quicksilver mines in California. From 1850 to 1900, California quicksilver mines produced half of the world's output. California mines were thus able to meet the rapidly increasing demand for quicksilver stemming from gold and silver discoveries in California, Nevada, other western states, Canada, Alaska, and Australia. In the late 1870s, California mines were producing two-thirds of the world's output of quicksilver and putting pressure on the Rothschild cartel. The cartel was unable to maintain price discipline, leading to vigorous competition for world markets in the early 1880s.[5]

Because cinnabar deposits at New Almaden tended to be erratic and illusive, output fluctuated through the years. But continuous production went on until 1927, and intermittent production continued until 1973. But by 1890, the rich cinnabar ores were exhausted. This exhaustion and the availability of data have limited the study here to the period 1850 to 1890.

CALIFORNIA QUICKSILVER EXPORTS?

Historians have generally linked the development of New Almaden and California quicksilver mining with the California Gold Rush and the Comstock silver boom. Rossiter Raymond cited reports in 1875 that "most of the metal [quicksilver] is consumed at the mines in the different mining states and territories, the Comstock mines using the largest amount of any one section" (Raymond 1875: 14). In *California Gold*, Rodman Paul wrote that at New Almaden,

> a small amount of mercury was secured in 1848. The mine did not come into production on a significant scale, however, until two and a half years after Marshall's discovery at Coloma. The Gold Rush gave the New Almaden company a huge local market for their product, and conversely, after 1850 New Almaden was able to provide the gold miners with an indispensable aid to their operations
>
> (Paul 1947: 273)

In *Mercury: A History of Quicksilver*, Leonard Goldwater expresses a similar view: "The discovery of gold in California in 1848 and subsequent gold discoveries in various parts of the West up to the 1870s created a huge demand for mercury to be used for purification of the precious metal by amalgamation" (Goldwater 1972: 48). He also claims that cinnabar had been discovered at New Almaden in 1834, or even earlier, and attributes the delay in developing the mine to a lack of demand and to a lack of zeal on the part of California's Mexican officials. To Goldwater, California's admission to the United States was therefore the crucial factor in developing California quicksilver because it brought American administration and American demand to New Almaden.

According to this view, the discovery of silver at the Comstock Lode in

Nevada in 1859 further augmented the domestic demand that began with the Gold Rush. In his extensive history of the New Almaden mine, Jimmie Schneider describes how Comstock Washoe mills placed "sizable orders" for quicksilver after 1873 (Schneider 1992: 115–17). Likewise, Henry Splitter describes the Comstock as a "very good customer" in the 1880s, when Nevada mills were taking an average of 3,299 flasks per year (Splitter 1947: 34). New Almaden received 60 percent of these sales, with other California mines picking up the remainder.

Chronology and proximity have caused most historians to view California and Nevada demand as the catalyst for developing California quicksilver. However, there are some hints in the literature of sizable California quicksilver exports. An early visitor to the mine in 1854, Mrs S.A. Downer, wrote that:

> The amount of quicksilver used in California, is much less than is generally supposed. Notwithstanding the increase in gold mining, the whole amount for home consumption, does not exceed one hundred flasks per month. The exports to Chile and China, are not large; much of that imported by the latter country, is mixed with sulfur and reconverted into the vermilion of commerce. Seven-ninths of the sales are made to Mexico, where it is extensively used in the silver mines of that country.
>
> (Downer 1854: 123)

Schneider also noted that New Almaden "freely supplied all of the Hispanic-American and California markets," and later referred to "excessive export sales" between 1865 and 1872 (Schneider 1992: 21). He added that there were 46,000 flasks awaiting consignment sale in China and London in 1865, an amount only slightly less than the record 47,194 flasks produced at New Almaden that year (Schneider 1992: 40). Splitter reports that exports to China were "heavy" in 1865, averaging about 3,000 flasks per month (Splitter 1947: 33). But like Schneider, he did not develop any data on exports beyond this isolated observation. Donald Brown repeats Splitter's observation about the size of China exports in 1865, but offers no additional data. He does, however, state that after 1884 quicksilver prices and the income of California quicksilver mines became "dependent upon the entire world consumption and not so much upon California and Nevada mines" (Brown 1958: 85).

This author challenges the view that California gold and Nevada silver were the principal catalysts to the development of the California quicksilver mines. California and Nevada were significant markets for California quicksilver, but Pacific exports were more important. The impetus for the development of New Almaden was Mexican demand for quicksilver, along with a bounty offered by the Mexican government for a Mexican quicksilver mine. After the US annexation of California, mercury exports to the

Pacific Rim usually exceeded domestic shipments. While not the catalyst for developing California quicksilver, California and Nevada gold and silver mines were significant beneficiaries of California quicksilver production.

Two lines of inquiry are developed here. First, the events surrounding the discovery of quicksilver will be reviewed. This is an important issue because it has been alleged that New Almaden development was delayed by a lack of demand or by lax Mexican government policy. Second, California quicksilver export statistics have been compiled. One important reason historians have neglected the study of exports has been the absence of comprehensive export data. Mine statistics have often been of little value because agents were used to handle sales. In addition, government reports often presented export data in a confusing and unusable manner. For example, export statistics usually included shipments to New York. While these shipments may have been exports from the Pacific economy, they were not exports in the traditional sense. The procedures used to compile export data are discussed in the Appendix (see p. 229).

WHEN WAS QUICKSILVER DISCOVERED AT NEW ALMADEN?

Was the development of New Almaden delayed in the Mexican period due to a lack of demand for quicksilver that was alleviated by the Gold Rush? Some scholars, including those cited above, have suggested that this was the case. This erroneous view can be traced in large part to confusion over when quicksilver was discovered at New Almaden. The cinnabar cave at New Almaden had long been mined by Indians seeking the red earth to use for body paint. They apparently traded cinnabar over a wide geographical area and had dug about sixty feet into the cave by the time padres from Mission Santa Clara were taken there, sometime around 1800 (Splitter 1947: 36). The red pigment from the cave was used to decorate the mission walls.

The cave was subsequently worked by Mexican miners as a gold and silver mine in 1824, and again in 1835. The gold and silver mine was never successful. Goldwater claims that cinnabar was recognized by at least 1834, but not developed (Goldwater 1972: 48). He also cites evidence that there were "hints" of mercury deposits in California as early as 1796, but that a lack of demand and the disinterest of Mexican officials stopped any development. Splitter also writes about a delay, but of a different kind (Splitter 1947: 37–8). He recounts a version of a popular story about how the padres who were taken to the mine immediately recognized the red rock as cinnabar. The Indians also told them of discovering "living water" in the rocks when fire was brought into contact with the red stones. The padres supposedly understood this to be quicksilver, but suppressed the knowledge, fearing an influx of the ungodly who would corrupt the souls of the Indians.

Neither of these very different accounts is very convincing. The story about the padres suppressing knowledge of quicksilver at the mine is implausible and irrelevant. The existence of the mine was never suppressed, so the real question is why didn't the miners work it for cinnabar? In any case, if the padres did suppress knowledge of quicksilver at the mine, slow development would not have been the result of any lack of demand or lax political officials.

Goldwater's argument is more serious and rests on his claim that cinnabar was identified by 1834. But Schneider provides a more compelling account of the discovery of quicksilver at New Almaden that contradicts this claim.[6] The miners who worked the mine in 1824 and 1835 were very puzzled by their inability to extract the gold and silver that they thought was responsible for the colour and weight of the rock. Since miners in Mexico had encountered similar problems with silver ores that defied recovery, it is easy to see why the New Almaden operators thought that they faced a similar problem.[7] On one occasion, the gold and silver miners at New Almaden applied quicksilver to the red ore, but became more confused when the quicksilver disappeared into the rock.

Schneider convincingly argues that cinnabar was never identified at New Almaden before 1845. It was identified in October of that year when General Jose Castro and Captain Don Andres Castillero were passing through Santa Clara on the way to Sutter's Fort to negotiate the purchase of Sutter's property on behalf of the Mexican government. Captain Castillero had some training in mineralogy and learned of the mine that had been abandoned because the silver could not be extracted. Castillero was taken to the cave, but was unable to solve the extraction problem. But he too was convinced that gold or silver was present, and he initially registered a claim for "a vein of silver, with a ley of gold" with the local *alcalde* (Schneider 1992: 13).

Sometime on the return trip from Sutter's Fort, Captain Castillero solved the mystery. The heavy metal had to be quicksilver. In an after-dinner experiment at Mission Santa Clara, Castillero heated the red rock and captured the vapor in a small glass. Quicksilver condensed on the inside of the glass, confirming his discovery.

Castillero immediately understood the value and implications of the discovery. A quicksilver mine could be far more valuable than a gold or silver discovery, and Castillero was convinced that he had found the basis for a "wedding" of Alta California with Mexico. In addition, a significant mercury mine in Alta California would qualify for a substantial bounty. In 1843, the Mexican government, through the Junta de Formento, had established a $100,000 bounty for any Mexican citizen who discovered and developed a quicksilver mine in Mexican territory. Castillero thus registered his quicksilver discovery with local officials and proceeded to produce about three hundred pounds of quicksilver a day. He followed the

Mexican custom of dividing interest in the mine into twenty-four *barras* or shares, keeping half for himself and distributing the rest to his partners at the mission, to the original miners, and to California officials.

In April 1846, Castillero returned to Mexico with ore samples that assayed at a remarkable 35 percent, far richer than Almaden. The Junta de Formento gave Castillero a nine-point program for meeting the bounty requirements. In the process of complying with the bounty requirements, Castillero was on a ship returning to California when he learned of the Bear Flag Revolt. Fearing that his claim would not be honored by the Americans, he cut short his journey and never returned to California. Moreover, since California had fallen out of Mexican control, the bounty would never be paid.

In this situation, Castillero sold part of his *barras* to the firm of Barron-Forbes of Tepic, Mexico. The owners of Barron-Forbes were British businessmen who had become naturalized Mexican citizens. With interests in Mexican silver mines, Barron-Forbes understood the significance of a California quicksilver mine. In addition to buying shares, they negotiated a contract with Castillero to develop the mine (Schneider 1992: 17–18).

Barron-Forbes operated the mine for the next fourteen years, extracting over 340,000 flasks of quicksilver valued at more than 18 million dollars, half of which was profit.[8] But they were quickly drawn into a long and bitter fight over ownership of the mine. The dispute grew out of the poorly defined boundary separating two Mexican land grants in the area. In addition, there were allegations that Captain Castillero had not properly registered his claim, and that he had engaged in fraud and land grabbing. The Barron-Forbes claim (based on the Castillero claim) was challenged by a group that held title to the adjacent land and claimed that the mine was on their property. At the same time, the United States government claimed that the mine was actually on public land. The US Attorney-General called New Almaden "the richest land on the globe," and the government sought to protect its interests with a court injunction in October 1858 that closed the mine for two years. President Lincoln also sent troops to seize the mine in 1863, but the order was quickly rescinded. The matter went through district and circuit courts before finally reaching the United States Supreme Court.[9]

The court proceedings lasted seven years and produced one of the most voluminous cases ever heard by the Supreme Court. The case took many twists and turns, but in the end the Supreme Court invalidated Castillero's claim in 1864. Barron-Forbes subsequently sold their interest in the mine to the Quicksilver Mining Company for $1.75 million. This Pennsylvania corporation had been organized by the opposing litigants. The Quicksilver Mining Company operated the mine into the twentieth century.

It is clear that cinnabar was not identified at New Almaden until 1845 and that there was no delay in developing the mine after that. Shipments were made to Mazatlan in 1848 and full production, under the auspices of Barron-Forbes, began in July 1850. Given the political and ownership uncertainties and the necessity of bringing in equipment and constructing the reduction works, it is remarkable how fast the mine was developed. Barron-Forbes was certainly aware of the demand for quicksilver in Mexico, and there is no evidence to suggest any delay due to concerns about insufficient demand. The California Gold Rush merely presented Barron-Forbes with an unexpected bonus. Given the history of quicksilver in Mexico and the bounty, it is hard to believe that New Almaden would not have been quickly developed into a world-class mine even in the absence of the Gold Rush.

CALIFORNIA QUICKSILVER AS AN EXPORT INDUSTRY

Table 13.3 presents a compilation of California quicksilver exports.[10] It is clear that exports, primarily to Pacific Rim countries, usually outpaced domestic shipments. For the entire period 1852–90, 57.1 percent of California quicksilver was exported. Exports were greatest during the first two decades, the period that includes both the California Gold Rush and the discovery of the Comstock Lode. Exports took 67.5 percent of output in the 1850s and 72 percent in the 1860s. Exports in the 1870s took 51 percent of output, with exports lower in the early part of the decade and higher in the second half. During the 1870–74 period, exports only took 34.9 percent of output. Overseas shipments recovered in 1875 and remained substantial through 1883. Exports in the 1880s amounted to 45.3 percent of output, but lower exports during this decade were due to the dramatic decline in exports after 1883. Exports in the period 1880–83 were 61.9 percent, but fell to half this rate thereafter.

Before 1870, exports always exceeded domestic shipments, often by a wide margin, except in 1859 when New Almaden was closed by court injunction. For the entire 1852–90 period, domestic consumption exceeded exports in only twelve years (1859 excluded). All of these years were in the period 1870–74 or after 1883.

New York "exports" are shown in Table 13.4. As noted above, shipments to New York were usually included in export statistics, and thus those figures had to be removed where possible (see Appendix, p. 229). New York shipments for years where data are available amounted to 68,648 flasks. This exceeded shipments to South America and all countries except China and Mexico. If New York exports are added to true exports, the percentage of California quicksilver "exported" out of the western United States during the 1852–90 period rises to 61.6 percent.[11] This left less than 40 percent of output available for use in California and Nevada.

These export figures confirm many of the export observations discussed

Table 13.3 California quicksilver exports, 1850–90 (in 76.5-pound flasks)

Year	*California*		*Exports as % of production*
	Production	*Exports*	
1850	7,723	n/a	n/a
1851	27,779	n/a	n/a
1852	20,000	900	4.5
1853	22,284	12,737	57.2
1854	30,004	20,963	69.9
1855	33,000	27,165	82.3
1856	30,000	23,740	79.1
1857	28,204	27,262	96.7
1858	31,000	24,142	77.9
1859	13,000*	3,149*	24.2
1860	10,000*	9,048*	90.5
1861	35,000	35,395	101.1
1862	42,000	31,482	75.0
1863	40,531	25,919	63.9
1864	47,489	35,223	74.2
1865	53,000	34,050	64.2
1866	46,550	30,287	65.1
1867	47,000	25,953	55.2
1868	47,728	40,006	83.8
1869	33,811	22,915	67.8
1870	30,077	12,788	42.5
1871	31,686	14,405	45.5
1872	31,621	11,896	37.6
1873	27,642	6,359	23.0
1874	27,756	6,455	23.3
1875	50,250	28,673	57.1
1876	75,074	38,046	50.7
1877	79,396	50,906	64.1
1878	63,880	33,365	52.2
1879	73,684	47,383	64.3
1880	59,926	37,210	62.1
1881	60,851	35,107	57.7
1882	52,732	33,875	64.2
1883	46,725	30,072	64.4
1884	31,913	10,874	34.1
1885	32,073	10,302	32.1
1886	29,981	6,091	20.3
1887	33,760	11,394	33.8
1888	33,250	10,684	32.1
1889	26,464	5,930	22.4
1890	22,926	3,425	14.9
Total 1852–90	1,532,268	875,576	

Source: See Appendix, p. 229
Note: * New Almaden mine closed by court injunction

Table 13.4 California quicksilver 'exports' to New York, 1859–90 (in 76.5-pound flasks)

Year	*Exports*	*Year*	*Exports*
1859	250	1875	287
1860	400	1876	3,094
1861	600	1877	n/a
1862	2,265	1878	n/a
1863	95	1879	n/a
1864	1,695	1880	n/a
1865	6,800	1881	n/a
1866	n/a	1882	n/a
1867	2,900	1883	3,100
1868	4,500	1884	8,350
1869	1,500	1885	9,055
1870	1,000	1886	600
1871	800	1887	8,370
1872	1,202	1888	2,320
1873	—	1889	7,030
1874	315	1890	2,120

Source: See Appendix, p. 229
Note: Total New York shipment for years where data is available = 68,648 flasks

above. Actually, Downer's 1854 figure of exports amounting to "seven-ninths" (i.e., about 78 percent) of production was very close to the mark. On the other hand, the marked reduction of the share of output going to exports in the 1870–74 period does not support Schneider's claim of "sizable" orders from the Comstock after 1873. "Sizable" is a relative term, and California quicksilver output did increase dramatically after 1875. Shipments to the Comstock may have seemed "sizable," but exports certainly remained greater. After 1875, exports greatly exceeded domestic shipments until the collapse of the export market in 1884.

The dramatic reduction in overseas shipments that occurred in 1884 followed record California production in the 1870s. This output effectively broke the price discipline of the Rothschild cartel and led to intense competition, especially for the China market.[12] Tables 13.5 and 13.6 show the steep drop in California sales to China in 1884, as the Rothschild cartel cut prices and captured the market. California producers lost the China market in 1884 and never recovered it, beginning a long period of distress for California quicksilver producers.

Splitter's observation about the Comstock being a 'good customer' in the 1880s probably refers to the increased importance of the domestic market after the collapse of exports in 1884. Likewise, Brown's comments about world demand becoming the primary determinant of quicksilver prices and profits after 1884 can only be understood in the context of reference to the loss of the China market.

Table 13.5 California quicksilver exports to selected Pacific countries, 1859–90 (in 76.5-pound flasks)

Year	*Total exports*	*China*	*Mexico*	*South America*	*Total Pacific exports*
1852–58			unavailable		
1859	3,149	1,068	103	1,634	3,149
1860	9,048	2,725	3,886	1,920	9,048
1861	35,395	13,788	12,061	5,030	32,895
1862	31,482	8,725	14,778	5,649	29,982
1863	25,919	8,889	11,590	4,036	24,857
1864	35,223	18,908	7,483	7,049	33,614
1865	34,050	14,250	2,650	7,750	23,650
1866	30,287		Unavailable		
1867	25,953	10,011	10,042	3,800	24,453
1868	40,006	17,785	14,120	2,500	36,005
1869	22,915	11,600	8,060	2,900	22,864
1870	12,788	4,050	7,088	1,300	12,747
1871	14,405	7,900	3,081	2,200	14,287
1872	11,896	4,810	5,038	1,300	11,793
1873	6,359	1,900	3,761	508	6,285
1874	6,455	1,200	4,104	884	6,455
1875	28,673	18,190	5,757	2,183	28,563
1876	38,046	24,526	7,400	3,804	37,396
1877	50,906		Unavailable		
1878	33,365		Unavailable		
1879	47,383		Unavailable		
1880	37,210	19,660	12,413	1,364	35,084
1881	35,107	17,031	15,256	1,171	35,107
1882	33,875	18,965	10,128	2,287	33,848
1883	30,072	16,356	10,157	1,452	30,054
1884	10,874	220	9,330	451	10,815
1885	10,302	233	9,277	361	10,288
1886	6,091	–	5,678	248	6,084
1887	11,394	3,323	6,920	212	10,593
1888	10,684	3,750	5,172	1,388	10,683
1889	5,930	–	5,660	111	5,922
1890	3,425	300	2,890	102	3,419
Total	576,726	250,163	213,883	63,594	549,940

Source: See Appendix, p. 229
Note: Destination of exports data is unavailable for 1852–58, 1866, and 1877–79. Exports for 1866 and 1877–79 are shown in the table but not included in the total

Tables 13.5 and 13.6 also illustrate the distribution of California quicksilver exports. For the years where data are available, China was the largest market, taking 43.4 percent of California exports. Mexico took 37.1 percent and South America 11 percent. Exports to all other countries were insignificant. China and Mexico combined accounted for more than 80 percent of California exports, and it is clear that California quicksilver exports were

Table 13.6 Exports of California quicksilver to Pacific countries, 1859–90 (as a percent of annual exports)

Year	*China*	*Mexico*	*South America*	*Australia*	*Japan*	*Canada*	*Total Pacific*
1859	33.9	3.3	51.9	10.3	–	*	100.0
1860	30.1	42.9	21.2	1.1	–	3.6	100.0
1861	39.0	34.1	14.2	5.2	*	*	92.3
1862	27.7	46.9	17.9	2.5	*	*	95.2
1863	34.3	44.7	15.6	1.2	–	*	95.9
1864	53.7	21.2	20.0	*	*	*	95.4
1865	41.9	7.8	22.2	*	–	–	69.5
1866				Unavailable			
1867	38.6	38.7	14.6	1.2	–	*	94.2
1868	44.5	35.3	6.2	3.9	–	*	90.0
1869	50.6	35.2	12.7	1.3	–	*	99.8
1870	31.7	55.4	10.2	2.3	–	*	99.7
1871	54.8	21.4	15.3	7.6	–	*	99.2
1872	40.4	42.4	10.9	5.4	–	*	99.1
1873	29.9	59.1	8.0	1.7	–	*	98.8
1874	18.6	63.6	11.4	1.5	–	*	100.0
1875	63.4	20.1	7.5	2.9	3.4	*	99.6
1876	64.5	19.5	10.0	2.1	1.1	*	98.3
1877				Unavailable			
1878				Unavailable			
1879				Unavailable			
1880	52.8	33.4	3.7	4.1	*	*	94.3
1881	48.5	43.5	3.3	3.8	*	*	100.0
1882	56.0	29.9	6.8	5.4	1.8	*	99.9
1883	54.4	33.8	4.8	2.6	4.3	*	99.9
1884	2.0	85.8	4.1	1.2	6.2	*	99.5
1885	2.3	90.1	3.5	*	2.9	*	99.9
1886	–	93.2	4.1	1.5	*	*	99.9
1887	29.2	60.7	1.9	*	–	*	93.0
1888	35.1	48.4	13.0	3.0	*	*	100.0
1889	–	95.4	1.8	2.2	–	*	99.9
1890	8.8	84.4	3.0	3.7	–	*	99.8
Total	43.4	37.1	11.0				95.4

Source: Derived from data in Table 13.4.
Note: * = less than 1 percent;
– = no exports. Data is unavailable for 1852–8; 1866 and 1877–9.

overwhelmingly destined for Pacific Rim countries. Over 95 percent of exports went to Pacific markets. Again, Downer seems to have been remarkably accurate in 1854 when she identified the importance of the Chinese and Mexican markets.

Shipments to South America also fell after 1883, and only shipments to Mexico fared well after that year. The Mexican market became increasingly important. We cannot tell from these data if Schneider was correct when he said that New Almaden freely supplied all of the Hispanic-American market, but it is clear that Mexico and South America were important markets for California quicksilver.

Shipments of California quicksilver to China and New York have something in common, both markets primarily supplied vermilion producers rather than precious metal refiners.[13] Vermilion is a manufactured sulfide of mercury, consisting of 86.3 percent mercury. American vermilion production was concentrated in four east coast firms that had mastered a secret and difficult manufacturing process. In 1883 and 1884, American producers consumed 14,102 flasks of quicksilver in the manufacture of vermilion. California quicksilver shipments to New York in 1883 and 1884 totaled 11,450 flasks, or 81.2 percent of the quicksilver used in producing vermilion in those years. American vermilion producers used both California and Rothschild quicksilver, depending on price, and California shipments to New York tended to be very volatile.

In shipping quicksilver to China, California mines were providing a raw material for a highly skilled Chinese manufacturing industry, the reverse of what one normally encounters today. Chinese vermilion was incorporated into products that were traded throughout the world. At one time, officials at New Almaden considered acquiring Chinese technology to enable them to produce vermilion themselves (Raymond 1877: 7). There is, however, no indication that this was ever done.

The demand for quicksilver from vermilion producers has usually been overlooked, but the size of China and New York shipments suggests that it was an important market. Indeed, the Chinese vermilion market was the main battleground in the struggle between California quicksilver producers and the Rothschild cartel.

THE IMPACT OF CALIFORNIA QUICKSILVER

Quicksilver was essential to the production of precious metals in the western United States. While the richest gold placers could be worked without quicksilver, mercury amalgamation greatly increased the efficiency of recovery and was indispensable after the early, rich deposits were depleted. Gold recovery from hydraulic and hard-rock mined ores was very difficult and impractical without quicksilver. This was even more true of silver refining. Mercury amalgamation was virtually the only practical technique available until the invention of the cyanide process in the 1890s. By supplying California and Nevada mills with mercury, California quicksilver mines made gold and silver production possible in the west.

Measuring the impact of California quicksilver on gold and silver output is difficult and clearly counterfactual. California was not the only producer of quicksilver, and it is likely that in the absence of local production Rothschild quicksilver would have been imported. But production at Almaden and Idria would have had to double in order to replace California quicksilver. There is no indication that this would have been possible, regardless of Rothschild intentions. Availability would have been a problem, and delays would have been unavoidable.

Still, some Rothschild quicksilver would have been available, but at what price? The Rothschilds had gone to great lengths to acquire what they had expected to be a virtual monopoly of the world quicksilver market. It is inconceivable that the Gold Rush and Comstock mining would not have driven prices higher. But how much higher? It will be recalled that the Mexican government had offered a bounty when quicksilver was selling for $150 per flask. This was before the California and Nevada discoveries increased demand. When serious production began at New Almaden in 1850, a flask of quicksilver sold for around $100. It would seem reasonable to expect that, in the absence of California production, quicksilver prices would have certainly gone back up to $150 per flask, and probably much higher.

Instead, California quicksilver production dramatically lowered quicksilver prices. Average annual quicksilver prices in San Francisco are shown in Table 13.7. In 1850, quicksilver sold at an average price of $99.45 per flask, with prices reaching as high as $114.75 that year. With full production at New Almaden, prices dropped quickly. In 1858, the average price was less

Table 13.7 Average San Francisco quicksilver prices, 1850–90 (dollars per 76.5-pound flask)

Year	*Price*	*Year*	*Price*
1850	99.45	1871	63.10
1851	66.93	1872	65.93
1852	58.33	1873	80.33
1853	55.45	1874	105.18
1854	55.45	1875	84.15
1855	53.55	1876	44.00
1856	51.65	1877	37.30
1857	48.73	1878	32.90
1858	47.83	1879	29.85
1859	63.13	1880	31.00
1860	53.55	1881	29.83
1861	42.05	1882	28.23
1862	36.35	1883	28.75
1863	42.08	1884	30.50
1864	45.90	1885	30.75
1865	45.90	1886	35.50
1866	53.13	1887	42.38
1867	45.90	1888	42.50
1868	45.90	1889	45.00
1869	45.90	1890	52.50
1870	57.38		

Source: California State Mining Bureau (1917: 47)

than half the 1850 level. In the 1860s, prices dipped to as low as $34.45 per flask. With lower prices, California gold miners were soon improving their yields by adding quicksilver to their pans, rockers, and toms. In the 1870s, Nevada Washoe mills were using California quicksilver that sold for as little as $25.25 per flask.

Lower quicksilver prices affected gold and silver refining costs in two ways. First, it reduced the capital cost incurred in acquiring the quicksilver to charge the mills and Washoe vats. Rossiter Raymond reported in 1871 that one pound of quicksilver was required to process 10 tons of gold ore (Raymond 1871: 29). At the Comstock, about 300–500 pounds of quicksilver were needed to process 3,000 pounds of ore, with one-to-ten apparently the most common ratio (Smith 1943: 43).

Second, lower quicksilver prices reduced the costs stemming from lost quicksilver. Only part of the quicksilver was recovered from the amalgam. Raymond put quicksilver losses in gold refining at between 60 to 65 percent of the quicksilver employed (Raymond 1871: 29). In silver refining, losses incurred with the Patio Process were about 1.5 pounds of quicksilver lost per pound of silver produced (Raymond 1869: 10). The Washoe process was more efficient, and Raymond estimated that Washoe losses might have been only one-third the level incurred with the Patio Process (Raymond 1869: 10). Grant Smith put Washoe losses at between 1.0 and 1.5 pounds of quicksilver lost per ton of ore processed, with richer ores incurring higher losses.[14] Smith considered Comstock quicksilver losses over the years to have been quite substantial, estimating that by 1943, 14 million pounds of quicksilver had been lost (Smith 1943: 257). The cost of this lost quicksilver had to be incorporated into milling prices, thus affecting the cost and profitability of silver mining.

But how great an impact would these higher costs have had on gold and silver output? Precise measurements are not possible at this time, but some estimates can be made. Price significance is essentially a question of demand elasticity for quicksilver. Elasticity in turn depended on demand characteristics such as the size of the input cost in the production process and the availability of substitutes. The price elasticity of quicksilver would therefore vary with its use; that is, it would depend on whether quicksilver was employed in the recovery of gold, in the refining of silver with the Patio Process, in the refining of silver with the Washoe Process, or used in the manufacture of vermilion. Each of these uses will be discussed in turn.

Gold

As noted above, Raymond observed that one pound of quicksilver was required to process 10 tons of gold ore, and that 35 to 40 percent of the quicksilver was recovered in the amalgam. At the same time, he presented data on mining and milling costs at the Ophir Mills in 1870 (Raymond

1871: 29). The Ophir Mills were located in Mariposa County, California, where they milled gold ores for $2.25 per ton. Quicksilver sold at an average price of $0.75 per pound in 1870. If we assume a recovery rate of 37.5 percent, quicksilver costs per ton of ore would amount to 4.8 cents, or only 2.1 percent of milling costs. Since mining costs (including milling costs) ranged from $6.75 to $9 per ton (depending on the mine where the ore was dug), quicksilver costs were a tiny fraction of production costs. They were an even smaller fraction of gold yields per ton.

Earlier, Raymond had characterized the cost of quicksilver lost in the amalgamation process as "very trifling" (Raymond 1869: 10). He did not distinguish between gold and silver amalgamation, but the figures presented here would tend to support his assessment regarding gold. Raymond concluded that quicksilver demand was therefore price insensitive (i.e., inelastic). He further concluded that higher quicksilver prices would not have seriously reduced the demand for quicksilver and gold production. The insignificance of quicksilver costs suggests that this is a warranted conclusion regarding gold refining. In the absence of California quicksilver production, the inelastic demand for Rothschild quicksilver would have driven prices up sharply. But even at $150 per flask, the price in effect when the Junta de Formento established the bounty for Mexican quicksilver, gold mining costs would not have increased very much. Rothschild income would have soared, but gold supply would not have been dramatically reduced.

Patio Process silver

While Raymond seems to have been correct about gold refining, silver presents a different picture. With 1.5 pounds of quicksilver consumed in the production of one pound of silver, quicksilver cost in the Patio Process were far more significant. For example, quicksilver exports to Mexico were highest in 1862 when the average quicksilver price had fallen to $36.35 (Table 13.7). The price of silver in New York in 1862 averaged $1.35 per fine ounce (US Commerce Department 1975: 606). While these are not Mexican prices, they are indicative of the Mexican situation. At these prices, 1.5 pounds of quicksilver would cost $0.713, while one pound of silver would be worth $16.20. Quicksilver costs would therefore amount to 4.4 percent of the value of the silver produced. Precise data on other mining and transportation costs are not available, but these costs were substantial. Quicksilver costs would therefore have had a significant effect on profit margins. In addition, quicksilver prices were quite low in 1862, and Comstock production subsequently lowered silver prices.

Higher quicksilver prices would certainly have cut into silver profits. If quicksilver had sold for $150 per flask, quicksilver costs would have amounted to 18.1 percent of the value of the silver produced in Mexico in 1862. This would have dramatically reduced or even eliminated operating margins and reduced silver production in Mexico and South America. Brading and Cross have stressed the importance of quicksilver price and availability in the colonial Mexican economy (Brading and Cross 1972: 562). While the analysis here is for a later time period, it supports their view.

Comstock silver

Comstock silver production, using the Washoe Process, was more efficient than the Patio Process, but quicksilver costs were still significant. As noted above, Smith put Comstock quicksilver losses at between 1.0 to 1.5 pounds per ton of ore processed. During the boom years of 1859 through 1881, Comstock mills processed 7,189,430 tons of ore that yielded about $320 million in silver and gold.[15] Profits amounted to about $20 million. This was a period of rich ores, so Smith's higher figure of 1.5 pounds per ton seems applicable. On this basis, 10,784,145 pounds of quicksilver would have been lost during these years. Smith estimated that the average price of quicksilver used on the Comstock was 60 cents per pound (i.e., $45.90 per flask). At this price, quicksilver costs would amount to $6,470,487, or 2 percent of revenues. This figure is roughly compatible with Raymond's observation that Washoe losses could have been as low as one-third of Patio Process losses.

Since profits on the Comstock were about 6.25 percent of revenues, quicksilver costs of 2 percent of revenues were significant. Smith called quicksilver costs "enormous" and "startling," and it is not hard to see why (Smith 1943: 254). At $150 per flask, Comstock profits would have been reduced by over 70 percent. It is inconceivable that this would not have affected silver output. The significance of quicksilver costs suggests a much greater elasticity than in gold refining. Raymond's characterization of quicksilver costs as "very trifling" does not seem valid in regard to silver production, either at home or abroad.

Vermilion

Two aspects of the vermilion industry suggest that its demand for quicksilver was far more price sensitive than even silver refining. Because mercury comprises 86.3 percent of vermilion, quicksilver price is the most important component of vermilion cost. Quicksilver prices therefore had a sizable impact on the cost and price of vermilion. For example, between 1882 and 1884, quicksilver costs constituted about 72 percent of the price of vermilion.[16] Even small changes in quicksilver costs had to be recouped through higher vermilion prices.

But vermilion producers were limited in their ability to raise their prices. American, European, and Chinese vermilion producers competed with each other and with producers of many substitute pigments (Williams

1885: 502). Most of the substitutes were inferior to true vermilion, but they still put pressure on vermilion prices.

The magnitude of quicksilver costs and the number of competitors suggest that quicksilver demand from vermilion producers was quite elastic. This would explain why American vermilion producers freely switched between Rothschild and California quicksilver, depending on price. It also explains why the struggle between the Rothschilds and California quicksilver producers was primarily waged in China. The Chinese market was acquired when New Almaden undercut Rothschild prices in China. Until 1884, the world quicksilver trade was often characterized as "an armed truce between Spain and California" (Raymond 1869: 10). But the truce collapsed in 1884 when the Rothschild cartel recaptured the China market through intense price competition.

CONCLUSIONS: WAS THERE A PACIFIC RIM ECONOMY?

This chapter has sought to show that the development of California quicksilver in the second half of the nineteenth century occurred in response to Pacific Rim demand, both foreign and domestic. While the demand from California gold and Comstock silver mining was important, it was the prospect of quicksilver exports to Mexico that sparked the initial development of New Almaden. And even as large quantities of quicksilver were being sent to California and Nevada, California quicksilver exports to Pacific Rim countries usually exceeded domestic shipments before 1884.

Is the notion of a "Pacific Rim economy," then, a useful way to understand the development of California quicksilver mining? It is, to a point. New Almaden was initially developed to serve Mexican and South American mines, and China quickly became a major customer. Pacific Rim exports exceeded domestic shipments. At the same time, California quicksilver facilitated the flow of US and Mexican gold and silver into the world economy. A Pacific Rim perspective seems to be a more accurate and more useful description of this process than does a domestic focus.

However, the Rothschild cartel must temper any Pacific Rim theme. California quicksilver broke the Rothschild monopoly, but with time, competition from this non-Pacific cartel became increasingly important. The battle with the Rothschilds was waged primarily in the Pacific, but it seems more accurate, especially after 1884, to speak of a world, rather than a Pacific, quicksilver market. Consequently, the concept of a Pacific rim economy must be used judiciously.

APPENDIX: THE COMPILATION OF EXPORT DATA

Annual California quicksilver exports and the distribution of those exports were compiled from many sources. No data were available on exports for the years 1850 and 1851, and it is not clear if there were no exports in these years or if there are simply no available data. Consequently, exports for these two years were not measured.

Exports for 1852–71 are found Raymond (1873: 523). The same figures, along with data for 1872 and 1873, are presented in Powell (1874: 81–2). Exports by destination are found in these two sources for the years 1868–73.

Exports by destination for the years 1859–64 are found in Browne and Taylor (1867: 176). Destination of exports for 1865 are found in Brown (1958: 65). His figures were derived from company annual reports.

Destination of exports for 1867 are found in Raymond (1871: 528). Exports by destination for 1874 and 1875 are found in Raymond (1877: 461).

No data on the destination of exports are available for the years 1852–58 and 1866. Consequently, no figures for these years are shown in Tables 13.5 or 13.6. In addition, export figures for these years in Table 13.3 may contain New York 'exports' and thus exaggerate true exports to the extent that New York shipments were not re-exported to Europe.

Exports for 1877–79 were calculated from Williams (1885: 500). Export figures that were expressed in pounds were converted to flasks by dividing by 76.5 (to yield exports in American flasks). These figures appear in Table 13.3, but are not in Tables 13.5 or 13.6 because destination of exports could not be determined with this procedure. New York "exports" may also distort these figures.

Exports and destination of exports for 1880–90 were calculated from Day (1892: 100, 108–9). Figures were derived by tabulating exports to individual countries from port records. New York 'exports' were not a problem here. Rail shipments to Mexico were added to the port figures when they could be specifically identified. The New York shipments shown in Table 13.4 were derived from the same sources discussed above in conjunction with destination of exports. However, data are not available for the years 1880–82, or for 1852–58, 1866, or 1877–79.

NOTES

1 Smith (1943: 296) estimates that the total profits of Comstock silver mines through the boom years from 1859–1881 amounted to about $20 million. Schneider (1992: 19) put New Almaden profits from 1850 through 1864 at $9 million. Day (1887: 167) lists profits for the New Almaden Quicksilver Company for 1871 through 1885 of about $4.3 million. Profits for the intervening years, including the profit from record production in 1865, are not available. Their inclusion would make New Almaden profits comparable with Comstock profits. The characterization of New Almaden as California's richest mine is found in Schneider (1992: ix), and Splitter (1947: 33).

2 For a description of the Patio Process and the problems encountered with mercury shortages and high mercury prices in colonial Mexico and Peru, see Bakewell (1971), especially chapters 6–8; and Brading and Cross (1972: 545–79).

3 The Washoe Process is described in Smith (1943: 41–5).

4 Calculated from Day (1888: 125) These figures do not include production at the Kwei-Chan quicksilver mines in China. Quicksilver had been produced at Kwei-Chan for centuries, but output figures are not available. The Kwei-Chan mines were generally characterized as inefficient and unable to satisfy the Chinese demand for quicksilver. For a description and history of major quicksilver mining regions of the world, see Goldwater (1972).

5 Day (1888: 125). For a discussion of the effects of record California production in the 1870s on the Rothschild cartel, see Brown (1958: 82). For a description of the Rothschild quicksilver cartel, see Goldwater (1972: 40 and 68).

6 The following account of the discovery of quicksilver at New Almaden is drawn from Schneider (1992: 9–18). With the exception of the story of the padres suppressing knowledge of quicksilver at the cave, Splitter is in essential agreement with Schneider's account.

7 See, for example, Bakewell (1971: 143) on the difficulties encountered with an ore called antimony (antimonia), from which silver could not be extracted until copper was added to the amalgam mix.

8 Schneider (1992: 19). The following account of the ownership dispute is drawn from Schneider (1992: 27–38). A fuller account can be found in Johnson (1963).

9 The comments of United States Attorney-General Jeremiah Black are found in Schneider (1992: 30–1). Lincoln's ill-advised order to seize the mine is discussed in Schneider (1992: 37) and Johnson (1963: 79–89). The court injunction closed the mine from October 30, 1858, until January, 1861. However, production records do record sales of quicksilver during the period of the injunction. The record is not clear if this was production in defiance of the injunction or permitted sales from stock. Figures for these years are consistently found in the record and are included in Table 13.3. The timing of sales versus production accounts for exports exceeding production in 1861. Consignment sales were especially troublesome in this regard.

10 Part of this article, including export data, appeared in St. Clair (1994–5: 278–95).

11 Some quicksilver sent to New York was subsequently shipped west to the Colorado mines because it was easier than shipping direct from San Francisco or San Jose. However, most of the New York shipments were destined for the vermilion industry.

12 Brown (1958: 80–2 and 118–20) describes the effects of California output on the Rothschild cartel and attempts by the Rothschilds to coordinate output with California producers. Schneider (1992: 119) also describes efforts by the Rothschild cartel to come to an agreement with California producers in 1881. All of these attempts failed.

13 The following discussion of vermilion is drawn from Williams (1885: 501–2).

14 Smith (1943: 43) put quicksilver losses at 1.5 pounds per ton. However, on page 257, he states that losses exceeded one pound per ton. There is no explanation for these different figures. It is likely that his lower figure may have related to total production through 1943 when tailings were reworked. However, this is only speculation and Smith's estimate is reported here as 1.0 to 1.5 pounds per ton.

15 The figures cited here on Comstock production and profits are from Smith (1943: 291–7). However, the calculation of quicksilver costs and the comments regarding their significance are the author's.

16 This figure is the author's calculation based on quicksilver prices in Table 13.7, and Williams (1885: 501–2).

BIBLIOGRAPHY

Bakewell, P.J. (1971) *Silver Mining and Society in Colonial Mexico: Zacatecas, 1546–1700*, Cambridge: Cambridge University Press.

Brading, D.A. and Cross, H.E. (1972) "Colonial Silver Mining: Mexico and Peru," *Hispanic American Historical Review* 52: 545–79.

Brown, D.C. (1958) "The New Almaden Quicksilver Mines," Unpublished M.Phil. thesis, San Jose State College.

Browne, J.R. and Taylor, J.W. (1867) *Reports Upon The Mineral Resources of the United States*, Washington, DC: Government Printing Office.

California Miners' Association (1899) *California Mines and Minerals*, San Francisco: Louis Roesch Company.

California State Mining Bureau (1917) *California Mineral Production for 1916*, Sacramento: California State Printing Office.

Day, D.T. (1887) US Bureau of Mines, *Mineral Resources of the United States, 1886*, Washington, DC: Government Printing Office.

—— (1888) US Bureau of Mines, *Mineral Resources of the United States, 1887*, Washington, DC: Government Printing Office.

—— (1890) US Bureau of Mines, *Mineral Resources of the United States, 1888*, Washington, DC: Government Printing Office.

—— (1892) US Bureau of Mines, *Mineral Resources of the United States, 1889 and 1890*, Washington, DC: Government Printing Office.

—— (1893a) US Bureau of Mines, *Mineral Resources of the United States, 1891*, Washington, DC: Government Printing Office.

—— (1893b) US Bureau of Mines, *Mineral Resources of the United States, 1892*, Washington, DC: Government Printing Office.

De Quille, D. (1973) *A History of the Comstock Lode*, New York: Arno Press. Reprint of the 1889 edition.

Downer, S.A. (1854) "The Quicksilver Mine of New Almaden," *The Pioneer*, or *California Monthly Magazine*. Reprinted in Eganhoff (1953): 113–23. All citations are to the reprint.

Eganhoff, E.L. (1953) *De Argento Vivo: Historic Documents on Quicksilver and Its Recovery in California Prior to 1860*, Sacramento: Supplement to the *California Journal of Mines and Geology*.

Goldwater, L.J. (1972) *Mercury: A History of Quicksilver*, Baltimore: York Press.

Johnson, K.M. (1963) *The New Almaden Quicksilver Mine*, Georgetown: Talisman Press.

Paul, R.W. (1947) *California Gold*, Lincoln, Nebr.: University of Nebraska Press.

Powell, J.J. (1874) *The Golden State and Its Resources*, San Francisco: Brown and Company.

Raymond, R.W. (1869) *Mineral Resources of the States and Territories*, Washington, DC: Government Printing Office.

—— (1871) *Mines, Mills, and Furnaces of the Pacific States and Territories*, New York: J.B. Ford and Co.

—— (1873) *Statistics of Mines and Mining in the States and Territories West of the Rocky Mountains*, Washington, DC: Government Printing Office.

—— (1875) *Statistics of Mines and Mining in the States and Territories West of the Rocky Mountains*, Washington, DC: Government Printing Office.

—— (1877) *Statistics of Mines and Mining in the States and Territories West of the Rocky Mountains*, Washington, DC: Government Printing Office.

St. Clair, D.J. (1994–5) "New Almaden and California Quicksilver in the Pacific Rim Economy," *California History*, LXXIII, 4: 278–95.

Schneider, J. (1992) *Quicksilver: The Complete History of Santa Clara County's New Almaden Mine*, San Jose, Calif.: Zella Schneider.
Smith, G.H. (1943) *The History of the Comstock Lode, 1859–1920,* University of Nevada Bulletin No. 3, Geology and Mining Series No. 37.
Splitter, H.W. (1947) "Quicksilver at New Almaden," *Pacific Historical Review,* XXV: 33–49.
US Bureau of Mines (1886) *Mineral Resources of the United States, 1885*, Washington, DC: Government Printing Office.
US Bureau of Mines (1908) *Mineral Resources of the United States, 1907*, Washington, DC: Government Printing Office.
US Bureau of Mines (1911) *Mineral Resources of the United States, 1910*, Washington, DC: Government Printing Office.
US Commerce Department (1975) *Historical Statistics of the United States, Colonial Times to 1970*, Washington, DC: Government Printing Office.
Williams, A., Jr. (1885) US Bureau of Mines, *Mineral Resources of the United States, 1883 and 1884*, Washington, DC: Government Printing Office.

14

ENVIRONMENTAL IMPACTS OF THE PACIFIC RIM TIMBER TRADE

An overview

Douglas Daigle

The forests of the Pacific Rim fall into the three broad global groups: tropical, temperate, and boreal, as well as many more specific categories. They include the tropical forests of Indonesia, Malaysia, the Philippines, and Papua New Guinea; the temperate forests of the American Pacific Northwest and Chile; and the boreal or northern forests of Siberia, the Russian Far East, and Canada. Regardless of their ecological differences, these forests and all others are now tied together in a single, global market. This process had its genesis in, and continues to receive much of its impetus from, the Pacific Rim, which has become the major arena for the global timber trade.

There are a number of reasons why this is so. Not only are the most extensive areas of remaining forests found in the Pacific Rim, but the world's fastest growing economies as well, in particular those of China and Southeast Asia. Most of these countries have acute timber shortages, which are being compensated for by increasing imports. The growth of the global timber trade, 300 percent since 1960 (Hagler 1993: 40), has become tied in large part to the economic growth of the Pacific Rim, with serious implications for the world's forests: "the economic development patterns in the countries of the Pacific Rim will largely determine the fate of remaining native forests both temperate and tropical, both hardwood and softwood" (Graham 1993: 36).

The Pacific Rim timber trade in its present shape is not an innocuous trend but a pressing problem, a key factor in a global forest crisis for which solutions need to be found and implemented. The crisis involves the loss of *native* or primary forests, their ecological values and biodiversity. For those concerned with saving native forests, it is vital to understand not only development patterns, but the flows of trade that connect and fuel them. The broad categories of forest types can provide a useful starting point.

Tropical forests have been particularly hard hit since the Second World War. The evolution of timber exploitation in the tropical Pacific, like that of its economic development, has been largely driven by Japan (Kuroda and Nectoux 1989). Japan earned hard currency in the 1950s by importing hardwood logs from the Philippines and exporting processed timber products to the US. Philippine dictator Ferdinand Marcos made a substantial part of his fortune by selling off his country's rainforests, similar to the way that later timber magnates have enriched themselves in Malaysia and Indonesia.

By the end of the 1950s, exports of timber products from Japan had declined because of competition in the US market from cheaper products manufactured in South Korea, Taiwan, and the Philippines. Cheap and abundant tropical hardwood logs were still in demand for Japan's own industrial development, and this continued the depletion of Philippine forests. Today, the Philippines are dealing with the aftermath of this exploitation, with periodic massive mudslides from denuded hills, and little in the way of remaining forests (Postel and Ryan 1991: 74).

Japan next turned to the Indonesian province of Kalimantan, focusing on importation of tropical hardwood logs from 1957 to 1985. During the peak years of 1973 and 1974, Japan consumed over 11 million cubic meters of Indonesian logs (Nectoux and Kuroda 1989). After instituting a ban on the export of raw logs in 1985, Indonesia focused on its domestic plywood and sawnwood industries as sources for export. The growth of Indonesia's domestic industries further strengthened timber concessionaires who controlled the Ministry of Forestry, and forests continue to be cut at high rates for plywood and converted to pulp plantations. With most profits going to timber "kings" and large corporations in Jakarta, the timber trade's role in Indonesia's development has become less attractive (Postel and Ryan 1991: 90).

Responding to the Indonesian export ban, Japan next focused on Malaysia, in particular the provinces of Sarawak and Sabah, to supply its demand for raw logs. Peninsular Malaysia was largely logged out by the late 1970s. Land use policies begun by the British to protect provincial resources from control by the peninsular government ironically allowed officials in Sarawak and Sabah to liquidate freely much of their forests. By 1991, Sarawak was the world's single largest exporter of tropical logs, but with only half of its original forest left. As in Indonesia, control of forest concessions was in the hands of a powerful few (Rainforest Action Network 1994b: 26).

Malaysian timber exports brought in a record $3.1 billion in 1989, but cutting has occurred at twice the level of sustained yield (Postel and Ryan 1991: 78). A 1990 report by the International Tropical Timber Organization estimated that Malaysia could run out of commercial timber by 2001 (World Resources Institute 1992–93). An economic shift to greater reliance on manufacturing is underway, but more than half of Malaysia's exports are still primary products such as timber and oil (World Resources Institute 1993).

With Malaysia's Sabah province instituting its own ban on raw log export, the timber industry's attention has shifted to Papua New Guinea (PNG). Japan and South Korea have been paying top dollar for whole logs after a worldwide rise in log prices during 1993. The spectacular rise in profits led the PNG government in 1993 to approve a 400 percent increase in log export volumes, but 80 percent of all PNG log exports are controlled by one Malaysian company.

Although little of the revenues are staying in PNG, the government has nonetheless allocated two-thirds of 'operable' forests for harvesting. Some government officials and tribal peoples are opposing the rapid increase in logging rates, but since timber companies have purchased over one-third of the commercially viable forests, those attempting to slow the pace of deforestation face an uphill battle (Rainforest Action Network 1994b: 5).

Countries with less extensive areas of forest, such as Australia, Vietnam, Thailand, Myanmar, and much of the rest of Southeast Asia are also being heavily impacted by the spread of the timber trade. Even countries with extremely limited forest areas have come under increased pressure. The volume of logs exported from the Solomon Islands, primarily to Japan and South Korea, doubled from 1991 to 1993 (Rainforest Action Network 1994b: 1).

Overcutting has turned one tropical nation after another into first a supplier of raw logs and then an importer, as its own forests and supplies have been depleted. Despite growing international concern and protection efforts, in most of these countries forestry laws, indigenous rights and claims, and compliance with royalty provisions have routinely been ignored. A particularly vivid exposé of these practices in Papua New Guinea, *The Barnett Report* (1990), summarized the findings of a commission of inquiry into lawless activity of the timber industry (Marshall 1990: 5). The effects of these practices on the native forests, tribal peoples, and endangered species of tropical countries have been overwhelmingly negative, especially when combined with pressures of local agriculture and population growth.

Tropical forests have had the lion's share of media and public attention over the past decade, but the focus of the timber trade has shifted north, and the Pacific Rim has led the way. Temperate forests in the US and Canada, significantly impacted by the expanding Asian markets, have also been the scene of some of the most intense social conflicts arising from the timber trade. The largest instance of civil disobedience in British Columbia's history has occurred at Vancouver Island's Clayquot Sound, one of the last extensive tracts of the coastal temperate rainforest that once stretched from Canada to northern California (Devall 1993: 50).

The political and social conflict over old-growth forests in the US Pacific Northwest received a great deal of media coverage. Export of raw logs from the Northwest to Pacific Rim markets played a significant role in this conflict, since the US domestic market had also taken up to a third of its softwood lumber and plywood from the forests of Washington, Oregon, and northern California during the 1980s. By some estimates harvests on private lands exceeded 'sustained yield' by more than 25 percent during the early 1980s, and cutting on the region's twelve national forests, where most of the remaining old growth is found, surpassed sustainable levels by 61 percent (Postel and Ryan 1991: 78).

The timber trade can now shift the location of its operations more easily, so the domestic American industry has responded to the declining wood supply in the Northwest by moving much of its production to the Southeast. By 1986 the southeast was already supplying 47 percent of the nation's timber harvest, compared to 25 percent in the Pacific Northwest (Postel and Ryan 1991: 78). The markets of the Pacific Rim have reached there as well: South Korea's Donghae Paper Company has been among the corporations seeking to open wood chipping mills in Alabama and Tennessee.

The growing significance of Chile's temperate forests as a source of wood for the Pacific Rim has received less attention. The Chilean timber industry was already exporting to five major wood-consuming countries by 1989: West Germany, Belgium, Brazil, the US, and Japan. Japan received almost one-quarter of Chilean wood fiber exports for that year. Wood from Chile, the US, Canada, and Australia now accounts for over 80 percent of Japan's wood imports (Hagler 1993: 41). Almost one-quarter of Chilean exports that year went to Japan. Chile now accounts, along with the US, Canada, and Australia, for 87 percent of fiber exports to Japan (Hagler 1993: 41).

Chile's forestry exports have more than doubled since 1983 (Hagler 1993). In response to this growth, and as part of a general push to increase its pulp and paper capacity, Chile has accelerated the conversion of its millennia-old native *alerce* forests to monoculture plantations slated for chipping and export. By 1991, Chile had planted 1.3 million acres of managed plantations, 85 percent of which relied on just one introduced (non-native) species, the Monterey Pine (Postel and Ryan 1991: 77).

UN Food and Agriculture figures suggest that in terms of *area*, temperate forests as a whole have been less hit by the timber trade than tropical ones, but considering impact in terms of area alone can be deceptive: large areas of temperate forest continue to be converted to managed monoculture plantations and stands (Dudley 1992). A marked loss of forest *quality* accompanies conversion of native forests into tree farms, even though temperate ecosystems are among the most resilient.

The ultimate 'wild card' in predictions of supply and demand for both the Pacific Rim and wider global markets are the boreal forests of Siberia and the Russian Far East. The *taiga* of the far north is the most extensive tract of forest left on the planet, stretching over 800 million square hectares, including northern permafrost regions as well as more temperate mixed forests, and amounting to 20 percent of global forest cover (Tracy 1994: 1).

Destructive and inefficient forest exploitation was practiced under the Soviet system. The devolution of power since the collapse of the Soviet Union has resulted in the rise of a timber "mafia," while fluctuations in price and supply have slowed exports (Rosencranz and Scott 1992: 294). The vastness of remaining tracts has attracted the notice of multinational timber giants such as Weyerhauser, Georgia-Pacific, South Korea's Hyundai, and a number of Japanese interests (Scott and Gordon 1992: 16). Joint ventures will become more common, and the nearness of the huge Asian markets of Japan, South Korea, and Taiwan virtually ensures greater exports of Siberian timber in the future (Cushman 1996).[1]

Just as Siberia figures prominently in projections of future timber supply for the Pacific Rim and global markets, China will play a major role in future demand for wood products. Rapid economic growth and overcutting of China's domestic forests have brought about an acute timber shortage. The economic reforms of the late 1970s resulted in a jump in domestic demand for wood. Annual harvests almost doubled from 1976 to 1988, but the area of timber-producing forests shrunk by almost 3 million hectares since 1980 (Postel and Ryan 1991: 76).

At the current rate of consumption, China will have harvested all of its remaining productive forests within a decade, but imports can be expected to rise substantially well before that. China has already become the major importer of plywood from Indonesia (Graham 1993: 62). The government has set a goal of planting 30 million hectares of trees by the year 2000, and has planted an estimated 10 million hectares of plantations in the hopes of doubling domestic wood production (Postel and Ryan 1991: 84).

The fragmentation of the Siberian timber industry is a notable exception to prevailing trends in the global timber industry. These trends, from increased integration and centralization in the industry to changes in the technology of wood processing, have had their impetus from Pacific Rim markets. The shift from tropical to temperate and boreal forests as major supply areas is one result. As one author argues:

> Changes in the structure and technology of both forestry and timber utilizations are causing major changes to the ways in which forests are used. In general, manufacturers can use a far wider range of species, ages, and qualities of trees, and demand is moving away from timber to pulp and cellulose. The increasingly international market means that new areas of forest are continually being utilized.
>
> (Dudley 1992)

These changes in structure and technology are in fact shaping the globalization of the timber trade. Raw logs have been replaced by wood chips and pulp in market dominance. A surge in pulp processing has followed on the spectacular growth of the wood fiber trade over the past three decades. In 1960, wood chips amounted to less than 10 percent of the fiber trade; by 1990 that amount had risen to 54 percent (Hagler 1993: 40). There are several reasons for this: wood chips are particularly advantageous for ocean trade, since the economics of shipping favor pulp and chips over raw logs – even where the latter are ridiculously cheap, as in Canada. The shift to pulp and chips has thus resulted in greater "substitutability" of wood, allowing comparable utilization of different species from different forest types. This technical change has in turn facilitated the move from tropical to boreal forests as supply areas.

The vicissitudes of the changing wood fiber market have shaped the strategies of importers to ensure access to supplies. Japan relies on Australia for over one-third of its imports of wood chips (Graham 1993: 43), mainly as a result of two "chip scares" in 1980 and 1987 which led them to broaden their sources of supply (Hagler 1993: 41). In the first, softwood chip prices doubled overnight, and Japanese importers found themselves completely dependent on US west coast exports, with no alternative sources of supply. After suffering significant losses, they diversified their supply sources by importing from Australia. When Australian supplies of eucalyptus chips were threatened by a proposed pulp mill in 1987, Japan looked to the US southeast as an alternative source (Hagler 1993: 41).

The Pacific Rim timber trade, like the global industry, shows two predominant characteristics: first, all of its forests, whatever their type and location, are tied into one market; second, that market continues to be basically colonial in character, with centers of demand drawing upon distant sources of supply.

This colonial model of resource use has also shaped what might be called the "institutional arrangements" by which the timber trade has worked with and through governments to ensure access to wood supplies. In the tropical countries, timber barons often control both logging concessions and revenues from export. Timber concessionaires in Indonesia gained control of the Ministry of Forestry to facilitate logging for the domestic plywood industry and conversion of native forests to pulp plantations, with most of the profits going to timber "kings" and large corporations in Jakarta (Rainforests Action Network 1993: 26).

"Institutional arrangements" of this sort are by no means limited to tropical countries, however. Forest liquidation in Canada has proceeded through a provincial tenure system that grants logging companies huge concessions on public lands at bargain prices that include some of the lowest stumpage fees in the world. In British Columbia, home-grown timber corporation MacMillan Bloedel has been given generous terms to clearcut native forests. In Alberta, Mitsubishi Corporation has been allowed to lease an area the size of Ohio to feed its pulp operations, and Daishowa

Pulp Company has built the world's largest disposable chopstick factory among old-growth aspen forests (McInnis 1994: 2).

When Daishowa Corporation's Peace River Pulp Company built a $579 million mill in Alberta in 1988, approximately $70 million of the infrastructure costs were borne by the province's taxpayers. Similarly, Alberta-Pacific Company, 85 percent Japanese-owned, finished construction of the world's largest bleached kraft pulp mill near Athabasca in 1993 with the province paying infrastructure costs of $75 million, with an agreement that the company need not begin repayment until the mill becomes profitable (McInnis 1994: 2).

These arrangements mean that the government is in effect a shareholder in timber operations, even though the terms of the agreements are not voted on by citizens. In British Columbia, the government *was* until recently an actual shareholder in MacMillan Bloedel, to whom it awarded the largest number of timber concessions. Canadian taxpayers thus find themselves paying the economic as well as environmental costs of a volatile market: a combination of oversupply of pulp and intense international competition has led the pulp industry in Canada to lose over $1 billion in the last few years (McInnis 1994: 3).

The degree to which industrial logging has been subsidized by national governments is especially striking. Industry's motivations are fueled by the volatility of the wood products market, which makes generous arrangements with compliant governments a virtual necessity. But access to timber supplies is not enough:

> despite all this fawning to international capital at the expense of our democracy and native forests, [the timber industry] still cannot get a competitive investment unless governments come to the party with large chunks of cash – infrastructure support, tax holidays, royalty discounts, and accelerated depreciation perks – and so spread the costs across the whole community.
>
> (Graham 1993: 56)

The motivations of governments to participate in such money-losing ventures may seem less clear. "Why [are] governments so eager to subsidize the production of more pulp, the liquidation of more taiga resources, more pollution, more incursion into aboriginal homelands?" (McInnis 1994: 3). The answer partly lies in a flawed system of natural resources accounting which has its roots in the colonial system of resource exploitation from which the Pacific Rim timber trade evolved.

In Canada, the tropics, Siberia, and many national forests in the US (such as Alaska's Tongass), royalties and taxes from timber concessions have tended to be set at unrealistically low rates, and government revenues have often amounted to only a fraction of their possible totals. Subsidies for harvesting and processing often compound the loss of timber revenues for local as well as national governments. Undervaluing the resource thus encourages overuse and depletion (Barbier *et al.* 1991: 55).

Correcting this flawed accounting system will necessitate a re-valuation of forest resources which reflects the full costs of their loss. Economists such as Robert Repetto have insisted that forests and the environmental services they provide be counted as capital assets *before* timber harvests, and that the depreciation of these assets be incorporated into any adequate accounting system (Repetto 1992: 96). The World Resources Institute has proposed a model for national budgets that integrates the full value of forests to a country's well-being to effectively eliminate most timber subsidies by making prices reflect environmental and social costs of logging *and* rewarding sustainable harvest practices through the use of market incentives (World Resources Institute 1992–93, 1994–95).

Can such reforms be implemented? Institutional attempts to impact the global market have so far been intermittent (Friends of the Earth 1992a: 7). International bodies such as the International Tropical Timber Organization and the UN Commission on Sustainable Development have an uneven record, and the UNCED Statement of Forest Principles is a non-legally binding agreement without mandatory obligations for member parties. The recently completed Uruguay Round of the General Agreement on Tariffs and Trade (GATT) could directly affect the ability of a country to restrict the flow of natural resources, as well as complicate the implementation of reform efforts such as a global system of wood certification based on economic and environmentally sustainable practices.

The main obstacle to any reform is the force of demand. Not only can demand now rise and fall on a global level, but the very structure of economic development is now tied to the global pulp market: per capita consumption of paper is a central indicator of the level of development (Postel and Ryan 1991: 87). Just as markets evolve through a combination of accident and design, fluctuations in demand are often manipulated as well. Some of the most promising tools for reducing both consumption of and demand for wood products are found in consumer-driven "demand management" strategies which specifically aim to change the marketplace. One example of this is the minimum recycled-content laws and requirements in the US, which have led to a rapid jump in the demand, price, and use of recycled paper.

The timber industry has promoted the expansion of plantations, especially in tropical countries, as one way to reduce market pressures on forests. Plantations have also been proposed as a tool in reforestation to offset climate change (Friends of the Earth 1992b: 8). This approach has its limits: substantial areas of native forest have already been converted to fast-growing, monoculture plantations, with a loss of habitat and biodiversity, and issues of local control have arisen as well. A preferable option is the growing use of "tree free" paper from plants like kenaf and hemp, which is just beginning to affect the market (Harsch 1993: 46). In the face of institutional inadequacy for addressing the scope and severity of the problem, consumer-driven strategies appear to be one of the most effective means for catalysing change.

The factor of demand on the level of global markets is providing an imperative for many options to be tried, because it compresses the time available for any of them to be effective. One author maintains that

> Present levels of, and rates of growth of, demand for wood products are so high that the chances of protecting large areas of remaining native forests of high conservation value are low unless major product substitution takes place, demand for virgin fibre is suppressed as much as possible, and rigorous conservation policies are put in place by countries and corporations alike and all very quickly indeed.
>
> (Graham 1993: 36).

This imperative is particularly critical in the Pacific Rim. The evolution of the region's timber trade has been a catalyst for the globalization of the timber industry and the wood products market. The environmental effects of this process include a pervasive loss of biodiversity and ecosystems as well as harmful impacts on local and indigenous economies and communities. Given the global reach of the timber trade, the increased emphasis on pulp and paper, the ability to use many different kinds of wood from a variety of regions, and the ever-growing demand in "developed" and emerging economies, there is great concern for the survival of native forests. Because the Pacific Rim holds the key to both future supply and demand, if effective change on both the regional and global levels is to happen at all, it must begin there.

BIBLIOGRAPHY

Barbier, E.B., Burgess, J.C. and Markanday, A. (1991) "The Economics of Tropical Deforestation," *Ambio*, XX, 2.

Belcher, M. and Gennino, A. (eds) (1993) *Southeast Asia Rainforests: A Resource Guide and Directory*, San Francisco: Rainforest Action Network, in cooperation with World Rainforest Movement.

Cushman, J.H., Jr. (1996) "Logging in Siberia Sets Off Battle in U.S.," *New York Times*, January 30.

Devall, B. (1993) "A Tree Farm is not a Forest," in *Clearcut: The Tragedy of Industrial Forestry*, San Francisco: Sierra Club.

Dudley, N. (1992) *Forests in Trouble: A Review of the Status of Forests Worldwide*, Washington, DC: World Wildlife Fund.

Dudley, N., Jeanrenaud, J.P. and Sullivan, F. (1995) *Bad Harvest: The Timber Trade and the Degradation of the World's Forests*, London: Earthscan Publications.

Flavin, C. and Ryan, M. (1995) 'Facing China's Limits,' *State of the World 1995*, New York and London: W.W. Norton & Company.

Friends of the Earth and World Rainforest Movement (1992a) *The International*

Tropical Timber Agreement: Conserving the Forests or Chainsaw Charter?, London: FOE Ltd.

Friends of the Earth (1992b) *Deserts of Trees: The Environmental & Social Impacts of Large-Scale Tropical Reforestation in Response to Global Climate Change*, London: FOE Trust Ltd.

"Global Perspectives on Pacific Rim Wood Supply," (1993) *Papermaker* 56, 4.

Graham, A. (1993) "Wood Flows Around the Pacific Rim (A Corporate Picture)," *Forestry, Pulp, and Paper.*

Grinnings, M. (1992) "Grim on the Rim," *Timber Trades Journal.*

Hagler, R. (1993) "Global Forest," *Papermaker* 56, 5.

Harsch, J. (1993) *New Industrial Uses, New Markets for U.S. Crops*, Washington: USDA.

McInnis, J. (1994) "The Great Alberta Giveaway: The Japanese Connection," *Taiga News* 9.

Marshall, G. (ed.) (1990) *The Barnett Report*, Hobart: Asia-Pacific Action Group.

Nectoux, F. and Kuroda, Y. (1989) *Timber from the South Seas: An Analysis of Japan's Tropical Timber Trade and its Environmental Impact*, World Wildlife International.

Noss, R.F. and Peters, R.L. (1995) *Endangered Ecosystems: A Status Report on America's Vanishing Habitat and Wildlife*, Washington: Defenders of Wildlife.

Postel, S. and Ryan, J. (1991) "Reforming Forestry," *State of the World 1991*, New York and London: W.W. Norton & Company

Rainforest Action Network (1994a) "Mitsubishi in Canada: The Fiasco Continues," *World Rainforest Report* XI, 1.

Rainforest Action Network (1994b) "Australian Forests Sold for Pulp," *World Rainforest Report* XI, 3.

Repetto, R. (1992) "Accounting for Environmental Assets," *Scientific American* 266.

Rosencranz, A. and Scott, A. (1992) "Siberia's Threatened Forests," *Nature* 355, 6358.

Scott, A. and Gordon, D. (1992) "The Russian Timber Rush," *Amicus Journal* 14, 3.

Tracy, L. (1994) "The Deforestation of Siberia: Economic and Environmental Problems in Russian Forest Management," *Forest Industry Lecture Series No. 32*, Edmonton: University of Alberta.

World Resources Institute (1992–93, 1994–95) "Forests and Rangelands", in *Guide to the Global Environment*, Oxford: Oxford University Press.

INDEX

NOTES

NOTES

NOTES

NOTES

NOTES

For Product Safety Concerns and Information please contact our EU representative GPSR@taylorandfrancis.com Taylor & Francis Verlag GmbH, Kaufingerstraße 24, 80331 München, Germany